RATTENBURY

RATT

ENBURY

Terry Reksten

SONO NIS PRESS
VICTORIA, BRITISH COLUMBIA

CANADIAN CATALOGUING IN PUBLICATION DATA

Reksten, Terry, 1942-2001
    Rattenbury

    Includes bibliographical references and index.
    ISBN 1-55039-090-2

    1. Rattenbury, Francis Mawson, 1867-1935. 2. Architects—
British Columbia—Biography. 3. Architecture—British
Columbia. I. Title.

NA749.R3R43 1998 720'.92 C98-910549-0

First Edition
First printing: September 1978
Tenth printing: January 1993
Second Edition
First printing: August 1998
Second printing: March 2005
Third Printing: August 2011

Sono Nis Press most gratefully acknowledges support for our publishing program provided by the Government of Canada through the Canada Book Fund and the Canada Council for the Arts, and by the Province of British Columbia through the British Columbia Arts Council and the Book Publishing Tax Credit, Ministry of Provincial Revenue.

Cover design by Jim Brennan
Interior design by Morriss Printing
Front cover photo and frontispiece: L. McCann photo collection

Published by
Sono Nis Press
PO Box 160
Winlaw, BC V0G 2J0
1-800-370-5228

books@sononis.com
www.sononis.com

Printed and bound in Canada by Houghton Boston.

The Canada Council | Le Conseil des Arts
for the Arts | du Canada

To my mother
FRANCES D. McVITTIE

Acknowledgements

I am especially grateful to the staff of a number of museums, archives and libraries; the British Library; the Newspaper Library at Colindale; Oxfordshire County Council Library; the General Register Office, London; Bradford Metropolitan Library; Washington State Library; Saskatchewan Archives Board; Glenbow-Alberta Institute; Archives of the Canadian Rockies; Victoria Public Library; Oak Bay Municipality and the Provincial Archives of British Columbia. Without their interest and helpful suggestions the research for this book could not have been completed. And I am most grateful to the Canada Council for providing the grant without which much of the research would have been impossible.

Many individuals gave invaluable assistance in the preparation of this book. I owe a special debt of gratitude to Frank B. Rattenbury and Mrs. E. Burton (Mary Rattenbury) for providing me with a highly personal view of their father. And to Ainslie Helmcken and Miss C. Maclure and many other long-time Victoria residents who shared their reminiscences with me. Thanks are also due to Ian Whitely of the *Bournemouth Daily Echo* who helped me find Stoner, to Bert Parsons and Dixie Dean for their recollections of Alma, to Martin Segger, Al Kerr and Leonard McCann for sharing their information and their photographs with me, to Carolyn Smyly, Joan Wright and Brian Smith who helped in the beginning when it was so important, and to Eric Tomlinson for helping to tie up loose ends. And to Jim Munro who gave me encouragement when I needed it most.

Candy Wyatt deserves special thanks. A constant friend and long-suffering sounding board, she also suggested changes to and then typed the final manuscript. I appreciate her help so much that someday I may find it in my heart to forgive her for the unbounded glee with which she pounced on yet another spelling mistake.

I hope Jane and Norah already know how much their patient acceptance of a slightly distracted mother has meant. And if my husband Don thinks for one moment that I could have completed this book without him, then he'd better think again.

ABBREVIATIONS

PABC Provincial Archives of British Columbia
VCA   Victoria City Archives

Contents

Introduction

Five years ago when I first became interested in Francis Mawson Rattenbury I knew only that he was the architect of British Columbia's Parliament Buildings and Victoria's Empress Hotel and that he had been murdered in England. In the beginning I was only mildly curious. This man must have been one of the most respected and successful architects of his day. Why had he chosen to leave Victoria to live in anonymity in Bournemouth, an English seaside town that was in many ways similar to Victoria? And why had he been murdered?

The second question proved the easier one to answer. Rattenbury's murder had resulted in one of the most celebrated trials to be held in London's Old Bailey in the first half of the twentieth century. A transcript of the trial, edited by F. Tennyson Jesse, had been added to the "Notable British Trials" series in 1935. Rattenbury, it appeared, had become entangled in a strange and unlikely *ménage à trois* and the jealousies and passions of that relationship had led to his murder.

But again why had he left Victoria, the scene of his success, to settle in Bournemouth where he became known as just another retired colonial with a few interesting stories to tell? By the time I discovered the answer to that question, learning more about Rattenbury, his life and his career, had ceased to be a part-time diversion and become a full time preoccupation. For at least twenty years Rattenbury had been British Columbia's most prominent architect. Even a partial list of his buildings was impressive; office buildings for the Bank of Montreal in Victoria, Nelson and New Westminster; courthouses in Vancouver, Nelson, and Nanaimo; Victoria's Crystal Garden, the Calgary home of cattle baron Pat Burns; B.C.'s Government House. All landmark buildings and all designed by a man who never thought of himself solely as an architect. A man who dabbled successfully in politics and who proved himself to be a sensitive and visionary town planner. A man who crossed the Chilkoot in 1898 to promote his transportation company and a man who dreamt of being an empire builder and who risked a fortune in an attempt to make that dream a reality.

It seemed to me that Rattenbury was a fascinating character whose story deserved to be told, but researching this book presented certain difficulties.

The Five Sisters block in Victoria which housed Rattenbury's office burned to the ground in 1910 taking with it many of his plans and sketches, his business records and his correspondence. Without those records it is impossible to know the full extent of his architectural practice. But fortunately a number of his plans and rough sketches have managed to survive — some in the files of the Department of Public Works and others found hidden away in the attic of his home years after his death. And they were enough to clearly indicate the impatient genius of the man who drew them, a man who sketched monumental buildings with quick bold strokes and who became bored with the careful and clever detail work on which other architects based their reputations.

And fortunately too, Rattenbury held his own opinions in such high regard that he could see no reason for keeping them to himself. He often rambled on happily to reporters from the Victoria newspapers about his ideas on town planning or about the assured success of his latest business venture. He was particularly sensitive to criticism and more than one "Letters to the Editor" column was enlivened by his aggressive and uninhibited letters. In 1903 he wrote an open letter to Alderman Yates. Yates, a Victoria lawyer for whom Rattenbury had designed a small office block five years earlier, had had the temerity to suggest that Rattenbury seldom completed a building within the estimated cost. "You have no more right, Mr. Yates, to make such a sweeping assertion as reported, than I should have to say that you have muddled almost every case you have ever taken into court, although I may think so." That kind of outspokenness was typical of Rattenbury and although none of his personal correspondence has been found, his public letters are more revealing of his character than might ordinarily be expected.

Many long-time residents of Victoria remember Rattenbury but they are contemporaries of his children and being a generation removed they lack the insight that would have helped immeasurably in understanding and exploring his character. During the course of many interviews, a surprising and disappointing consistency emerged. Rattenbury was remembered as a man who doted on his children, particularly his daughter, but who felt a contemptuous dislike for his wife; a bad tempered man who became increasingly so as the years passed. Without exception the people I interviewed told me that their fathers had considered Rattenbury a genius but that they, as children, had found that he wasn't a very nice man to know. It was a distressingly one-dimensional picture. There is some evidence to suggest that in his younger days Rattenbury's fellows had found him rowdy good company and at least one man had benefited from his generosity but otherwise his character has received unanimously bad reviews.

And yet I can't help but admire him and feel some sympathy for him. If, as his competitors charged, his cunning rather than his talent accounted for much of his success then one must at least give him credit for having a finely calculating mind, for while his commission-winning tactics could be devious, there is no evidence to suggest that they were dishonest. His one true ambition was to be a man who counted. He wanted prominence, fame and wealth. He wanted to be someone who mattered and it made little difference to him whether he achieved his goal through architecture or by building a northern empire. To appreciate his passionate need to succeed is to begin to understand the narrow single-mindedness with which he pursued his goal.

I have avoided a detailed critical analysis of Rattenbury's buildings for two reasons. As someone with a general, rather than a specialized, interest I find the vocabulary of architectural criticism confounding and the subject both technical and complex. Even so, such an omission might be unforgivable were it not for the fact that Rattenbury simply wasn't a particularly original architect. He broke no new ground. He was never considered by himself or by others to be avant-garde or daringly creative. He succeeded by giving people what they wanted and despite changing tastes many of his buildings continue to be objects of public admiration. Rattenbury's skill lay not in attention to the finer details of design but in his ability to envision monumental buildings in spectacular settings, buildings which would have an immediate and unforgettable visual impact.

Rattenbury and Sam Maclure were Victoria's two most prominent architects. They worked out of adjacent offices in the Five Sisters block and they worked together on at least two projects; Cary Castle and Dr. Jones' home on Island Road in Oak Bay. But while Maclure's work has been the subject of books, photographic displays and numerous articles, Rattenbury's buildings have been virtually ignored by architects and art historians. The reason for this, according to Martin Segger, an acknowledged expert on Victoria's early architects, is that Rattenbury isn't particularly interesting from an architectural historian's point of view. What Rattenbury looked for was the opportunity to design huge, powerful buildings, impressive monuments which would dominate town and cityscapes. He worked at a time when the creation of a fine and impressive skyline was the mark of a good designer and many of his buildings could be considered good in that respect, says Segger. But in creating that impressive skyline he often produced buildings that lack dimension. Segger cites the Empress Hotel as an example of a building which appears like a cardboard cut-out against the sky. Rattenbury was a great dreamer and a monumental planner and while that might be great romantic stuff his buildings won't stand intensive scrutiny, whereas Maclure's can and do. The major difference between the two architects, according to Segger, is in their treatment of interior spaces and their attention to detail. Rattenbury's interiors tended to be confined and restricted not so much in terms of size but according to use. Maclure, by thinking in terms of volume rather than floor area, designed interiors which seemed much larger than they actually were, one room flowing into another creating a grand dramatic space in an otherwise modest house. Maclure was known to design every last moulding, developing a theme which would be carried throughout the house, while Rattenbury often left this kind of decision up to his contractor. Maclure visited his construction sites at least once a day, carefully checking all the work that had been done. His attention to detail was almost obsessive. Hatley Park, his largest commission, nearly drove Maclure berserk, says Segger. He couldn't leave well enough alone and Hatley Park was just too big.

Thinking big was Rattenbury's forte. He was not an architect who grew in ability, who gradually refined a style or a technique. His buildings were symbolic of his towering self confidence, products of a forceful personality rather than contemplative artistry. And so while his buildings might not bear close inspection, the man who designed them certainly does.

Part I

FRANCIS MAWSON RATTENBURY

1

Family Background and Training

Arrogant and boastful, driven by ambition, Francis Mawson Rattenbury was a talented architect who easily rose to the top of his profession. A visionary capitalist and skilled promoter, he pictured himself as an empire builder and if fate had not intervened he might well have achieved his goal of becoming one of British Columbia's richest and most powerful men. Residents of Victoria, B.C. who remember him are quick to admit that he was a genius, but he made few real friends, more than his share of enemies and those who became close to him were left embittered by the experience. And when he was murdered there were many who secretly felt that he had got what he deserved.

Yet things might have turned out differently. His grandfather, with whom Rattenbury shared many of the same talents and many of the same faults, made a success of both his public and private life. Both men were tall, blessed with a commanding physical presence and almost hypnotic powers of persuasion. They brought to their work the same single-minded enthusiasm and insatiable desire to succeed, combined with a sometimes selfish disregard for the welfare of their families. But his grandfather, John Rattenbury, died a contented and revered man for he had devoted his life to God rather than the pursuit of personal success and his excesses were praised as evidence of exceptional religious ardour rather than condemned as signs of ruthless personal ambition.

As a boy living in Manchester, John Rattenbury had fallen under the spell of the local Methodist preacher. In 1825 when he was nineteen and after the death of his unsympathetic father he had thrown himself into preaching with an almost fanatical dedication. As a brother minister recalled, "No minister ever felt the call to preach more loudly than he . . ."[1]

3

And apparently few ministers had come so well equipped for their chosen vocation. "His physical advantages were great. Tall, with an abundance of flowing dark hair, he had a 'pulpit-presence' of the finest kind. His mobile features, his large, expressive, lustrous, yet dreamy eyes, quivering lips, and unspeakably tender, persuasive and pathetic utterance, were wonderfully in his favour."[2]

Reverend John Rattenbury knew instinctively how to manipulate his audience. He would begin quietly, seriously, earnestly "but soon kindled with his subject; and his hearers soon caught the contagion of his fervour, and broke out at first into low murmurs of delighted assent, which soon swelled into shouts of rapturous exclamations, so that the preacher's words were over and over again drowned by many-voiced bursts of Hallelujah! Glory! Praise the Lamb!"[3]

His religious ardour was not confined to the pulpit. Upon entering a drawing room and finding the inhabitants happily engaged in gossip or carefree repartee, he would determinedly steer the conversation to more sober topics and end by leading the chastened assembly in prayer. And when it came to Sabbath-breaking his outrage knew no bounds. Whether the guilty parties were hapless shopkeepers peddling their wares of a Sunday or drunkards turned out of a local gin-palace, he would accost them on the spot and gently but persistently lecture to them until their indignant oaths became cries for mercy.

His ministry was centred in the West Riding of Yorkshire, an area beset by social problems as the result of sudden change. For centuries the Riding had been the site of a flourishing cottage industry, wool being spun and woven into cloth by hand in scattered villages and lonely farmhouses. But now towns located in river-filled valleys near beds of waiting coal had become centres of the new industry created when steam power was adapted to the processing of wool. Farm workers, encouraged to leave the countryside by an agricultural depression, had flocked to these growing cities, spurred on by the promise of plentiful work. Almost overnight sleepy market villages became squalid cities, their skies leaden with the smoke from a growing forest of chimneys. Disease was rampant, the result of fouled streams, long hours of backbreaking labour in the mills and overcrowded, unsanitary living conditions. While many turned to drink to escape the grim realities of their existence, others found solace in religion. They filled the chapels on the Methodist circuit eager to hear the inspirational words of the travelling preachers.

A minister on the circuit was allowed to stay in any one place for no more than three years before being required to move on to the next town on the circuit and so Reverend Rattenbury's life became a succession of one grim industrial city after another. He was fortunate that when he married he chose a wife whose dedication to God's work matched his own.

During his stay in Sheffield from 1831-1833 he married Mary Owen, a pious and devout woman who had been attracted to the young preacher by his habitual godliness, his Christian simplicity and cheerfulness, and his natural and unpretentious courtesy — the same qualities that helped him rise from obscurity to his church's highest position, President of the Conference, some thirty years later. The daughter of Samuel Owen, a successful coal merchant and influential Methodist, Mary Owen accepted their transient life without complaint even though the family moved so often that no two of her children were born in the same place. Their first child, John Owen Rattenbury (Francis Rattenbury's father) was born in Macclesfield in 1836. Three years later Samuel was born in Leeds, followed by Sarah Anne in 1841 in York. Henry was born in Manchester in 1843 and Catherine in 1846 near Bradford.

In his home Reverend Rattenbury set an example of solemn prayerful piety. In his musical and powerful voice, with his pale handsome face lifted toward heaven, he prayed daily for each of his children in turn, listing their individual faults and needs and pleading with God to give them guidance. Although his easy understanding of their problems filled them with awe and at times covered them with embarrassment, his children, with one possible exception, adored him.

His third son, Henry, born with his feet firmly planted on the road to righteousness found his father's presence "pure sunshine in the house"[4] and never deviated from his life's ambition to follow his example. Becoming a minister at the age of twenty, Henry laboured on the Methodist circuit for forty years and while he could never match his father's dynamic appeal, he did become known as a conscientious pastor and just administrator.[5] Inspired by his example, two of his sons became Methodist ministers and his younger son, Harold Burgoyne Rattenbury, was elected to fill his grandfather's position as President of the Conference in 1949.

Henry may have found that his father's prayers at the family altar seemed to bring him "beneath the very wings of the holy and loving

God.''[6] But for his older brother John, who all too often found himself the subject of those fervent prayers, they were an uncomfortable experience. John Owen Rattenbury seemed so out of place in that reverent family that his mother became more than a little concerned that he might follow in the footsteps of a quite different John Rattenbury — one to whom, she shuddered to think, her family might be related. In 1836 this John Rattenbury, a reluctantly reformed smuggler, had given up the sea and fondly recounted his boisterous career. He called his book *Memoirs of a Smuggler* and proudly reminded his readers that he had been known as the "Rob Roy of the West." So much did he enjoy smuggling that he had introduced his sons to the trade and proclaimed that while smuggling might be fraught with difficulties and danger it was a career "calculated to gratify a hardy and enterprising spirit, and to call forth the latent energies of the soul . . .''[7]

When Mary Owen Rattenbury read John's *Memoirs* she hurled the offensive book into the fire, for as well as sharing the same name, the portrait grinning merrily from the book's frontispiece showed that the "Rob Roy of the West" bore a distinct resemblance to her husband.[8] The fear that her oldest child might take after this roving pirate seemed to be confirmed when, at the first opportunity, John Owen Rattenbury cast himself loose from his family and sailed for New Zealand. But his restlessness was easily overcome and his desire for adventure easily met for in 1861 when he was twenty-five John Rattenbury returned to England and settled in Leeds where he met and courted Mary Anne Mawson.

The Mawsons, a large, solidly middle-class family, had made the most of Yorkshire's expanding economy. Mary Anne's father owned a prosperous printing business in Leeds and in the same city her uncles and cousins were engaged in the textile trade marketing the products of the busy woollen mills. In Bradford two of her brothers, William and Richard Mawson, were working with Henry Francis Lockwood in an architectural partnership which was proving to be outstandingly successful. It seemed likely that Mary Anne and her industrious family would have a steadying influence on John Owen Rattenbury.

On March 12, 1862 they were married in the Wesleyan Chapel in Leeds, John gaining both a devoted wife and a partnership in the firm of Mawson and Dewhirst, woollen merchants in the city. The couple settled down on Hyde Park Terrace in Headingley, a pleasant residential section of Leeds favoured by moderately successful business and professional men and for a time John Rattenbury tried to fit into the place that had been made for him in the world of commerce. When his first son, John, was born in 1864 he still listed his occupation as cloth merchant, but by the time his second son, Francis Mawson Rattenbury, was born on October 11, 1867 he had severed his connection with Rattenbury, Mawson and Dewhirst and become the local manager of the General Assurance Company. Ten years later, in a move that earned him the reputation of the family's black sheep, John Rattenbury gave up the role of a man of business and eased himself into the life of a self-styled artist and the family found it necessary to move down the street into a more modest, severely plain house. Francis Rattenbury's enrollment the following year in the Leeds Free Grammar School is a further hint that the family suffered financially from John's decision to devote himself to art. Affiliated with the Church of England, the school had been founded in the sixteenth century and under headmaster Reverend William Henderson it continued to perform its original function — providing, without fee, a classical education for those boys of the parish whose parents could not afford to pay for it.

Mary Anne may have been disappointed by her husband's apparent lack of ambition, but at least she still had the Mawsons on whom she could rely. It seems that they were prepared to offer Francis Rattenbury his father's former position with the firm of Mawson and Dewhirst for after completing the course of studies at the Leeds Free Grammar School, he was enrolled at Yorkshire College, a vocational school founded in the 1870's to channel students into the textile industry. But like his father, Francis Rattenbury found that learning the techniques of processing, dyeing and marketing wool held no appeal for him and he left the college without a diploma.

As well as an aversion to the textile trade, he had inherited from his father a facile ability to draw, to cover page after page with sure, accurate sketches. Hoping that he would learn to use this skill in a practical way, Mary Anne arranged for her bachelor brothers, William and Richard Mawson, to take him under their wing and in 1885, when he was eighteen, Francis Mawson Rattenbury left Leeds to become an articled student with the firm of Mawson and Mawson, architects in the city of Bradford.

7

It cannot have taken long for Rattenbury who was later to become an architect of imagination and vision, a dreamer of grand architectural dreams, to realize that the firm he had joined was now producing buildings of only mediocre quality. It had not always been so. In Bradford, Rattenbury was surrounded by the firm's past glories, the much admired public buildings designed by the Mawsons when they had been partnered with Henry Francis Lockwood. Later when he struck out on his own as an architect in Canada it was to these buildings designed long before he joined the firm that Rattenbury would point as evidence of the excellence of his training and of the wide range of his experience.

The association of Henry Lockwood and the Mawsons had begun in 1849 when William Mawson, who had just completed his articles in Leeds, and Lockwood, who had been practicing for some fifteen years in Hull, decided to form a partnership and move to Bradford where they felt the opportunities for enterprising architects were unsurpassed. While the booming textile industry had encouraged the growth of many towns, Bradford's growth had been explosive. In the fifty years since the turn of the century the town of 13,000 people had mushroomed into a city with a population of 103,000. In 1850 there were few large buildings in Bradford and Lockwood and Mawson knew they would have to be built soon.

They had completed work on their first Bradford commission, a workhouse for the Bradford Board of Guardians, and were preparing plans for the city's concert hall, when one winter afternoon in 1850 a certain Titus Salt called at their offices and told them of his plans to build a new mill at Shipley Glen some four miles from the centre of Bradford. Lockwood set to work on the preliminary sketches without suspecting that they would lead to the single most important commission the firm would ever be given.

The owner of several local textile mills, Salt was a capitalist with a conscience. During his term as mayor of Bradford in 1848 he had been confronted by the many social problems he, as an industrialist, had helped to create. Ignored by mill owners in their scramble for profits, the textile workers led squalid lives, blighted by disease, drunkenness, and deplorably inadequate housing. As mayor, Salt had found that there was little he could do to allay their suffering. Now he had decided to lead the way. He would build a model community, a showplace of enlightened capitalism on the banks of the Aire.

8

Calling at the architects' offices a few days later, Salt approved of the sketches and found his admiration increasing for Henry Lockwood, a cultured, quietly diligent man whose Liberal political views matched his own. The plan he gradually unfolded astounded the architects in its scope. As well as a factory equipped with all the modern inventions to combat the twin evils of air and water pollution, Salt proposed the building of an entire town complete with attractive homes for his workers and including many social amenities, such as schools, churches, a library, alms houses, a hospital and parks. It would not, however, boast any public houses or inns as Salt remained convinced that Demon Drink was at the bottom of all the ills of the nation. The community was to be planned down to the smallest detail, even to the prohibition of washing lines and hoardings. Nothing quite like it had ever been attempted before.[9]

The architects chose the same Italianate style for all the buildings, from the mill, its 250 foot chimney resembling an Italian bell tower, to the workers' houses with their gracefully arched windows and to further unify the design of the community they decided that all the buildings would be constructed of the same cream coloured brick and stone. Salt, proud of the new town, christened it Saltaire and both Lockwood and Mawson were honoured to have streets named after them.

As well as establishing their reputation, Saltaire would keep Lockwood and Mawson busy for the next twenty years. When William Mawson's younger brother, Richard, joined the firm in the mid-1850's he was a welcome addition to an extremely busy company. As well as their ongoing work on Saltaire, they were, with ecumenical enthusiasm, designing churches for the Congregationalists in Cleckheaton, the Methodists in Harrogate, and the Baptists in Scarborough.

Adding to the firm's prestige was the selection of Lockwood as one of the seven architects invited to compete for the design of the new Law Courts to be erected in London, placing him in the heady company of such well-known men as Barry, Scott, Waterhouse and Street, the top echelon of English architects of the time. The fact that he lost the contest to Street did little to diminish his reputation locally. The opinion voiced in Bradford was that Lockwood's design had shown "the greatest power, the greatest skill as an architect for arrangement, and the greatest idea of beauty as an artist."[10]

9

Lockwood and Mawson's guess that Bradford would engage in a madly energetic building boom proved correct. During the 1860's they won a wide variety of commissions ranging from the Victoria Hotel and the Kirkgate Market to the Wool Exchange, their success culminating when they were selected as architects for Bradford's Town Hall in 1870.

When the Town Hall was officially opened in 1873 all Bradford turned out to celebrate. An elaborate procession of eighteen bands and a great display of flags and standards, somewhat sodden by a heavy downpour, wound through the town. So important was the event in Bradford that the Prime Minister, Mr. Gladstone, had been invited to attend and, while he found better things to do, the guest list did include four members of parliament.

An impressive mixture of Franco-English and Italian Gothic styles, with statues of the thirty-five English monarchs from William the Conqueror to Queen Victoria peering down from niches in its second floor arcade, the Town Hall was the pinnacle of Lockwood and Mawson's career.

Their early success had been due to three factors: as Yorkshiremen they appealed to the regional loyalties of local concerns, they were on the spot when Bradford needed architects most, and they worked well together each providing necessary ingredients for a successful client-attracting formula. Lockwood was the most architecturally talented of the three and was recognized as the foundation of the firm's success.[11] William Mawson was an efficient business manager known for his practical ability.[12] Richard Mawson was a social asset, a well known sportsman[13] who made many important friends and connections through his many club memberships and who carefully eschewed political affiliations to counteract the effects of Lockwood's vocal Liberalism.

Encouraged by local success, they opened a branch office in London. And from 1871 when Henry Lockwood moved to the sunnier climes of Surrey, his health broken by the damp, dirty Bradford air, it was from this office at 10 Lincoln's Inn Fields that he practiced. With Lockwood's removal to London and all major buildings in Bradford completed, two necessary ingredients of the firm's success were gone. Business fell off as commissions they might have won in Leeds went to Cuthbert Broderick, an architect who had trained under Lockwood in Hull and whose Gothic designs had a wider appeal than did Lockwood and Mawson's Italianate.

When Henry Francis Lockwood died in 1878, he took with him the firm's creative spark. The two brothers formed a new partnership under the title Mawson and Mawson but in 1886, a year after Francis Rattenbury joined the firm as a student, William Mawson, his health failing, retired and Robert Hudson who had laboured anonymously with the Mawsons and Lockwood for 17 years was elevated to a full partnership.

During the six years Rattenbury spent with Mawson and Hudson the architects were engaged in projects of little impact or importance either locally or nationally. Later in an attempt to establish his credibility as an architect in Canada, Rattenbury could name with pride only two buildings on which he had worked and in both cases he found it necessary to exaggerate both his role in their design and the critical acceptance they had enjoyed.

One was the Town Hall of Cleckheaton, a mill town near Bradford. In 1887 after casting about for a fitting way to celebrate Queen Victoria's jubilee, the city fathers decided that the Queen would best be fêted by the erection of a new building to house municipal government. A competition was held to select the best design and Mawson and Hudson's entry entitled "Light and Air" was judged to be the most suitable. Rattenbury would later claim dual authorship of the design with his uncle, but he certainly received no credit for it at the time. And perhaps in later years he would just as soon not have been reminded of it, for Cleckheaton's Town Hall is an odd, strangely out-of-proportion building — not one of Mawson and Hudson's greater successes.

Contemporary opinion was not so harsh, but neither was it overly enthusiastic. When a professional journal, *The Architect*, noted that "The architects have sought to obtain picturesque grouping without excessive ornamentation, and the sketch plans show this desirable result has been achieved,"[14] Mawson and Hudson were so encouraged by this mildly favourable praise that they decided to submit their plans to the Royal Academy in 1891, hoping they would be selected for display at the Academy's annual exhibition of British architecture. Rattenbury would later boast about the Academy's ultimate selection of their design, but this honour wasn't necessarily all that it seemed. While other buildings brought effusive praise, little was said about their design. "The town-hall of Cleckheaton, by Messrs. Mawson and Hudson, is shown on too small a drawing. The architects have produced a very effective building without imposing a burthen on the inhabitants,"[15] *The Architect* damned with faint praise.

And the whole method of selection and the quality of the exhibits shown at the Academy was beginning to be questioned. The following year the display was roundly condemned by *The British Architect*. "The annual farce had once again been enacted. Some architects having again elected to send specimens of their work to Burlington House to uphold the credit of British Architecture, a certain number have been selected, and having been mixed up with studies of old works and drawings of stained glass, have produced a totally inadequate and misleading record of the quality of British Art in this department."[16]

Rattenbury also claimed to have made a substantial contribution to Mawson and Hudson's design for the municipal buildings to be erected at Oxford. The firm did not win the design competition, nor did it place among the five finalists, but Rattenbury, finding a way of turning a company failure into a personal success took comfort in the fact that their design had been highly recommended[17] by T. E. Collcutt, contest judge and architect of the buildings housing the Imperial Institute in London. Some would have found this cold comfort indeed for while Collcutt was a well-known architect, he was not universally admired. In commenting on his entries at the Royal Academy's exhibition of 1892, *The British Architect* was most uncharitable. "Mr. T. E. Collcutt gives a coloured view of the upper part of his Imperial Institute Tower, in which the want of force and substance is more apparent than ever." Another Collcutt design was found to be "an unpleasantly spotty ink view" and "one of those instances where variety is *not pleasing*."[18]

By the spring of 1892 Rattenbury had become convinced that there was nothing more his uncle could teach him. He was chronically ambitious and sure of his own abilities. Just slightly under six feet tall, he carried himself well, his erect bearing a clue to his belief in his own importance and his red hair hinting of an inner impatience to get on with the job of realizing his potential. He knew that the firm of Mawson and Hudson was going nowhere and he no doubt chafed under the tutelage and advice of his bachelor uncle. He was certainly shrewd enough to have correctly assessed the reasons for the early success of Lockwood and Mawson. He was sure that he was at least as architecturally talented as Lockwood had been. All that was left was for him to find the right place for his time. He could certainly eliminate Bradford. What he hoped to find was a town such as Bradford had been some thirty years before — new and growing, anxious to erect substantial buildings as evidence of its prosperity. He doubted if he could find such a city in all England which was beginning to draw a more relaxed breath after the hectic building boom which had accompanied the industry-spurred growth of the preceding decades. Encouraged to look further afield by the same early restlessness that had afflicted his father, in 1892 he set sail for Canada. But not just any part of Canada. He was bound quite purposefully for Vancouver, British Columbia.

2

A "B.C. Architect" and the Parliament Buildings
pleasure and pardonable pride

For most of the twenty-five years that had passed since 1867 when "Gassy" Jack Deighton had beached his canoe, his Indian wife and a case of rum at a tiny clearing in the rain forest bringing civilization to the shores of Burrard Inlet, any suggestion that Vancouver might one day become a great west coast seaport would have been greeted with hilarity. While the city of Victoria was bent on spreading over the southern tip of Vancouver Island and industriously establishing itself as the centre of business and commerce, the little settlement that grew up around "Gassy" Jack's saloon was a community without ambition or dreams of future glory. Given the unpromising name of Gastown,[1] it seemed content to remain a nondescript backwater, the home of a few mill workers and a motley company of sailors who had jumped ship and found safe haven at Deighton House. For eleven years Gastown dozed on but then with a treachery that long rankled Victorians, the Canadian Pacific Railway reneged on its commitment to make Victoria the western terminus of the transcontinental rail line, deciding instead to end the tracks at Burrard Inlet, and the little town shook itself awake and began to think about its future. Victorians were indignant when, at the suggestion of C.P.R. Vice-President Cornelius Van Horne, Gastown appropriated the name of their island and Victoria's businessmen sensed that the upstart town would soon compound that affront to local pride by stealing their city's commercial eminence.

In 1886 a major fire cleared the townsite of all but a few of the wooden frame buildings, many little more than shacks, that had sprung up in boom town fashion since the C.P.R.'s announcement. The building spree that followed was only slightly less exuberant as Vancouverites, sobered by the fire and finally aware of their city's potential, erected less combustible and more dignified buildings of brick and stone.

The Vancouver to which Rattenbury was attracted in 1892 had experienced six years of growing prosperity and unchecked optimism. The frontier shanty town had become a cosmopolitan city of 15,000 residents, a city billed in England as the "Constantinople of the West," a city of long streets, big blocks, handsome churches and elegant villas.[2] But it was also in the spring of 1892 a city on the brink of recession. Within a year, an economic depression in the United States would spread to British Columbia, the elegant mansions of "Blue Blood Alley" would be boarded up and all over the city land values would plummet. But in May when Rattenbury took rooms at Mrs. Morency's boarding house at 617 Richards, pleasantly situated in a quiet part of the city, only the most cautious suggested that the city might be already overbuilt and that progress and prosperity might not be endless after all.

Making himself known in a strange city presented no problem to Rattenbury who enjoyed the promotion of himself and his schemes as much as, if not more than, he enjoyed the practice of architecture. He called at the offices of the *Vancouver Daily World* and on July 5, 1892 a friendly article appeared on the pages of that paper.

Attention is directed to the advertisement of Mr. F. M. Rattenbury, architect, who has opened an office in the New Holland Block, Cordova St. He has been for ten years erecting all classes of buildings in conjunction with the well-known firm of Lockwood and Mawson — Bradford Town.

It was the first, but not the last, time that Rattenbury would consider it prudent to improve his reputation by claiming to have trained under Henry Francis Lockwood. Lockwood, who had died when Rattenbury was 11 years old and before that had practiced out of the firm's London office for seven years, enjoyed a wide reputation — a reputation from which Rattenbury was determined to benefit until he had established one of his own.

Just how many clients were attracted by Rattenbury's first foray into self-promotion via the newspapers is unknown, but soon after he arrived in the city he designed a house for Gustav Roedde on Barclay Street in the city's prestigious West End. And whether German-born Roedde was attracted to the architect by his puffed up reputation or by the common misspelling of his name as "Rattenberg," the building was a success, remembered many years later as a happy, comfortable house; the stairs winding up its many windowed tower, an exciting place to the Roedde children and grand-children.[3]

There are no records of Rattenbury's having designed any other buildings during his stay in Vancouver, but if he found that he had time to spare, he had no trouble in deciding how to fill it. He may have considered it a good omen when he noticed that the same page of the *Vancouver Daily World* that announced his presence in Vancouver carried a "Notice to Architects" announcing that a competition would be held for the design of new buildings to house the Legislative Assembly in Victoria.

Although it had only been fifty years since the first permanent European settlement had been established on Vancouver Island, the new legislative buildings would be the fourth in the series of buildings used to house government.

Meeting for the first time in 1856, the members of the House of Assembly had gathered around a dilapidated and picturesquely bulging[4] iron stove inside the Bachelors' Hall, a building constructed of squared logs within the walls of the Hudson's Bay Company fort. After several meetings in these spartan surroundings, the House had removed itself to a more noble building which also served as a jail and courthouse and settled in for a long stay. The discovery of gold on the Fraser River changed their plans.

During the summer of 1858 a swarm of 20,000 gold hungry prospectors and American merchants, wise to the ways of business after the California rush of '49, had transformed Victoria from a lonely Company outpost to a bustling city. While they pocketed the extravagant sums these foreigners were prepared to pay for their town lots, Victorians felt a certain uneasiness about this sudden influx of Americans with their republican ideas. The time seemed ripe for the construction of government buildings suitable to the maintenance of British law. Herman Otto Tiedemann was retained as architect and under his direction a group of most unusual buildings had begun to rise, across the harbour from the city, in the autumn of 1859.

Their construction had delighted William Alexander Smith, an eccentric Nova Scotian who had arrived in Victoria in the gold-mad year of 1858, changed his name to Amor De Cosmos, founded a newspaper, the *British Colonist*, and appointed himself editor. Nothing pleased De Cosmos more than an opportunity to rail in print at the follies of the colonial administration, and the new government buildings became the favourite target of his enthusiastic barbs. "No one competent to draw a plan or accept one would have hesitated one moment in rejecting the contemptible design which is now being carried into execution,"[5] he crowed in an editorial.

While some found their design to be Elizabethan and tasteful, De Cosmos saw them as something between a Dutch Toy and a Chinese Pagoda and condemned them as gingerbread contrivances. But whatever one thought of their design it had become apparent that some thirty years after their construction the "Birdcages" as everyone called them were no longer a suitable home for the government and its burgeoning bureaucracy. Clerks in the Colonial Secretary's office reported they could see through the walls and it was no surprise to anyone when in 1893 the Legislature found it necessary to adjourn for a week because it was impossible to keep the Legislative Hall at anything like a temperature at which a man could work.[6]

And then there was the question of the province's image. As the Victoria *Colonist* pointed out, "Mean and insignificant public buildings are outward and visible signs of a sordid, narrow-minded and uncultivated State or Province. Visitors are sure to judge the whole people by the buildings they erect for public uses. Those buildings ought to be handsome as well as commodious."[7] Premier Theodore Davie couldn't have agreed more. Under his leadership the Legislature passed the necessary monies and the Chief Commissioner of Lands and Works announced the competition to select the design of the new buildings. And Rattenbury, although only he would have considered it even remotely possible, was on his way to pulling off the most astounding architectural coup in the province's history — a feat due in no small part to his talent for self-promotion.

Two non-competing architects from eastern Canada, Curry from Ontario and Taylor from Quebec, had been chosen to judge the competition. They settled in to the homelike comforts of the Roccabella Guest House and began the prodigious task of selecting five preliminary winners from among the 67 sets of drawings the government had received. The judges were aware that the new legislative buildings should be symbolic as well as practical — they must be functional, of course, but they should also serve as a showpiece, an example of what British Columbia craftsmen working with local building materials could accomplish. It would be something of a set-back to provincial pride if none of the finalists in the architectural competition were from British Columbia. But Curry and Taylor's decision must be seen to be unbiassed and so all entrants had been asked to submit their designs identified only by a nom de plume.

Most of the competitors complied with the spirit of this rule showing a stunning lack of creativity in their choice of name. "Hopeful" and "Patience" were two uninspired and unhelpful choices. Some like "Utility and Dignity" were more ponderous than descriptive. One wit threw all caution to the winds and signed his drawings "Ta-ra-ra-boom-de-ay" convincing the judges that even he wasn't optimistic about his chance of winning.

Rattenbury gave his choice of nom de plume a great deal of thought. Guessing that both the government and the judges would be somewhat discomfitted if a local man was not among the finalists, he cast about for a name which while retaining his anonymity would give the contest judges a most welcome piece of information. His final choice left no room for doubt. "B.C. Architect" he signed himself and he must have been overjoyed and maybe even a little surprised when, on November 11, 1892, he received a letter telling him that he was one of the five finalists in the first phase of the competition.

As might have been predicted the local press found reason to be smugly proud. "British Columbia architects have to be especially congratulated in having taken two out of the five prizes out of the 67 sets submitted from all parts of North America. This speaks well of the skill of the profession in the Province,"[8] the Victoria *Colonist* bragged.

With the energy of a young man just four weeks past his twenty-fifth birthday, Rattenbury set to work enlarging and elaborating his drawings for the final phase of the competition. As the *Colonist* had noted two of the winning designs had been submitted by local architects, Rattenbury of Vancouver and Thomas Sorby of Victoria. The other finalists were Brown of Toronto, Garden of Chicago and Corner and Skillings of Boston and Seattle. Perhaps working on the theory that it was a shame to let a good opportunity go to waste and that it was foolish not to hedge his bets, Rattenbury identified his second set of drawings with a nom de plume which provided the useful information that their author was one of the British Columbians. "For Our Queen and Province" was certainly a title calculated to gently nudge the judges in his direction and it really needed to do little more for Rattenbury had submitted a fine set of drawings. While the judges deemed the designs of other competitors to be correct but somewhat commonplace, or picturesque . . . but wanting dignity, Rattenbury's design variously described as "Renaissance Revival," "neo-classical" and "a blending . . . of the Romanesque, Classic and Gothic," was pronounced by the judges to be very dignified and effective . . . from all points of view.[9]

On March 15, 1893 he received a telegram from W. S. Gore, Deputy Chief Commissioner of Lands and Works, "Accept congratulations come to Victoria by tomorrow's boat if possible."

To Rattenbury his presence in the province's capital when the government announced his name as winning architect was not only possible — it was essential. He realized that the judges' decision might be questioned when it was discovered that the "B.C. Architect" who had submitted his design for his province was an unknown twenty-five-year-old Yorkshireman and the following day he was not only in Victoria but was also a resident of the Driard, the city's best hotel. And he was prepared to meet the press with a short history of his professional career guaranteed to consolidate his position. His credentials, as they were reported in newspapers in both Vancouver and Victoria, sounded so impressive that awkward questions were answered even before they had been framed.

When he began the profession of architecture he entered the office of his uncle, Richard Mawson — the firm being the well-known one of Lockwood and Mawson of Bradford, England. This firm was one of the seven chosen out of all England to compete for the great Law Courts in London, and they it was who built the grand Town Hall of Bradford and most of the other great public buildings of the town. They built the whole of the model town of Saltaire — churches, mills, universities and markets. On many of these Mr. Rattenbury worked, after having served his articles for six years, gaining great practical experience from them.[10]

The last statement was, quite simply, untrue. The contest to select the design of the Law Courts had been held in 1867. The construction of Saltaire had begun in 1850 and all the town's major buildings had been completed long before Rattenbury joined the firm. Likewise he had had nothing to do with the design of Bradford's town hall which had been officially opened in 1873 when Rattenbury was a child of six. But to Rattenbury it was at most a white lie born of the knowledge that while he possessed exceptional ability and talent his true experience sounded distressingly meagre. He could and did mention his design of the Cleckheaton Town Hall which had been displayed at the Royal Academy and his losing entry in the competition for the municipal buildings at Oxford which had been highly recommended by the judge but these two achievements alone would hardly have convinced the government that he could be entrusted with the construction of buildings for which they had voted what was then the enormous sum of $600,000.

The improved version of his professional career was accepted without question, the press noting with "pleasure and pardonable pride" that the winner was a British Columbian and except for a few disgruntled local architects, whose professional jealousy was to plague Rattenbury over the years, Victorians were simply relieved that they had succeeded in anchoring the province's capital in Victoria, and they no longer had to fear the agitation of vocal mainlanders.

Many residents of Victoria had come to suspect that the continued presence of the provincial government would prove essential to the economic survival of their city. As late as 1889 an observer had been able to state, quite truthfully, that Victoria was the largest and wealthiest city in the province.[11] That wealth had come from the city's bustling harbour, the home of the sealing and whaling fleets and a prime destination for coastal shipping, and from a strong manufacturing base. On the coast only San Francisco had an iron foundry larger than Victoria's Albion Iron Works. From his factory on the banks of James Bay, William Pendray shipped his soap as far east as Calgary and the 120,000 gallons of beer produced annually by Loewen and Erb's brewery slaked thirsts all over the province. Half a dozen factories manufactured cigars and another made the boxes to put them in. Four companies made carriages and wagons and five produced boots and shoes. With a sawmill, a planing mill, two book binderies, a meat packer, a vinegar factory, a corset maker and a flour mill, Victoria in 1889 gave every evidence of being a growing city of promising prospects and over the next two years more than a dozen new business blocks rose in the commercial district close by the harbour and the tram cars of the Electric Railway Company began to rattle through the town and out to the countryside of Oak Bay.

But by 1891 the picture had begun to change. The dominion census of that year revealed that Vancouver's population had equalled Victoria's and Victorians were forced to face the fact that Vancouver, as a mainland city and as the terminus of a transcontinental railway, enjoyed advantages which would make its commercial pre-eminence inevitable. By 1892, while Vancouver continued to boom, the pace of Victoria had already begun to slow. "I found in that quiet English town of beautiful streets quite a colony of old men doing nothing but talking, fishing, and loafing at the Club,"[12] wrote Rudyard Kipling. But Kipling, who seems to have spent most of his brief visit within the walls of the Union Club, was overstating the case. For Victoria was the home of the province's oldest and wealthiest families and their presence in the city, their grand homes set in sprawling park-like grounds, had given it a unique style, which combined with its mild climate and the natural beauty of its setting, would soon promote the growth of a new and prosperous industry. Atop the Fort Street hill surrounded by ten acres of terraced gardens was "Craigdarroch," the half million dollar Scottish baronial dream castle built by coal magnate Robert Dunsmuir. "Pentrelew," the Crease family's eighteen room Italian style mansion, "Gonzales," the Pemberton home facing the sea and set in 1,200 acres, "Hollybank," the Rithet home near Beacon Hill Park, "Cary Castle," the residence of the province's Lieutenant-Governors — these and other fine homes with their extravagant decoration, their studied elegance, their carefully laid out croquet lawns and tennis courts, suggested a life of ease punctuated by gay and glittering social events. They lent to the city an air of charm and grace and gave the impression that Victoria was a very desirable place in which to live — and, more than a few shrewd entrepreneurs thought, an equally desirable place to visit.

Since 1858, when the first brick hotel had been built to accommodate those passing through the city on the way to the gold fields, Victoria had taken pride in its hotels. By 1889 the city had been able to boast of more than a dozen hotels which enjoyed almost a world wide reputation for the excellence of their accommodations. But they had been built in the heart of the city, built for people who were travelling for business rather than solely for pleasure. In the early 1890's a new kind of hotel had begun to appear on the scene, one removed from the business district, sited to take full advantage of the scenery and designed to appeal especially to tourists. The "Dallas," on the waterfront near the city's outer wharf, faced south across the straits of Juan de Fuca and offered its clientele a breathtaking view of the Olympic Mountains. And the "Mount Baker" built at the end of the streetcar tracks on the beach at Oak Bay drew customers with the equally awe-inspiring sight of the snow-capped peak of the dormant volcano in Washington State.

By 1893, when Rattenbury closed his Vancouver office and moved to Victoria, the city's future had become clear. While industries slipped away to the mainland, prosperity would hinge on the growth of the provincial civil service and on the number of tourists that could be lured to the city. And Rattenbury would find that despite its quietness and the secondary role it was forced to play, Victoria suited him very well for in Victoria he was in continuing contact with the men who ran the government's Works department and with the men who were investing in the tourist industry and over the next thirty years these men would give him the commissions on which he based the most successful architectural practice in the province.

Rattenbury moved out of the Driard and into a boarding house on Menzies Street in the James Bay district only a few minutes' walk from the Birdcages and set to work preparing the specifications for the foundation of the Parliament Buildings.

The commission he had won was one of such complexity and symbolic importance that it would have been a sobering prospect for an experienced architect and it might be supposed that Rattenbury experienced more than a few sleepless nights when he considered the problems that would have to be faced in seeing a building of almost 600,000 square feet through to completion. But Rattenbury seemed immune from the anxiety of self-doubt. Instead he soon proved that as well as having sublime confidence in his ability, he was also quite recklessly ambitious.

The work on the foundation of the buildings had begun in the summer of 1893 and Rattenbury was preparing the detailed drawings and specifications for the second and largest part of the contract when he did something quite extraordinary considering the circumstances — he entered another competition.

Not to be outdone by the Canadian province to the north, the legislators of Washington State had voted one million dollars for the construction of new Capitol buildings to be erected in Olympia and in August of 1893 invited architects to enter the competition. Rattenbury was one of the 188 architects who accepted the invitation and submitted plans. How he thought he could have coped with two huge projects in two different jurisdictions with no experience in seeing any building nearly so large or complex through to completion is hard to fathom. But it seems he gave little thought to the problems he might encounter if he won the competition or to the fact that he might lose and that failure to win would dull the brilliance of his local success by suggesting that what was good enough for B.C. was second rate in Washington. It seemed that whether he won or lost Rattenbury stood to find himself in an unpleasant position — but events proved otherwise.

Shortly before the Washington Capitol Commission announced in April 1894 that Ernest Flagg of New York City had won the competition, a rumour which was attributed directly to Rattenbury began to circulate in Victoria. Rattenbury, the story went, had been contacted by the Commission and informed that his drawings had placed first. But when he had travelled to Olympia to meet with the Commissioners he had been greeted with the question, "Well, Mr. Rattenbury, if we give you first place what is there in it for us?"[13] Rattenbury had refused to bribe the Commissioners and lost the competition.

When the story reached Seattle and Olympia it was vehemently denied. Rattenbury was branded an unmitigated liar by the Commissioners. He had reached the very pinnacle of meanness and baseness, the Seattle press stormed. The story that the Commissioners were open to bribery amounted to nothing more than shameless abuse at the hands of a disgruntled architect.[14] For his part Rattenbury too denied the rumour. "The whole story is absurd,"[15] he said but then, should anyone take his denial too seriously, he was careful to add that he had been told by people in Victoria and Seattle that there was little use in sending in plans unless he was prepared to offer a consideration for their acceptance. Whether the Commissioners had attempted to line their own pockets or not, it was a nice exercise in face saving.

Any disappointment Rattenbury felt at having lost the competition must have been tempered by some feeling of relief for work on the Legislative Buildings was not progressing as smoothly as he might have hoped.

When the tenders for the second phase of construction had been opened, it was discovered that the lowest bid exceeded by more than $17,000 the amount allocated by the government for the completion of the entire project and to make matters worse it had been submitted by an American contractor from Tacoma. The next lowest bid had come from a Victoria man, Frederick Adams, and as Rattenbury hastened to assure the government, "Should it be desired to let the Contract to the local man, Mr. Adams, he would doubtless reduce his estimate considerably ... to conform to the other Tenders."[16]

Adams, a man in his fifties who had had considerable experience as a contractor in Ontario and Quebec before coming to Victoria, should have known better but he agreed to do just what Rattenbury suggested and won the contract. Bursting with pride he ordered new stationery proclaiming that he was "Contractor for the Parliament Buildings" and he must have felt that his reputation was made and his future secure. What he had not counted on was Rattenbury's tendency to refine and improve his original plans by designing on the spot as the work progressed. Nor could he have known that Rattenbury would disregard the fact that he had agreed to court financial disaster to bring in a tender which more closely matched the architect's estimates.

Two months into the contract Adams realized he was in trouble. Adams had gone along with the government's decision to use stone from two different quarries in the construction of the buildings. But when stone from the Koksilah quarry was delivered to the site, Rattenbury ordered the entire shipment rejected claiming that it was full of flaws and that the stability of the building would be imperilled by using it.[17] Although Adams had inspected the stone and found that only 27 out of 170 pieces were unsuitable, he dared not risk challenging the architect's decision for he had been warned by the government that he would be held responsible for unsound construction. The problem for Adams lay in the fact that the stone from the second quarry on Haddington Island was more expensive and so the substitution would add to the cost of the buildings. Adams had contracted to construct the buildings for a fixed price. Any increased expenditure would eat into his profits and eventually into his capital unless he received a note from the architect releasing him from his original contract price by stating that substitutions or additions not included in the contract had added to the cost of the building. Had Adams received such a paper regarding the Haddington Island stone his problems would have been solved. But Rattenbury was most reluctant to give him the written order he had requested because the true reason for his rejecting the stone from Koksilah was becoming all too apparent and he did not want to admit that a mistake of his was adding to the cost of a building already threatening to go considerably over budget.

Rattenbury had visited the Koksilah quarry and approved the stone before Adams had contracted to use it, but when the stone had been delivered to the building site he had seen at once that it was a much darker shade of grey than he had envisioned, so dark that even if used only on the sunny southern elevation it would not blend in with the lighter stone from Haddington Island. He had rejected the stone because of colour, not because of quality and his claim that the stone was flawed had become immediately suspect when John Teague, an architect who had practiced in the city for twenty years, decided to use the rejected stone from Koksilah which still lay in piles around the site for his addition to the Jubilee Hospital. Rattenbury was unwilling to admit that an aesthetic misjudgment of his was costing the government extra so Adams went without his paper, hoping that he could recoup his increased expenditure by cutting costs elsewhere. But rather than saving on other facets of the buildings' construction, Adams found his costs mounting there too as Rattenbury continued to insist on making changes to the original plans.

Adams, becoming quite desperate, insisted that Rattenbury give him a written order for the extra work and when the architect refused, saying he would not do any such thing, he threatened to go to the Attorney-General and request an investigation into the conduct of the contract. That he had badly underestimated his adversary became obvious to him a few days later when he received a letter from the Attorney-General. Rattenbury, outmanoeuvring him, had called at the Attorney-General's office himself and complained to him that Adams had "in a manner offensive to him, disputed his authority in matters coming within his jurisdiction."[18] The Attorney-General was not pleased. "I trust that he will not have cause in the future to complain of offensive references to his position,"[19] he chided Adams.

Adams now took his case to the Chief Commissioner of Lands and Works. He had not disputed the architect's authority, he said. Neither had he been offensive to him. But Haddington stone was costing 50 per cent more than stone from Koksilah and the stonework on the south side of the building was costing more than double due to changes Rattenbury had made to the original plans.

Rattenbury lost no time in giving the Chief Commissioner his version of the controversy. "I can assure you," he said, "that Mr. Adams has no real cause for complaint." In tones of pained patience he continued, "Mr. Adams alleges I refused to give him an order for a certain comparatively small alteration . . . I told Mr. Adams I would at once measure and value this work and give him an order — but Mr. Adams informed me that he would accept no valuation of mine for the work — and then broke into a storm of abuse directed against my authority and even the Government's."

Rattenbury dismissed Adams' complaint that the Haddington stone was proving to be even more expensive than he had anticipated. "This, even if true, which I doubt — is Mr. Adams' own lookout — Surely Mr. Adams does not suppose a Committee is going to investigate into the causes and results of his own lack of business knowledge."

Ending with a veiled threat, Rattenbury suggested to the Chief Commissioner the only course of action he felt appropriate. ". . . unless Mr. Adams is given peremptorily to understand that he is subject to my authority and that no attention will be paid to his complaints against myself . . . I cannot see how the work can proceed."[20]

And taking Rattenbury's advice the Chief Commissioner did adopt a peremptory tone when he wrote to Adams telling him exactly where he stood. The architect's decisions were final, he wrote, and his orders must be obeyed. In addition he must be treated with courtesy. Unless Adams could prove that Rattenbury was guilty of misconduct "it will be useless for you to prolong the complaint, as contempt of the Architect's authority will not be tolerated."[21]

Adams should have realized that he was finished but he hung on hoping he could salvage his reputation and preserve his solvency. The final blow came when he submitted for Rattenbury's approval an accounting of what was owing to him for work already completed on the buildings. Rattenbury refused to sign it, insisting that Adams had already been paid in full and maintaining that, rather than payment due, Adams was asking for an advance or a loan.

"If we advance Mr. Adams money beyond what is earned where are these advances to end?",[22] he wondered to the Chief Commissioner.

Adams had exhausted his capital and his credit had run dry. He was, as he put it to the Chief Commissioner, "in the unpleasant position of not being able to pay my weekly wages."[23] He had no choice but to give up the contract.

Rattenbury felt the controversy over, the issue closed. But to Adams the dispute was far from settled. And the government, although they had consistently defended their architect to Adams, suspected that the contractor had not been dealt with altogether fairly. John Turner, who became premier in 1895, later remembered, "It was evident that the architect was very anxious to keep down expenses to the lowest point. He had boasted that there would be no extras and he was evidently trying to keep to that statement." And as for the differences that existed between Rattenbury's and Adams' valuations of the work completed, "The government was not very confident of the architect's figures," Turner said, "for they had found very serious clerical errors in the figures sent in by the architect."

The government had arranged several meetings between Rattenbury and Adams in an attempt to reach an agreement but some of these meetings were "quite hostile" and both men had become "exceedingly excited neither willing to admit the statement of his opponent."[24] And Rattenbury had hardly endeared himself to the government when he submitted a bill for $3,000 for attending these meetings.

Adams was not going to let the matter drop. He intended to remain a persistent thorn in the architect's side, pestering both Rattenbury and the government until he was vindicated. But then a tragic accident removed him from the scene. On the night of March 22, 1895 three months after he had given up the contract, Adams sailed out of Victoria aboard the little forty-nine ton steamer *Velos* bound for Haddington Island. Caught by a southeast gale an hour after leaving port, the *Velos* refused to answer to her helm, was struck broadside by a heavy sea and thrown onto a ledge of rock near Trial Island. Adams and four members of the steamer's crew were drowned. The day after his death a chilling discovery was made — the afternoon of the day he sailed, Adams, perhaps as the result of some strange premonition, had written his will.

Eighteen months after Adams' death the stonework, under the direction of a new contractor, was completed and to mark the occasion the government treated the workmen to a celebratory dinner at the Mount Baker Hotel. Amid the general bonhomie cries went up for the architect and Rattenbury toasted the assembly saying, "The pleasantest part of this work has been that it has gone through with such good feeling that there is not a man employed on it that I cannot tonight shake hands with."[25] A statement that no doubt rung true since he could scarcely shake hands with Adams.

3

Rattenbury versus the Chief Commissioner
I beg to remind you . . .

Commissioner of Lands and Works George Bohun Martin joined in the applause that greeted Rattenbury's friendly remarks at the Mount Baker Hotel but he might not have felt so inclined to cheer had the dinner been held a year later for by then he had found himself cast in the role of the architect's adversary and had learned that it could be an aggravating experience. So aggravating that in 1898 at the age of 57 Martin would resign from public life.

A successful cattleman from the South Thompson district first elected to the legislature in 1882, he had had little practical experience to equip him to handle the problems which would arise in the Works section of his ministry. Justifiably modest about his unspectacular political career, Martin who had served as a midshipman in the navy during the Crimean War, remained proud of his family's military tradition and somewhat wistful that he had been the only son to break with that tradition. His fondest memory was of pacing the decks of the *Victory* with his father, Flag Captain G. Bohun Martin, and his grandfather, Admiral Sir Thomas Briggs, and his real interest lay not in politics or the parliament buildings but in Victoria's still busy harbour.*

Martin, as a member of the legislature, had voted against the construction of the new government buildings. And Rattenbury bore this fact in mind as he prepared to do battle over the parliament buildings' marble — a battle in which, Rattenbury made sure, Martin would remain unaware that he had been engaged.

In 1893, when even the lowest tender submitted for the second phase of construction had proven to be much higher than he had estimated, Rattenbury had suggested to the government that $44,000

---

* Martin died in 1933 at the age of ninety-one. "He refused to go to the hospital," the *Colonist* reported, "insisting that he be allowed to remain in his home, overlooking the sea he loved so well." *Colonist*, August 30, 1933.

worth of marble might be omitted "without injuring the . . . appearance of the building."[1] To the former Chief Commissioner Forbes G. Vernon and his deputy this had seemed an eminently sensible suggestion and they must have felt gratified that their architect had shown that he was willing to compromise his original artistic decisions in the cause of budgetary responsibility

But Rattenbury had had no intention of omitting the marble from the completed building. Biding his time, waiting for two years until November of 1895 when the much-admired magnificent pile was rising grandly above the shores of James Bay and a general election had resulted in the appointment of a new Chief Commissioner, he reintroduced the subject of the marble in a letter to Chief Commissioner Martin.

I have ventured to place in the Executive Council Room, the samples of marble and stained glass which I have received. So beautiful are these in themselves, and so much time and money has been expended by the firms sending these samples that I trust you will at least examine them before coming to an irrevocable decision.

The Marble is so urgent a matter, and the omission of it would be so serious an injury to the building, that I trust you will reconsider this matter.

The Legislative Hall is the most important feature in the Interior of the building and is the leading "Motif" of the whole design. The exterior suggesting and emphasizing this feature. The Grand Entrance has been made rich and ornate — as an appropriate entrance — through this you pass into the great Domical Hall surmounted by the Dome — then onwards to the Legislative Hall.

The grandeur of the whole scheme would be absolutely ruined should the culminating feature "the Legislative Hall" be poor and commonplace, and it would be so if the Marble is omitted, for the whole character of the Hall depends entirely on the rich and massive marble columns and we cannot in any adequate way replace these with any cheaper imitation material. No future expenditure, however large, could in any way compensate for the omission — and the amount, in comparison to the cost and character of the buildings, is comparatively small, considering the marvellous improvement it would effect.[2]

Members of the government, perhaps unaware that Rattenbury had assured their predecessors in 1893 that the same marble could be omitted without injury to the appearance of the building, had viewed the samples and capitulated — just as Rattenbury had guessed they would.

By 1897 Rattenbury had been hovering over the construction of the buildings for four years and his patience had worn thin. With the buildings only a few months away from completion, he had neither the time nor the self-control to humour the Chief Commissioner or to travel circuitous routes to get his own way. When in the spring of 1897 Rattenbury was informed by Chief Commissioner Martin that the government had decided to use the East Block, designed to house the Land Registry Office, as a Museum and place the laboratories of the Mining Bureau in the basement, Rattenbury wasted no time in letting Martin know what he thought of politicians who dabbled in design.

"I firmly believe," he wrote to Martin, "that to carry out the instructions I have received from you in regard to these alterations will result in an extremely inconvenient, unsanitary, and evil-smelling arrangement, bad at any time, but almost ludicrous when occuring [*sic*] in a new and large building of the costly character of the New Parliament Buildings."

He was convinced, he told Martin, that "these arrangements will receive the universal condemnation and ridicule which they will merit.

"I speak strongly, because I feel strongly in this matter, and I must clear myself from all appearance of concurring in the suggested arrangement, for should I do so my reputation as an Architect will inevitably suffer."

Should Martin refuse to accept his advice "the responsibility (of what I consider will be spoiling the buildings) will rest on you,"[3] he warned.

Martin responded coolly, telling Rattenbury that he saw no reason to alter his decision as regards to the location of the Museum but he would reconsider siting the Department of Mines below it.

This did little to appease the architect and he answered with a letter of such passionate indignation that the Executive Council meeting on May 19, 1897 decided that the most charitable course would be to permit him to withdraw his "highly intemperate" letter as it had been intimated he wished to do.[4]

But if Rattenbury had wished to reconsider his intemperate language of May, by September he was again in high dudgeon when he discovered that the fittings of the Museum he had been asked to design had not only been designed without his knowledge but had also already been ordered without his approval.

Furious, he threw off a stinging letter to Martin, a letter alive with the impatient dashes with which he habitually littered his writing and which seemed to increase with his level of exasperation.

As Architect of the Parliament Buildings — pardon me for reminding you — that the design of all work that enters into the buildings, must pass through my hands — *so long as I am in charge and responsible for the work.*

After I have delivered up the buildings to you, as absolutely completed according to existing Contracts — you may introduce any materials or workmanship you may deem fit — but I strongly object to receiving the credit for workmanship that I have never even seen —

Should it be, Sir, that you decide that my professional advice & recommendations are not worthy of confidence —

Believe me — much as I would regret, to sever my connection with the Parliament Buildings especially after having for so many years — exerted every faculty — and made such painstaking endeavours — to carry out the works to as perfect and satisfactory a conclusion as possible — Still — I am ready to resign my position as Architect of the Buildings a position no longer tolerable, if not accompanied by confidence — and so afford you the opportunity of obtaining other professional advice and assistance — in which you could place confidence.[5]

Rattenbury knew that his reputation as an architect depended on the favourable critical acceptance of the Parliament Buildings and while the changes approved by Martin might not be drastic, they were highly visible. Convinced that Martin would ruin the buildings, Rattenbury, always quick to anger, had reacted with sputtering indignation. But when his blood had cooled, he realized that Martin's actions had been prompted not so much by an irresistible urge to improve on the original design but rather by a new-found determination to assert his authority. Rattenbury, with self-assured arrogance, had all but taken over the Department of Lands and Works and Martin, perhaps feeling rather sheepish, had decided that it was time for him to regain control now that the buildings were near completion and he could safely risk precipitating the architect's resignation. The more Rattenbury protested and the more insistently he demanded the right to exercise artistic control, the more determined Martin became to put him in his place. Rattenbury would have to curb his impatience and control his temper if he hoped to regain the upper hand.

A few weeks later when he received a letter from W. S. Gore, Martin's deputy, informing him that the Superintendent of Education was unhappy about the architect's intention to remove a partition wall in his office, Rattenbury faced the new confrontation with uncharacteristic composure.

Gore described himself as being somewhat surprised to learn of these changes. "I have not heard you mention the matter," Gore wrote, "and I must request you to call at my office and show me what you propose doing before you take any steps in the matter."

"I beg to remind you," Gore continued, "that as the professional deputy head of the Department I expect you to consult me on any material changes in connection with the building. . . ."[6]

Rattenbury's answer was prompt, politely hostile, and imperiously detached.

"In response to your rather peremptory demand that I should call at your office and show you what I propose doing before I take any steps in the matter — I have to inform you that I have already let the contract for this work."

Rattenbury, who understood well the psychological advantage of engaging in a battle of wills on his home ground continued, "Should you desire any information on this matter I shall be happy to make an appointment with you at my office. . . ."

In the meantime he requested that Gore "be good enough not to issue any instructions in the Buildings . . . as such instructions confuse and lead to endless trouble.

"As regards your desire that I should consult you in respect to every small change rendered necessary in my opinion to insure the due and satisfactory completion of the Parliament Buildings, I am afraid were I to do so I should take up more of your time than you could spare. I have been accustomed therefore to rely upon my own judgement and I think it wiser to do so as I have found that non-professional interference in technical work produces costly and disastrous results."[7]

This time it was Gore's turn to be vexed. Although he might not be an architect, Gore who had studied civil engineering and had served as the Surveyor General of British Columbia before becoming Deputy Commissioner, would hardly have considered himself as a non-professional. He wrote to Martin, enclosing his original letter and Rattenbury's reply which, he complained, "is not only framed in language discourteous to me but sets at defiance the authority of the Department in connection with the expenditure of public money on the Parliament Buildings."[8]

Martin apparently felt that the only course left to him was to take direct action. Howell, a government employee who was serving as Rattenbury's Clerk of Works and who had been taking his orders directly from the architect, was called to the Chief Commissioner's office and told to ignore Rattenbury's instructions regarding the removal of the wall.

If Martin had expected an explosion when Rattenbury discovered what had taken place, he must have been rather nonplussed by the mildness of the architect's response:

I understand from Mr. Howell, that he was imperatively ordered by you ... to make certain alterations in the Education Dept according to your Instructions — Knowing that you were acting without professional advice — and convinced that you were making a serious blunder — I had previously instructed Mr. Howell not to make any change in the Contract work except with my sanction — As Mr. Howell — in my agreement with the Government — is expressly stated to be under my orders — I was very much surprised to hear of the Government giving orders to him direct — I consequently asked Mr. Howell to produce them — He informs me however — that altho the work has been carried out — that you refuse to issue the order to him in writing —

In addition to the above matter — the Government on previous occassion [sic] have insisted — in spite of my advice & remonstrations — in making several very serious changes in the arrangement of the Parliament Buildings — which changes will eventually entail costly expenditures.

I feel it therefore due to myself — that the responsibility of these changes shall rest upon the proper shoulders — at such times — when all matters — pertaining to the Parliament Buildings are brought before the Legislature.[9]

Martin, it seems, was about to be hoist on his own petard. It was November 1897, less than three months away from the buildings' official opening. So little work was left to do that Rattenbury now had no cause to concern himself with the possibility of Martin's further interference in design matters. It seems likely that Rattenbury, in order to estimate the total amount of commission due him, had begun to study his accounts and had calculated that the actual cost of the completed buildings would be close to one million dollars. By insisting on changes Martin would now have to share with Rattenbury any blame that might be attached to the expenditure of almost $400,000 over the amount voted by the Legislature and by refusing to give a written order for those changes he had confused the issue by making it difficult for any future investigation to ascertain just who had altered the original plans.

Martin, finally appreciating the problems he had created for himself flew, rather belatedly, into action.

On December 3, 1897 he wrote to the architect informing him that he would refuse to pay the contractor for any work done that had not first been sanctioned by the Works Department. And as Rattenbury soon discovered when he submitted a personal account, he had decided to hold back any further payments to the architect for services rendered.

Although irritated by this turn of events, Rattenbury seems to have enjoyed witnessing Martin's rather frantic attempts to assume control. When he learned that the contractor had been ordered by Martin to stop work on a sidewalk until he had received a written order from the Department, Rattenbury couldn't resist the temptation to needle the Chief Commissioner.

"As regards this sidewalk," he wrote, "as a matter of fact — it was ordered by me — at the request of yourself and Mr. Turner (the Premier) — of course — However — if you desire me not to take any instruction from you — unless in writing — I am quite prepared not to do so — But if you will permit me to remind you — that on a previous ocassion [sic] — on which you issued orders — which you insisted should be carried out — You refused to give those orders in writing — and I wrote to you about the matter ... with no avail." And on two separate occasions, Martin had named two different individuals from whom Rattenbury should seek final approval before proceeding with any work.

"There certainly seems to be a little confusion in these various mandates," Rattenbury sighed.[10]

It is not too difficult to guess what Martin's reaction to this letter might have been, but publicly he had no choice but to grit his teeth and feign equanimity, for while Rattenbury might scorn his authority and try his patience, even he had to admit that the architect had produced buildings which did the government proud.

Just how he had managed to do it is hard to explain. There had been little in his early training to equip him for a project of the magnitude and complexity of the Legislative Buildings. And the buildings were designed in a style with which Rattenbury was not really enamoured, a style which he seldom used again. After the Legislative Buildings almost every major building that he designed was a variation on French château architecture, a style with which he never tired of experimenting.

A persistent and tantalizing rumour insists that the Legislative Buildings were inspired by the palace of an Indian prince and a variation of this story has it that they are a direct copy of that building. Like other long lasting rumours this one probably contains a grain of truth but it is not necessary to look to India or an Indian prince for the possible genesis of the story. When Lockwood and Mawson entered the competition for the design of Bradford's Town Hall they submitted two designs. Their gothic design won the contest but both architects admitted that they preferred the second design which they described as classical. It is possible then that Rattenbury's design for the Legislative Buildings, which he himself described as free classical, was an adaptation of Lockwood's losing design for the Bradford Town Hall. Richard Mawson felt that the firm of Mawson and Hudson should have received a percentage of the fees Rattenbury collected for the design of the buildings and his refusal to pay resulted in strained relations that lasted for many years. But whether this was because Rattenbury had used a design belonging to the firm or whether it was because Mawson felt it only fair that Rattenbury should share part of his first large commission in payment for the training he had received, is unknown.

Whatever the case, the Parliament Buildings were a stunning achievement.

Just as the government had hoped they were seen as "an imposing monument to the architectural skill, natural resources and commendable enterprise of this most western Canadian province."

The Victoria *Colonist* was decidedly enthusiastic. "The beauty of the structure calls forth the admiration of everyone who has seen it, while the perfection of the work and the thoroughness in which the details have been carried out is a surprise to visitors. In general design and in choice of the stone for the buildings the good taste and judgement displayed has been decidedly happy, the result being a harmonious picture delightful to the eye."

Obviously impressed by the buildings' size as much as their appearance, the *Colonist* informed its readers that the buildings covered an area of more than an acre. "The front of the building including the wings is 500 and the central building is 200 feet deep. To the top of the gilded figure of Captain Vancouver which surmounts the dome is a distance of 165 feet ... if the outside walls were all placed in a straight line they would extend half a mile in length."

The completed buildings proved, the *Colonist* said, that the choice of Mr. Rattenbury as architect had been a wise one.

Only later, after the buildings had opened, would it be discovered that Rattenbury's design had been guilty of singular faults and omissions.

Soon after they moved into their new meeting place it became evident to the Members of the Legislative Assembly that while the new hall might be grand and imposing it was also a room in which it was very difficult for them to hear one another. Some resourceful soul suggested that the bad acoustic properties of the hall might be corrected by hanging salmon net from the ceiling on a framework of steel wires and the members noted with some relief that this humble addition resulted in a marked improvement.[12]

Strangely, the members of the press, whom Rattenbury would assiduously court throughout his career, had been treated in a rather offhanded way in his original plans. Around the upper level of the Legislative Hall, Rattenbury's plans called for three spectators' galleries for the public, ladies and reporters. It seemed that Rattenbury, if he had considered the matter at all, felt that reporters were perfectly capable of taking notes with their papers balanced on their knees. Reporters who covered the first session in 1898 grumbled loudly and were far from mollified when at the next session they were seated on the floor of the house behind the legislators. The situation was corrected in 1900 when the Speaker's Throne was moved forward to allow the construction of the press' own gallery which reporters found to be fairly acceptable except for several glaring errors such as the provision of sloping desks and stationary seats "which can never be satisfactory to people doing much writing."

Apparently Lieutenant-Governors were not so likely to be vocal about their complaints and it was not until 1913, fifteen years after the buildings were opened, that it was brought to the government's attention that another Rattenbury omission was greatly inconveniencing the Lieutenant-Governor and his guests. To entertain visiting dignitaries and to play host at other social functions more properly held at the Legislative Buildings than at his official residence, the

Lieutenant-Governor had been provided with a suite of rooms on the third floor which offered a fine view of the harbour, the city and the Sooke hills. What they didn't have, according to a memo from a most sympathetic and understanding caretaker, was anything in the way of washroom facilities. "As the rooms now occupied by the Lieutenant-Governor are liable to always remain such," he wrote, "I would respectfully draw your attention to the entire absence of anything in the shape of Lavatory accommodation for either Ladies or Gentlemen, it has been found very akward [sic] at times when Entertainments were in progress we are compelled to furnish the crudest kind of accommodation for the Ladies and Gentlemen have a long way to travel before reaching a Lavatory, which on such occasions are always crowded."[13]

As opening day approached, these deficiencies, if they had been known, would have been dismissed as irrelevancies for the whole province was agog at the grandeur of the new government buildings.

Seven thousand invitations described as being ornate in the extreme had been issued and as people began to flood into Victoria filling every available hotel room a plea went out to Victorians to open their homes to accommodate the visitors. The official opening of the buildings had been timed to coincide with the opening of the legislative session of 1898 but, as the *Colonist* promised its readers, elaborate preparations had been made and the ceremonies would be far more imposing than anything hitherto seen and 4,000 people clamoured for one of the 650 tickets which would permit them to occupy a seat in the house.

On opening day, February 10, 1898 the sun shone, albeit intermittently, military bands played, crowds cheered, "the brave new flag of Canada fluttered from the giant flagpole" and the government closed the schools and presented each happy youngster with a picture of the new Parliament Buildings.

Inside the Legislative Hall the cream of provincial society, vying for breathing space yet unwilling to sacrifice any part of the proceedings to personal comfort, listened to inspiring patriotic anthems sung by the Arion Choir, to prayers offered by the bishops of the church and to the reading, by the Lieutenant-Governor, of a Speech from the Throne of welcome brevity.

Celebrations continued into the night. While a display of fireworks brightened the night sky, Lieutenant-Governor McInnes hosted a grand dinner at Government House. Inside the new buildings the band of the Fifth Regiment entertained the crowds that had accepted the government's invitation to come and explore the buildings and to peruse the collections of special historical interest displayed in various government departments.

It had been an exciting, gala day but as the *Colonist* put it "one factor appeared wanting to satisfy the public sense of the fitness of things" — the architect had not been present to accept the honours of his authorship.

Neither shyness nor humility had dictated Rattenbury's absence. Nor was he a magnanimous soul likely to modestly step aside so that his assistants could receive the praise and congratulations. Only one thing could have prompted his absence that day. He had, quite simply, more important things to do.

4

Klondike
the air is so exhilarating

On July 17, 1897 the steamer *Portland* sailing out of St. Michael, Alaska docked at Seattle and off-loaded sixty-eight prospectors and two tons of gold and the stampede to the Klondike was on! For years tales of the gold that was to be found along northern rivers had filtered down to the south. But the rumours had been so vague that only seasoned prospectors, men who felt at home with Yukon loneliness, had drifted about the territory studying gravelly river banks for the tell-tale glint of yellow. Now, suddenly, everyone knew that the stories had been true. There was proof — two tons of it — on the docks at Seattle. As the electrifying news spread up and down the coast, across the continent and around the world, thousands of men and women prepared to take part in what would become the greatest gold rush in history.

Ho for the Klondike! was the cry that rang out as west coast cities leapt joyously into competition each claiming to be the best jumping off place for the northern goldfields. While San Francisco and Seattle both proclaimed that they were "The Gateway to the Klondike," Victoria enjoyed a distinct advantage over the American cities. As the B.C. Board of Trade pointed out in a widely circulated pamphlet, Victoria was the gateway to "The quickest route, The nearest route, The safest route, The cheapest route," and most important of all, "The Duty Saving Route."

The goldfields were in Canada and Canadian law required that each prospector entering the territory bring with him enough supplies to make him self-sufficient for a year. Prospectors could avoid import duties if they purchased their supplies in a Canadian city and soon Victoria's Johnson and Yates Streets became clogged with piles of carefully packed supplies ready to be hauled down to the docks for loading aboard a Klondike-bound steamer.

Tappan Adney, a correspondent for *Harper's Illustrated Weekly,* observed that as early as August the streets of Victoria were thronged with strange men.

They are buying horses, and watching men who in front of stores explain the "diamond hitch"; they are buying thick warm woolens; belts that go round the waist, with flaps that button down over little compartments; little bags of buckskin, with gathering-strings at the top; heavy iron shod shoes ... and moccasins of moose hide ...

During the winter of 1897 Klondike gold and the business it could attract to the city became Victoria's preoccupation.

Victoria sells mittens and hats and coats only for Klondike. Flour and bacon, tea and coffee, are sold only for Klondike. Shoes and saddles and boats, shovels and sacks — everything for Klondike![1]

It seemed as though everyone wanted to get in on the act. "Don't go to the Klondike without an Albion stove," the Albion Iron Works warned and introduced three new portable models. Thomas Earle, "Wholesale Grocer," became Thomas Earle, "Klondike Outfitter" and only the most foolhardy would have dared venture north without first stopping at Thomas Shotbolt's drugstore to pick up a supply of Vasoline after reading that "It cures Coughs, Sore throats, Cuts, Burns, Frostbite. It is the best Lubricant for Metal Implements. It softens and preserves leather."

Some Victorians were content to remain in town, making their fortune by supplying prospectors. But for others this wasn't enough. For a time they struggled to control their growing excitement, but in the end they gave in to feelings that the world and opportunity were passing them by. Like the proprietor of the San Francisco House who announced in December 1897 that his large and well assorted stock of Gentlemens Furnishings would be absolutely sold at cost as he was leaving for the Klondike in January, they sold their businesses or quit their jobs, bought their miner's licence at the Customs' House on Wharf Street and boarded the first boat bound for Skagway or Dyea.

Rattenbury's seething impatience to be part of the adventure had added to his choler during the autumn months of 1897 and his threat to resign as architect of the Parliament Buildings had not been altogether empty. It was impossible for anyone with even the slightest imagination or adventurous spirit to avoid being caught up in the excitement and it was worse for Rattenbury who had hit upon a scheme for making his fortune — if only he could find the time to organize and promote the enterprise.

Recalling this period some years later, Rattenbury made what was for an architect a rather strange boast. During the winter of 1897, Rattenbury said, he had purchased some sixty head of cattle which after a perilous expedition had arrived in Dawson City in the Yukon just in time to prevent the residents from starving. Altruistic though it may sound, it was a venture motivated almost solely by profit for in Dawson that hungry winter cattle brought as much as a thousand dollars a head. It was a shrewd but rather improbable investment for him to have made since he had had no past experience in shipping cattle and while Rattenbury had a fertile imagination, a busy brain his friends said, it seems unlikely that the idea would have occurred to him if he had not met Pat Burns, a man who would play an important role in his career over the next few years.

A short plump little man with an amused twinkle in his eyes, Burns, through a combination of good luck, good humour, imagination and honesty, was already well on his way to earning his reputation as a man who became a millionaire without losing a friend. Born into an Irish Catholic family in Ontario in 1856, at twenty-two Burns had come west to homestead at Minnedosa some 150 miles outside Winnipeg. An unenthusiastic farmer, he soon set up a freight business, hauling supplies from Winnipeg to Minnedosa and trailing cattle back to the city. In 1885 he won the contract to supply fresh meat to railway workers constructing a line from Regina to Prince Albert. In 1890 he turned up in Calgary supplying workers on the new line being built between that city and Edmonton and a few years later he followed development into the interior of British Columbia establishing his headquarters in Nelson and shipping fresh meat to Rossland, Kaslo, Greenwood and other towns in the Kootenays.

During this time Rattenbury, too, was in the Kootenays working for a new client, the Bank of Montreal. In 1896 he had won a competition sponsored by the bank for the design of their head office in Victoria. The building, reminiscent of a French château, had pleased the company so well that they had asked Rattenbury to design buildings for their planned expansion into the interior of the province.

It seems likely that in some Kootenay town, probably Nelson or Rossland, Rattenbury and Burns' paths had crossed and each had recognized the other as a man with an eye to the main chance. And in 1897 the main chance was the Klondike.

From past experience Burns knew that he would find a ready market for his cattle in Dawson City. On August 4th, just two weeks after the *Portland*'s arrival signalled the beginning of the gold rush, Burns purchased eighty-five head of cattle in Alberta and shipped them to Vancouver where they were loaded aboard a steamer bound for Skagway. They crossed the White Pass in the last days of August and were driven overland to the Yukon River where they were slaughtered, tied on to rafts and floated down the river to Dawson arriving there on November 4th.

Encouraged by Burns, Rattenbury probably invested in this venture and his boast years later that he had saved the inhabitants of Dawson from starving was very near the truth for as early as October of 1897 it was reported that the stores had nothing to sell and a famine was predicted by early spring. With beef selling at $1.25 a pound healthy profits would have been absolutely guaranteed if it had not been for the losses faced on the last leg of the journey. The Yukon River could be unpredictable and a hurriedly constructed raft piled high with quarters of beef was not the easiest craft to handle. More than one of Burns' makeshift scows had lost their cargo of meat in the icy waters when they had been caught by the swift current, dragged into the wrong part of the river and dashed to pieces on the rocks. What was needed was a reliable system of water transportation, one which could guarantee the safe arrival of an entire herd of live cattle at Dawson. Knowing that if he could devise such a system he would be assured of large contracts from the P. Burns Company, Rattenbury set his busy brain to work on the problem.

For cattle and for men, the safest and most direct route to the Klondike began aboard a steamer sailing out of Vancouver or Victoria for the Lynn Canal and the Alaskan ports of Skagway or Dyea. From there the trail led through the coastal mountains over the White or Chilkoot passes to Lake Bennett and the headwaters of the Yukon River. From Bennett, the rest of the journey could be made by water — across Lake Bennett, known for its cold winds, across warmer Tagish Lake and the shallow waters of Marsh Lake to Miles Canyon where the river narrowed and boiled through sheer rock walls, over the White Horse Rapids and on to Lake LaBarge, Thirty Mile River and the Five Finger Rapids, where 250 miles upriver from Dawson, the waters flowed into the main stream of the Yukon River.

What was needed, Rattenbury decided, was a fleet of sturdy river boats, large enough to shoot the rapids but with a shallow draft to enable them to ply the boggy waters of Marsh Lake. They could be built in Vancouver or Victoria, knocked down and carried over the White Pass and re-assembled at Lake Bennett.

The honour of being present at the opening of his Parliament Buildings had paled beside the excitement of establishing this business and the anxiety that some other entrepreneur might have had the same idea. A week before the great ceremony took place Rattenbury left Victoria for London hoping that he could convince British capitalists to invest in his "Lake Bennett and Klondike Navigation Company."

In London it seems his salesmanship failed him, but by the spring of 1898 the construction of his first steamer, backed at least in part by local capital, was well underway. Rather than build a complete boat in Vancouver, parts and equipment had been packed in to Lake Bennett where, in some secrecy, the company established a mill a few miles along the shore from Bennett where thousands of Klondikers were encamped by the lake, building an oddly assorted fleet of rafts, canoes, skiffs and kayaks as they waited for spring melt.

When Pat Burns, as good as his word, announced in May that he and Rattenbury had signed a contract for more than forty thousand dollars to ship his cattle to Dawson, the success of the venture seemed assured. But Rattenbury was not satisfied. As manager of the Lake Bennett and Klondike Navigation Company he was determined to tap every possible source of profit. His steamers were fitted out for passengers as well as cargo but he knew that he would not find customers among the desperate, driven men who had spent their savings on supplies and arrived on the shores of Lake Bennett penniless. Instead he would have to sell his steamers' service to businessmen and monied adventurers — just the people who might be discouraged from venturing north by the stories of horrible hardships endured the previous winter.

The way in to Bennett lay over the White and Chilkoot passes. The White Pass was lower and wider but the journey was some ten miles longer than the trail over the Chilkoot. At the summit of both

44

passes the North West Mounted Police waited, ready to turn back anyone who had not brought with them the ton of supplies calculated to make them self-sufficient for a year. For well-heeled Klondikers this presented no problem. They simply paid for their supplies to be packed in over the White Pass while they walked the Chilkoot unburdened and without too much difficulty. Thousands who couldn't afford this luxury went through hell upon earth and by the spring of '98 tales of the suffering they had endured had made the Chilkoot synonymous with inhuman toil, defeat and death.

From Dyea to Lake Bennett over the Chilkoot was a distance of only thirty-five miles and on thousands of mass produced Klondike maps it seemed to represent nothing more than a good, stiff hike. The first thirteen miles, from Dyea to Sheep Camp seemed easy enough, especially in winter when the trail led up a frozen creek bed. At Sheep Camp a stampeder cached his first load and returned to Dyea for the second, shuttling back and forth between the two some thirty-five to forty times until by the time he had packed all his supplies into Sheep Camp he had travelled over seven hundred miles, half of them staggering under the weight of a sixty to eighty pound pack. The next four miles gave him a real taste of what was to come. The trail rose steadily upward until a mile from the Scales, the stopping-off place at the base of the pass, the incline became a steady twenty-five degrees. Stumbling and cursing, with straining muscles and aching backs, stampeders trudged up that last mile and then, at the Scales, they had their first look at the summit. Many went no further. They sold their gear for whatever it would bring and returned home — for the trail over the pass seemed to lead straight up. Twelve hundred steps, the "Golden Stairs," had been hacked into the frozen snow and over the pass struggled an endless line of men, each burdened with a heavy pack. Locked in step, they plodded up the thirty-five degree incline toward the notch high in the towering wall of blinding white snow that marked the summit of the pass. Bad enough to have to cross the Chilkoot once, it required almost inhuman fortitude to face crossing and recrossing it, over and over again. A man who had crossed the Chilkoot was a man who had proved his mettle, a man who had passed a supreme test of his body and spirit. And when he finally reached Bennett he was anxious to talk, eager to compare stories with other stampeders who had crossed their Chilkoot too. Reading these stories in outside newspapers, many people began to wonder if even a fortune in gold was worth the risk. Then in April of '98 even more alarming news reached Victoria. A spring blizzard followed by a warm spell had brought an avalanche thundering down into the pass. Hundreds had been buried, more than sixty killed and it was suspected that still more bodies were trapped beneath the snow.

Rattenbury knew that while some would be undaunted by this latest news, other less intrepid adventurers would decide against venturing north unless, of course, they could be encouraged by a first-hand account of a journey over the Chilkoot by someone who would not seek to dramatize himself with stories of danger faced and hardship endured. Being able to think of no one who fitted that description better than himself, Rattenbury decided to walk the route in the summer of '98 and to underline the fact that he viewed the journey as little more than a pleasant jaunt he took with him his bride, Florence Eleanor Nunn, who surely must have been one of only a few women to find herself honeymooning in a tent at Sheep Camp surrounded by dirty, dog-tired men and the stench of rotting horses appearing from beneath the melting snows.

But then Florrie at twenty-seven was a mature and not particularly attractive bride who might have counted herself lucky to have married any man at all, much less a handsome, ambitious man of some wealth and great promise.

They were married in a very quiet ceremony on Saturday evening June 18, 1898 exchanging their vows in the presence of a few friends at Christ Church Cathedral, Florrie proudly wearing a handsome crescent of diamonds presented to her by the groom and carrying a bouquet of white roses and stephanotis, a gift of Rattenbury's older brother, John,[2] now a sea captain who had come to Victoria to attend the wedding and to travel north with the couple to inspect his brother's fleet of steamers.

The next morning the party sailed for Vancouver to begin their journey to Dyea and the Chilkoot Pass. It was, of course, more business trip than honeymoon and a week after their marriage Rattenbury took time out to write a letter, which duly found its way onto the pages of the *Colonist*, in which he described their crossing of the Chilkoot Pass in terms that would have encouraged even the faintest heart.

"There were really no difficulties on the trail," he wrote. "We simply strolled along and actually did not know that we had come to the dreaded part of the Pass until we were told that we were at the summit. You can judge by this how ridiculous and exaggerated the accounts we have read of it must have been."

Florrie, he reported, had declared that she had often found the walk to Oak Bay and back more tiring and as for himself, well, ". . . really the air is so exhilarating that I myself did not feel the slightest fatigue."[3]

Martha Louise Black, a truly redoubtable woman, who would later deliver her baby alone in a Dawson cabin, become manager of a Dawson sawmill and win election to the federal parliament, crossed the pass two weeks later and described her experiences somewhat differently.

"I was straining every nerve, every ounce of physical endurance in that upward climb," she wrote. "There were moments when, with sweating forehead, pounding heart, and panting breath I felt I could go no farther.

"— stumbling — staggering — crawling — God pity me!

"Another breath! Another step — God give me strength. How far away that summit! Can I ever make it?"[4]

". . . the scenery is so interesting," Rattenbury wrote, "that if people only knew how insignificant the trip was, they would run up here for a day or two, just for the fun of it."

There were some nasty places on the trail, he admitted and it was hard to imagine horses picking their way along the boulder strewn path. "But when walking these places present no difficulties, but are simply good fun . . ."

For the less easily convinced Rattenbury provided an explanation for previous accounts which had stressed the rigours of the journey. "I fancy the descriptions of the hardships and terrors of the trail must have been written at so much a line."

Employees of the Lake Bennett and Klondike Navigation Company had made careful preparations for Rattenbury's visit and when his party walked into Bennett on the evening of June 25th they found everything in readiness for their arrival. Five tents, "capitally arranged" with terraces in front, had been pitched on the shores of Lake Bennett and after a good dinner in the dining tent and "a hearty laugh over the insurmountable perils we had overcome," Rattenbury listened with satisfaction to the news that his company promised to be at least as successful as he had hoped.

Their first vessel the *Ora* had created quite a sensation when she had steamed unannounced and at full speed up to Bennett from their mill camp. As well as being a great surprise to everyone, the company's steamers were looked upon as splendid craft, the topic of conversation from Bennett to Juneau. In testament to their reliability and the speed with which they could complete the journey from Bennett to Dawson they had been entrusted with the mail and, even more impressively, with the supplies for the Mounted Police.

If the trip left something to be desired as a honeymoon, it did provide Florrie with one sentimental moment. Rattenbury had decided to name two of his steamers after his wife using the short and familiar version of her given names Florence Eleanor. The *Flora* had been launched sometime earlier but Florrie was there to christen the latest addition to the fleet the *Nora* and then climb aboard her for the trip to Dawson.

The *Nora* steamed through Bennett, Tagish and Marsh Lakes at a steady nine and a half knots arriving at the entrance to Miles Canyon eleven hours after leaving Bennett. Although the *Ora* and *Flora* had managed to get through the canyon safely, shooting the White Horse Rapids, Rattenbury said, without so much as removing even a scrap of paint from their bottoms, the passage through the treacherous waters was both difficult and dangerous and, thanks to another enterprising Victorian, Norman Macauley, no longer necessary. As she neared the mouth of the canyon the *Nora* pulled into shore where passengers, baggage and freight were transferred to Macauley's horse-drawn tramcars which ran on wooden rails parallel to the river. Below the rapids, they boarded the *Ora* and two and a half days later arrived at Dawson.

Staying in Dawson for two weeks, Rattenbury collared anyone who had a moment to spare and a story to tell, eager to pick up any scrap of information that might help him to plot his company's future. Everything he saw and heard seemed to indicate that the Yukon was on the verge of unprecedented growth and development. That summer of '98 Dawson was reputed to be the largest city west of Chicago and north of San Francisco. Upwards of forty thousand people were milling about in its streets, town lots were changing hands for as much as five thousand dollars a front foot and merchants were finding plenty of customers ready to pay even the most exorbitant prices for anything from nails to French champagne. All the way down from Bennett Rattenbury had observed iron-stained rock and his opinion that the area was well mineralized had been confirmed when he learned from Captain Rant, the B.C. Gold Commissioner, that valuable quartz discoveries had been made at Tagish, one claim alone being worth an estimated $150,000. Already experimental oats and vegetables had been sown in the warmer regions around Marsh and Tagish Lakes and the agricultural possibilities of this area were thought to be very promising. With the booming city of Dawson, hungry for fresh vegetables, only three days down river, the profits for farmers, and for the riverboats which would carry their produce to market, could be nothing short of enormous.

He left Dawson in July, his mind racing as he considered a variety of schemes which would allow him to capitalize on northern expansion. With evangelistic zeal be began expounding on his vision of the Yukon's future the moment he stepped off the boat in Victoria. After taking care to let it be known that he carried with him twenty thousand dollars in gold, he hammered away at his constant theme that life in the north was not as rigorous as people had been led to believe. Reproaching a reporter he said, ". . . the very fellows you have been warning and advising and trying to frighten with stories of hardship, the class known as 'tenderfeet', are the very beggars who stand the hardships best. Your old-time prospector is always growling and grumbling at the country, but the undismayed tenderfoot takes the whole thing as a joke and continues to laugh at the hardships."

He praised the scenery. The journey up the coast to Dyea was a "most delightful four days voyage . . . the countless small islands rising out of the sea, and the icebergs and glaciers being picturesque in the extreme, with an Italian sky overhead and a deep blue sea." Lake Bennett might be cursed with cold winds but soon one reached the Tagish, the garden valley of the Yukon, and here the country was "park-like, with grass meadows beautifully adorned with brilliant tinted wild flowers innumerable."

He dismissed the competition. ". . . the two rival steamboat lines on the lake . . . each own a little wretched 50-foot boat, and one of these recently got wrecked on the rapids, and yet they are accepting contracts for freight and passengers, demanding payment in advance and guaranteeing to land the men and belongings at Dawson by their lines. Many unfortunates have thus got stranded half-way on the journey, and they simply have no means of redress. It is deplorable." He ran things quite differently, Rattenbury said. His company did not ask for payment until freighted goods had arrived at their destination.

49

Others shared his conviction that steady and orderly development would follow on the heels of the gold rush. Already construction had begun on a railway which would push its way through the mountains from Skagway to Bennett over the White Pass. Requiring a huge investment, the railway represented great confidence in the future of the Yukon. In some places the roadbed had been blasted out of solid rock and in others the tracks had to cross deep ravines. ". . . the whole work," Rattenbury said, "is of the most permanent and durable character."[5]

What Rattenbury didn't realize was that the gold rush was coming to an end with the same abruptness that had marked its beginning. The same psychology that had led to the boom, would soon lead, just as inevitably, to a bust. One hundred thousand people had streamed into the Yukon. All but a few had arrived too late. At Dawson they soon discovered that the promising claims had already been taken, staked before the gold rush had really begun. Stunned at first by the realization that they had come so far for nothing, they had wandered about in the streets of Dawson without quite knowing what to do next. A few stayed in the town finding jobs or opening businesses, others pursued vague rumours of rich new strikes, but as winter approached with its prospects of dark cold days and soaring prices, most admitted defeat and prepared to return home.

Without knowing it Rattenbury had visited the north just as the flood of gold hungry men and women to the Yukon was peaking. By the time the tide had turned and the signs that the rush was over had become unmistakable, he was back in Victoria preaching the gospel of the soundness of northern investment with an enthusiasm which proved to be unfortunately infectious.

On August 19th, two weeks after his return to Victoria he announced that he had formed a new company, the Arctic Express Company, backed with a capital of $100,000 which, Rattenbury said, he had raised in Victoria in only two days. To overcome the problem of Dawson's isolation once the rivers and lakes froze, immobilizing the river boats, the company would build a string of relay stations, log houses spaced thirty miles apart all the way from Dawson to Skagway. An agent of the company would be posted at each station ready to provide every comfort and convenience for the traveller; a warm shelter, a comfortable bed, and good food. Once the line was completed a man wanting to leave Dawson during the winter would no longer find it necessary to make the journey encumbered with a tent and bedding, a stove and all his food. Instead he could leave Dawson empty-handed, "carrying nothing with him save the clothes he stands in," knowing that after each day's walk he would find an Arctic Express Company station ready to see to his every need.

As well as providing wayside stations for travellers, the company proposed to set up a reliable and efficient express service, purchasing hundreds of sled dogs to carry the mail, newspapers and packages between Dawson and the coast. A businessman would no longer have to spend an anxious winter wondering how his investments on the "inside" were faring, Rattenbury said.

Already the company had secured an eighty thousand dollar yearly contract to carry the U.S. mail, supplies and equipment were on their way north and construction of the relay stations would soon begin. The opportunities for profitable business, Rattenbury reported, appear to be practically limitless.

But by October the Arctic Express Company was in trouble. Ice had formed on the rivers and lakes and the steamers were "snugly stored away for their winter rest"; the shelters were built and fully provisioned; the company's agents were poised to greet the first traveller; a "small army of Manitoba dogs" waited to be strapped into harness, but still the Yukon remained cut off from the outside world. Except for a few hurrying dashes there had been no snow. Until it came no sleds could move and men postponed setting out on the six hundred mile trek, knowing that a thick blanket of snow would make the trail more easily passable. The success of Rattenbury's system of relay stations, promoted as being "second in extent and completeness to none in the world, not even excepting the famous Siberian relay," depended on careful and constant organization. As the days passed with no Skagway bound travellers to provide the necessary incentive to maintain that efficient organization, the system began to fall into disarray.

The mail did go through, but no thanks to the Arctic Express Company. Rattenbury's contract called for the delivery of mail in Dawson every two weeks, but as Lieutenant-Corporal Sam Steele of the North West Mounted Police observed, ". . . there was no sign of the contractor or his men" and "no mails came through unless we undertook to bring them."[6] Rather than leave the inhabitants of Dawson cut off for another winter Steele and his men assumed the responsibility for carrying the mail. Corporal Richardson walked the route from Skagway to Dawson, recording a description of the trail and blazing trees as he went, covering the six hundred miles in just twelve days. Police detachments were already in position up and down the Yukon River at posts thirty miles apart. Men and dogs would be relieved at each post, Steele decided, and the mail was to be kept going and coming day and night. The first mail left Dawson on December 1 and soon a brisk competition sprang up among the men, each trying to cover his thirty mile stretch in the fastest possible time, the record going to a constable who covered the distance in four and a half hours, running behind his dog team all the way.

The Arctic Express Company did make an attempt to live up to its contract. On December 8 an agent for the company set out from Dawson but he reached no further than the Mounted Police station at Stewart River, seventy miles upstream from Dawson, where he gave up and handed the mail over to a police corporal who sent it on with one of his own dog trains. As Steele dryly noted, "All attempts made by others during the winter to send out mails were failures."

Failures too were the Arctic Express Company way stations. Anyone leaving Dawson that winter was more likely to be heading in the opposite direction — north toward the rumoured new strike at Nome. Government officials who travelled between Skagway and Dawson were provided with free food and lodgings by the police and sometimes even hitched a ride with one of their dog trains. Others leaving Dawson for the outside found that in return for an hour's work chopping wood they would receive a night's bed and board with each police detachment along the route. With an elite company of superbly conditioned and strictly disciplined men, who benefited from a very special esprit de corps, ready to leap into the breach when his company showed the first sign of faltering, Rattenbury was given no second chance.

The Lake Bennett and Klondike Navigation Company still promised success and when the ice broke up in May the following spring, the *Flora* was one of the first river boats to reach Dawson, triumphantly depositing thirty sacks of mail on the city's docks. But few booked passage aboard her for the return voyage to Bennett. The insubstantial rumours of the winter before had now taken form. There was gold at Nome, gold waiting to be scooped up from the sand of the beach! Eight thousand clamoured for a space aboard steamers bound for the mouth of the river and the port of St. Michael on the Bering Sea. By the end of the summer more than half of Dawson's population had left the city forever.

Rattenbury, warned by the failure of the Arctic Express Company, turned his back on the Klondike before this final disaster scuttled his steamers. But he could hardly admit that he was scrambling to divest himself of his northern interests and still hope to retain his reputation as an enterprising and canny businessman. The previous summer he had described his design work as a leisure time activity but now in April of 1899 he calmly announced that he was so busy with his architectural career that he had been forced to sever his connection with the Lake Bennett and Klondike Navigation Company. "Ratz," as people had come to call him, had invested his own money in the Arctic Express Company and his "busyness" with architecture was prompted by necessity rather than by a reawakening of the urge to create. But fortunately for Rattenbury his reputation as the province's premier architect, won for him by his design of the Parliament Buildings, stood him in good stead and soon he was at work on so many different commissions that what had been, in the spring, a face-saving excuse had become, by December, an accurate description of the facts.

5

Cary Castle
a personal and malicious attack

By the winter of 1899, Pat Burns alone had given Ratz enough work to occupy the full attention of any architect. Burns, who had made a fortune following the trail of western expansion ready to fill the need for fresh meat almost as soon as it arose, was no longer content to act only as a middle-man, buying beef from ranchers and selling it to retailers. Perhaps savouring his title of Klondike Cattle King, he had decided to become the ruler of a kingdom, in fact as well as by repute. Raising beef on his own ranches, slaughtering and delivering it to his own string of butcher shops, he would control the business from beginning to end. He purchased vast acreages of range land in Alberta, closed down his Nelson office, moved his headquarters to Calgary and asked Rattenbury to design the cold storage warehouses and other buildings required to house his expanded operations. And perhaps as an inducement for Eileen Ellis of Penticton, whom he married two years later, he also commissioned the architect to design for him a grand and impressive residence to be erected in Calgary. Built of sandstone quarried near the site, as were most other buildings in the "Sandstone City," it was the largest residential building Rattenbury had ever been asked to design. An eighteen room mansion boasting ten bedrooms and the almost unheard of luxury of four bathrooms, Burns' home set him back $32,000, some $7,000 more than Rattenbury had estimated. A mixture of French château and Irish castle, it was completed in 1901, just in time to receive Burns and his new bride.

In addition to all the work he was doing for Pat Burns, Rattenbury had, in the autumn of 1899, more than a score of other buildings in various stages of construction; offices for the Bank of Montreal in Rossland, New Westminster and Nelson; hotels at Greenwood and Rossland; office blocks in Vancouver and New Westminster; a residence at Deer Park on the Lower Arrow Lake; and two residences in Victoria, one of them his own home on the water-front in Oak Bay. Even for a man who thrived on an almost manic level of activity, Ratz should have been content. But he had set his sights on yet another commission — one that threatened to elude him and one that he was prepared to go to almost any lengths to win.

In the spring of 1899, Cary Castle, the official residence of B.C.'s Lieutenant-Governor, had been destroyed by fire. An eccentric building with an equally eccentric history, Cary Castle was a familiar Victoria landmark, a well-loved oddity, and a very special building would be required to replace it.

It had been built as the home of the first Attorney-General of the colony of British Columbia, George Hunter Cary. Cary was more than just a little mad and his credentials were questionable, but well-placed relatives in England had recognized in the post of Attorney-General in a far flung colony a god-sent opportunity to remove a potential embarrassment from the bosom of his family and pressed for his appointment. So in 1859 Cary had arrived in Victoria, armed with "six law books, a carpet bag and a tooth brush," in search of colonial experience and alert to the possibilities of pickings unknown.

Cary dreamt of building a castle and when certain mining specula-tions seemed about to pay off he began to scour Victoria looking for a perfect site. When he stood on a bleak, windswept, rocky hill at the top of Belcher Road, he knew that he had found it. In the best tradition of castle-building, the location allowed for a commanding view, not just of the growing settlement of Victoria, but also out across the Straits of Juan de Fuca to the towering peaks of the Olympic Peninsula.

Designed by Fred Walter Green who later found his true calling as a city engineer, Cary's medieval fantasy had slowly begun to rise, "a queer architectural intrusion of the wild landscape," but after the completion of one wing and a tower, three stories high topped with battlement-like crenellations, Cary, discovering that he had over-estimated the returns from his investments and underestimated the costs of castle building, had been forced to face reality and com-promise his dream. Rather than completing the building according to the original plans, he could only afford to add a squat one storey wing with matching crenellations and featuring a most unlikely bay window to take advantage of the view.

Cary was not to be king of his abbreviated castle for long. He had been accused of handling cases in a hot impulsive wayward manner and by 1864 his mental condition had deteriorated to such an extent that friends urged him to resign. Cary sold his castle and returned to England where he died in 1866 of an "overworked brain and a weak constitution" at the age of thirty-five.

In 1864 when Arthur Kennedy arrived to assume the post of Governor, he had been encouraged by the enthusiasm of his welcome, but he soon found that while the people might be prepared to accept him, they weren't about to house him. During James Douglas' tenure as Governor, Government House had been Douglas' own home adjacent to the legislative buildings. But Douglas was still in residence and the House of Assembly had been of the opinion that Kennedy or the British Parliament should be responsible for providing an official residence. For a while Kennedy bided his time, but finally growing tired of rented accommodations, he had purchased Cary Castle.

Architects Wright and Saunders set to work replacing the old crenellated roof with a Gothic roof broken by finialed dormer windows. The exterior walls were shingled or plastered to keep out the weather and the *Colonist* voiced popular opinion when it stated, "From the southern elevation the improvements to the old building appear to the best advantage, none of the old castle being visible except the tower."

Having finally voted funds for the provision of an official residence and faced with a fait accompli, the Assembly purchased Cary Castle and for more than thirty years the official representatives of the British Throne were housed in a medieval-cum-gothic castle, "an unsightly pile of buildings on the summit of a great rock . . . exposed to every wind that blows."

Kennedy's personal philosophy was that "It is better to be decidedly wrong than undecidedly right." Many Governors and Lieutenant-Governors would come to be of the opinion that in the case of Cary Castle, Kennedy had been most decidedly wrong. For Cary Castle was damp, draughty and bone-chillingly cold. Fires burning in every room did little to counteract the icy wind that found its way through the cracks in the walls. On at least one occasion the annual ball was advanced to October so it wouldn't be too cold and the ladies wouldn't catch pneumonia.

Governors and later Lieutenant-Governors grumbled and complained and balked at moving in. But one royal visitor housed at Cary Castle while its official occupants willingly vacated to the warmth and comfort of a local hotel had found the castle strangely agreeable. "This place is half way between Heaven and Balmoral,"[1] Princess Louise wrote to her mother Queen Victoria.

With its cold draughts and steeply banked fireplaces Cary Castle had displayed an alarming, if not surprising, penchant for catching fire. Lieutenant-Governor McInnes, a dour Nova Scotia-born doctor who took up residence in the castle in 1897, must have been particularly susceptible to the cold. More than half the fires at the castle occurred during his tenancy, and it was he who had been awakened from his sleep on the morning of May 18, 1899 and escaped from the house with no more than the clothes on his back as sparks from an overworked chimney ignited the roof and the wind from the sea fanned the smouldering embers into a roaring blaze.

The government moved McInnes into Mrs. Green's elegant home "Gyppeswyk" on nearby Moss Street and then became hesitant and indecisive, unwilling to commit itself to the unexpected expense of a new Government House.

Rattenbury was not the only architect who waited impatiently for the government to reach a decision. The new Cary Castle, and no one ever suggested that it could be called anything else, would have to be a very special building, recalling the traditions of the old but on a grander scale. As the home of the Lieutenant-Governor and the home-away-from-home of visiting royalty, it was expected to be the most imposing residential building in the province. To architects it was a coveted commission. After a year passed with no official government announcement, Ratz felt he could wait no longer.

In June 1900, shortly after assuming the office of premier, James Dunsmuir had appointed as his minister of lands and works Wilmer Cleveland Wells, the sixty-year-old owner of a sawmill on the Kicking Horse River who had first been elected to the legislature in 1898. On August 27, after allowing Wells a scant two months to settle into office, Rattenbury wrote two letters to the new Chief Commissioner.

Although more than two years had passed since the completion of the Parliament Buildings, Rattenbury was still at odds with the government over the amount of commission due to him. His commission was based on a percentage of the buildings' final cost and the government continued to pore over accounts, work orders and memos determined to ensure that the architect would not profit from increased expenditures caused by his own mistakes or by extras he had ordered without government approval. While Rattenbury was not prepared to give up his claims against the government, he understood that, if he hoped to win another important government contract, it would be politic to remove himself somewhat from the unpleasantness engendered by direct confrontation. This he accomplished in his first letter to Wells. Written in his handwriting but signed by his wife Florrie, it read,

I hereby notify you that Francis M. Rattenbury of Victoria, B.C. has assigned to me, all his claims against the Government of British Columbia, for services rendered as Architect on the Parliament Buildings of British Columbia at Victoria B.C.

Having settled that matter to his satisfaction, he wrote a second letter to the Chief Commissioner in which he made a direct appeal to be engaged as architect of Government House.

Unless you have already made other arrangements I should be very happy to lay before you, for your consideration some designs for the rebuilding of Government House —

At sundry times during the past year, I have prepared designs suitable for the exquisite site on which the building will be erected. And I have, I think, evolved a plan which would result in a picturesque and stately residence suitable for the purposes for which it will be used.

It is such a charming subject for an Architect to design that, should you entrust me with the work, I can assure you, I should spare no pains to render the building a credit to the Government and to myself.

If the Government desired, I would prepare a full set of plans specifications and full size details of every part, and the Government could engage another architect to carry out the work from the plans — as I myself am desirous of travelling abroad this winter.

Rattenbury, who owed his reputation to the winning of one competition warned Wells about the dangers of holding another.

I have heard it rumoured that there may be a Competition for this particular Government work. I sincerely hope, however, that you will not so decide, for I do not think it is a class of building suitable for competition and I think all other architects will agree with me on this.

The charm of a Residence, as you are aware, lies in its harmony with the surroundings, and in broad and picturesque groupings and choice of materials — qualities not particularly observable in geometric drawings

In a competition a more showy and ornate elevation on paper would most likely be sent in — which whilst more attractive on paper, would in execution look commonplace and tawdry —

He ended by offering his services in a manner calculated to completely disarm the Chief Commissioner by demonstrating that he sought to gain no personal or professional advantage.

Should the Government however decide on a Competition, I should be most happy, not being a Competitor, to render any assistance I may be able, in getting out the particulars or in assisting at the selection of a design. Should you desire me to do so.[2]

But Rattenbury's was not the only letter the Chief Commissioner received. Thomas Hooper, an architect who since his arrival in Victoria in 1890 had built for himself a considerable reputation, had learned of Rattenbury's letter and the following day he wrote to Wells on his own behalf. "I have the honour to make application to you to be retained as Architect for the proposed new Government House,"[3] he wrote and then listed four prominent citizens, who also happened to be members of the Provincial Parliament, who would bear witness to his abilities. Quite understandably Wells decided to hold a competition.

The "Notice to Architects" released on October 31, 1900 made it clear that the government did not intend to provide the Lieutenant-Governor with lavish accommodations. The building was to be plain though dignified, built of wood on a stone foundation and the entire cost was not to exceed fifty thousand dollars. Entrants were to use a nom de plume and two non-competing architects would judge the competition which was to close on December 22.

The matter seemed settled when on January 16, 1901 the judges, local architects W. Ridgeway-Wilson and J. C. Keith, announced their decision. The winners were Byrens and Tait of Vancouver. Since the *Colonist* found their design to be imposing, dignified and most picturesque, and considering that Byrens and Tait estimated that it could be constructed for four thousand dollars less than the sum budgeted by the government, Wells was quite unprepared for the storm of protest that broke about his head.

The *Colonist* received a flood of angry letters to the editor and if Rattenbury was not the author of one or more of them there can be little doubt that he agreed wholeheartedly with the sympathies expressed. The government had stipulated that the ground floor plans should be so arranged that all the rooms, or as many as possible, be thrown open en suite with the ballroom. This condition was conspicuous by its absence, "Architect" grumbled in a letter dated January 18. "Fair Play" agreed. Any person could see at a glance that only three entrants had complied with the government's specifications and the Byrens and Tait design was not among them, he wrote. Adding his voice to the chorus, "A Citizen" heaped abuse on the judges, claiming that they had not judged according to the conditions given. The winning design would cost closer to seventy-five thousand dollars, he maintained. And it had been drawn on a larger scale than that called for by the government and the details of the interior and exterior were incomplete. He went on to question the judges' honesty as well as their competence saying that the plans should have been judged by experts from outside the province "who do not know the different styles of drawing of the local men."

Finding himself in somewhat of a quandary, Wells turned to Rattenbury who had been waiting patiently in the wings anxious to play his promised role of disinterested advisor. Would he meet with Byrens and Tait, Wells asked, and study their design to determine if the charges made against it were valid.

On August 14, 1901 Rattenbury wrote to Wells reporting on the meeting he had had with the two architects. He had gone over the plans with them and together they had calculated the area of the building and found that it would contain some 935,000 cubic feet. At a cost of eight cents per cubic foot the building would cost seventy-five thousand dollars to construct. Byrens and Tait would have to go back to the draughting table for as Ratz carefully pointed out "the changes to be made to come within the Government estimate of $50,000 will have to be radical." But, he hastened to assure Wells, the government should not think that their original budget had been impractical. "I think there should be no difficulty in building a very good and suitable residence for the sum of $50,000,"[4] he wrote.

When Byrens and Tait received a copy of Rattenbury's letter they sensed, quite correctly, that he was out to trump their ace. They did not agree with Rattenbury's estimate of cost, they protested to Wells, and they questioned the accuracy of arriving at the cost of a building based on its cubic content. But their protests were to no avail. Wells, quailing at the very thought of approving a design that might cost $25,000 more than the sum set aside by the government, awarded them the $250 prize for placing first in the competition and began to look elsewhere for a design that could be built for a more modest price.

Again Byrens and Tait wrote to the Chief Commissioner charging that Rattenbury's estimate was deliberately misleading. On September 11, when he responded to these charges Ratz assured the Chief Commissioner that in rejecting their plans he had made the right decision.

"As a matter of fact," he wrote, "I measured the cubical contents of the building in conjunction with Mr. Sait (as he consistently referred to Tait) and we did agree that it would not be possible to erect a suitable building for less than 8 cents per foot.

"As regards the accuracy of arriving at an Estimate of Cost of a building by cubing it, and then pricing it out proportionately with other buildings of a similar character, I may say that I have used this system for many years, and found it to work out almost invariably with the contract price."

He had really gone out of his way to be fair to the architects. After all a recently erected Victoria home had cost fifteen cents per cubic foot. That house had "a good deal of hardwood panelling on the ground floor, and whilst I understand that Messrs. Byrens and Sait had specified similar work in their Design, I only estimated in my Report to you for a simply finished Interior executed mainly in Cedar.

"I should very much regret that Messrs. Byrens and Sait should suppose, that my very moderate report to you, should have been written with any intention of prejudicing them. It seemed to me a moderate statement of facts."[5]

Rattenbury could afford to be patient and reasonable. Five days before he wrote this letter, the government had invited contractors to submit sealed tenders for the construction of Government House and it seems more than likely that the plans they studied in order to estimate their costs were Rattenbury's.

After deciding against using the Byrens and Tait plans, Wells had asked Rattenbury to design the building. But Ratz had demurred, pointing out to Wells, who seems to have been politically naive as well as quite spectacularly malleable, that both he and Wells would be open to criticism if he were given the commission after having scrutinized and evaluated the plans of the winning architects. There was, however, a much more acceptable solution. He would agree to serve as supervising architect, if another architect were named as the designer. Perhaps Samuel Maclure might be interested. Maclure was indeed interested. An architect who excelled in residential design, he had already built several large homes for members of Victoria's aristocracy. A commission like Cary Castle would go a long way to solidifying his position as the city's most sought after domestic architect. For an equal share of the commission, he agreed to work with Rattenbury on the building.

Maclure may have provided the designs for the building, but as only three weeks passed from the time Rattenbury was first asked to study the Byrens and Tait plans until tenders, based on the new plans, were called there had been scant time for an architect to draw new plans complete with specifications, especially an architect who showed such painstaking attention to detail as Maclure was wont to do. It seems more likely that the two architects agreed to share the design work, Rattenbury using the plan he had described the year before as one which would result in a picturesque and stately residence for the exterior and Maclure assuming the responsibility for the interior.

It happened that during the early stages of the building's construction Maclure fell ill and while Rattenbury may have been secretly delighted that this turn of events gave him the full control he had always wanted, later it would be Maclure who would be grateful that poor health had removed him from the scene.

When the new Cary Castle was ready to receive its official occupant in August of 1903, Rattenbury was given sole credit for its design. As he had predicted, it was both picturesque and stately. Its *porte cochère* and centre block were of rough stone recalling the old castle and so there could be no mistake as to the building's antecedents, Rattenbury had added a fat round tower, built of wood and shingled but topped with the same battlement-like crenellations that had adorned Cary's tower. Then he had crowned the building with the closed-in gables which were becoming an unmistakable Rattenbury stamp, the same château-like gables that adorned Pat Burns' Calgary home and which he would later use on the additions to his own home in Oak Bay. Describing the building as "baronial English," the *Colonist* deemed it to be one of Mr. Rattenbury's happiest creations, a building which appeared both imposing and noble while at the same time retaining a look of cosiness and comfort.

Through a nice combination of tactics and luck Ratz had achieved his ends. He was now architect of the two most important government buildings to be built in British Columbia during his lifetime. But trouble was brewing and he was to find his reputation tarnished by charges of incompetence, dishonesty and downright thievery, charges that might have remained unspoken if it had not been for the resentment caused by his arrogance and the jealousy engendered by his success.

George Jeeves who as Clerk of the Works had the responsibility of supervising the supervising architect on the government's behalf had become concerned about the number of extras Rattenbury was ordering for the interior of Cary Castle. He felt that the plans that had been approved by the Chief Commissioner should be followed more closely and he was disturbed by Rattenbury's habit of making changes in the design as the work progressed. Ratz, who felt he was a law unto himself when it came to government contracts, resented Jeeves' poking about the building asking bothersome questions and he told the contractor to ignore him. This advice the contractor followed, for when Jeeves asked why a window which had been shown on the original plans did not appear in the almost completed building he was told to "go to h . . . and find out."

After inspecting the building shortly before the Lieutenant-Governor was due to move in, Jeeves, who admitted that he didn't care for Rattenbury any more than Rattenbury cared for him, had written to the architect protesting that the interior finishing of the castle was "the worst piece of work I ever saw." And when the contractor's bill came in at $30,000 over the contract price, the preservation of his own reputation became Jeeves' prime concern. When the new premier, Richard McBride, asked him what he knew about the extra work done at Cary Castle, he replied, "practically nothing" and asked that an investigative committee be appointed "as I desire to protect my Reputation as an Honest Citizen."

Faced with contractor Richard Drake's bill for $75,000 for a building which he had contracted to build for under $45,000, McBride felt it wise to grant Jeeves' request and he appointed a three-man board of arbitration to decide how much the contractor deserved to be paid. Unfortunately for Rattenbury, the board included two Victoria architects, Thomas Hooper and A. Maxwell Muir, whom he described as professional and personal opponents, and they had in mind an inquiry of a much broader scope than that considered by McBride.

It may have been impossible for Rattenbury to receive a completely fair and unbiased hearing from any board that included local architects. During the ten years he had spent in Victoria, he had built up the largest practice in the city. Many of his fellow professionals were jealous of his success not only because he possessed an almost uncanny ability to win commissions, but also because so few commissions, however insignificant, escaped his attention. In 1900 he had been awarded the work of designing a home for the Royal Jubilee Hospital's resident medical officer. Rattenbury had designed and supervised the construction of the building but had graciously declined to accept the commission of $127.57 — an act of generosity which may have endeared him to the hospital board but not to the city's architects many of whom were hungry for work.

It could be very frustrating to compete with Rattenbury and there were few Victoria architects who did not take some comfort from their suspicion that superior tactics rather than superior talent accounted for his success. And yet at the same time they resented his competence. Even Sam Maclure, whose residential practice was secure and who saved his spleen for contractors guilty of shoddy workmanship, experienced some pangs of envy when he saw the lightning speed with which Rattenbury could complete drawings. Others, more threatened than Maclure, found that Rattenbury, who seldom felt the need to hire assistants, was greedy rather than gifted and they complained about his unwillingness to share his good fortune with others by spreading the work around.

Outclassed by Rattenbury for reasons they felt had very little to do with talent, most Victoria architects harboured varying degrees of ill-will toward him but Hooper and Maxwell Muir were two of those who had felt sufficiently aggrieved to attack him publicly.

Thomas Hooper, a man as ambitious and intemperate as Rattenbury, had more than one axe to grind. A native of Devonshire, Hooper had worked as a joiner in Ontario before moving to Winnipeg in 1878 where he had become an architect and a contractor. He had arrived in Vancouver shortly after the great fire of 1886 and four years later at the age of thirty-three he had moved to Victoria where he enjoyed a wide and varied architectural practice. Hooper had asked to be retained as architect for Government House but had found himself outmanoeuvred by Rattenbury. And Rattenbury had beaten him out of another commission in a way Hooper found highly suspicious.

In June of 1901 the City of Victoria had announced a competition for the design of a new high school building. Entrants were to submit their plans anonymously together with an envelope containing their name. The plans and the envelopes would be marked with corresponding numbers as they were received. After the winning design was selected, the envelope carrying the same number would be opened and the winning architect identified. The School Board's decision was announced on August 16. Rattenbury had won the contest, Thomas Hooper had placed third. Four days later the *Colonist* reported that quite a controversy had arisen over the selection of Rattenbury's plans, adding that "some of the unsuccessful architects have gone so far as to make charges against the trustees."

It was rumoured that certain members of the School Board had decided in advance to give the contract to Rattenbury, that they had ignored the advice of an assessor who had recommended the selection of another set of plans, and that the final choice of a design had been made only after the plans had been identified. And Rattenbury with a notable lack of discretion had lent credence to these charges when, the day after winning the contest, he called for tenders for the construction of the building, having with either reckless confidence or guilty foreknowledge, taken the time to produce detailed drawings and the list of specifications in advance of the official announcement.

The School Board Chairman's vehement denial of these charges confirmed Hooper's suspicions. The fact that he had "waxed thus indignant" suggested to him, Hooper said, that all was not "square and above-board." A. Maxwell Muir had been even more to the point. "I think," he wrote to the editor of the *Colonist*, "that my plans should have placed first."

Muir, who had begun his career in his native Glasgow and who had worked in John Teague's office until 1891 when he had established his own practice, had been just as direct but much more impassioned when, two years later, he locked horns with Rattenbury over the question of the design of the Carnegie Library.

In March 1902 Andrew Carnegie had offered to give the city $50,000 for the purpose of erecting a public library and for the next twelve months an embattled city council had found itself at the centre of a heated debate. Was it proper, some Victorians asked themselves, for a Canadian city to accept the gift of an American millionaire? And was his money tainted because, as some said, he had made his fortune by the exploitation of human labour? And if the city did accept his offer where should the building be sited? On Government Street opposite the Post Office? On Cathedral hill? On Fort or Yates streets? Two plebiscites were necessary before it was finally decided on April 3, 1903 that the city would take Carnegie's money and that the building would be located at the corner of Blanshard and Yates. Weary of the whole subject of the library, the aldermen welcomed a petition signed by local architects Hooper, Watkins, Muir, Keith and Maclure praying that one of their number be appointed to prepare plans. Relieved that this issue could be resolved amiably and expeditiously, Council voted to select an architect by secret ballot. But the aldermen were soon disabused of the notion that they might avoid bickering and contention by following the advice of the city's established architects. At a council meeting on April 20th a letter from Rattenbury was read into the record and the aldermen were thrown "all in a heap."

Gentlemen,

I regret to learn that you propose obtaining designs for the Carnegie library by appointing an architect by secret ballot, opening the way to favoritism, in place of having a competition: giving a fair field to all and no favor.

In a competition each man has a chance of showing the best building he can design. In the ballot system only one man has this chance, and the city does not know what kind of building they are to have, whereas in a competition they do.

In order that the aldermen may select the most competent man to erect this building, it must be assumed that the aldermen are competent themselves to judge the professional abilities of the several architects of the city: but are they?

I cannot see how you can be any more qualified to give an authorative decision on this point than I am to judge of the professional attainments of musicians, and I should think myself impertinent if I attempted to do so.

I certainly must decline to allow my name to be balloted for in any such manner.

It is generally supposed also that the amount of canvassing that has been going on, and I think you must have all been canvassed, must thwart your judgement. In fact, I have heard it said that several aldermen have already pledged themselves, and had done so before this system of secret balloting was adopted.

The aldermen should know that all the finest buildings of modern times have been erected by competition, and whilst it is possible to get unsatisfactory results, it is generally owing to unfair conditions, or poor judgement in choosing an assessor, or some such cause. There is no reason why these conditions cannot be satisfactory if a little care is exercised.

But if there are to be no competitions in Victoria, and as we are always debarred from competing for civic buildings in Vancouver or elsewhere (owing to being non-resident) what inducement is there to practice in Victoria?

There is very little private practice here. Personally I have not made office rent in Victoria, out of my private practice in the last ten years, except for competition work. At the same time I have a large practice outside the city, for which I purchase supplies and men are employed here to the extent of many thousands of dollars a year. If it becomes so much more advantageous to open an office in Vancouver this business naturally follows.

I am not advancing all this as any reason for entrusting the Carnegie library to me. I don't care tuppence about it, but you are adopting a principle which will cause trouble all the time.[6]

If his letter had been enough to throw Council in a heap, its effect on the city's architectural community must have been awe-inspiring. For, although Rattenbury may not have been aware of it, the contents of his letter to the Chief Commissioner in which he had advised against holding a competition for the design of Government House were well known.* What wasn't understood was how he had come to be given that particular work but, as in the case of the high school, the feeling was that all had not been square and above-board.

It was all more than Maxwell Muir could take. His career spanned twenty-five years but compared to Rattenbury, his success had been modest. As Muir himself said, "Mr. Rattenbury has been more fortunate in his efforts than any other man, perhaps in this country."

* As a correspondent to the *Colonist* who chose to hide behind the pen name "Ratepayer" put it ". . . how does this argument of Mr. Rattenbury coincide with the previous opinion of his given to the provincial government a little over two years ago. At that time Mr. Rattenbury strongly urged the government to discard competitive plans, and appoint an architect to carry out the work of building a new Government House. Notwithstanding this advice, a competition took place and Mr. Rattenbury did not compete, but nevertheless we find that subsequently Mr. Rattenbury got the work and is today, as architect, superintending the operations of the contractor." *Daily Colonist,* April 26, 1903.

In an unguarded letter to Council, Muir gave full reign to his hostility and bitterness. Particularly incensed by Ratz' claim that he had not done enough local work to pay his office expenses, Muir wrote, "(Rattenbury) has done more local work in this city during the last ten years than any other man." What more did he want, Muir demanded. Especially since he employed no assistants and spent no more money in the city than he could possibly avoid.

"... he declares he does not care 'tuppence' for the library," Muir sputtered. "Why then does he worry himself so much about it as to write? The truth is, he is anxious for the almighty dollar, aye, more so than many of his professional brethren, who if they had made as much by a fortuitous set of circumstances, rather than by pre-eminent ability, would have retired long ago and left the field to others less fortunate."[7]

Muir must have come to regret that he had so openly identified himself as one of those less fortunate who couldn't hope to compete with Rattenbury. Especially since the aldermen proved the extent of Ratz' influence over them by reversing their earlier decision and voting in favour of holding a competition.

"... it appears to me," grumbled architect Edward Mallandane, "it was the intention of Council to select Mr. Rattenbury by ballot, and now they hope to get him by sidewind."[8] And, as illogical as that charge might be, it was the commonly held belief.

Rattenbury, perhaps welcoming the opportunity to prove his adversaries wrong, did not enter the competition. On June 18, 1903 it was announced that Thomas Hooper's plans had won first prize. But if either Hooper or Muir felt any satisfaction at seeing Ratz beaten out of a commission it proved to be short lived.

A new wing was to be added to the Jubilee Hospital and both Hooper and Muir submitted plans for the hospital board's consideration. Rejecting Hooper's design because it included wider corridors and fewer rooms, the board's building committee had given Muir to understand that his plans would be accepted. But on July 24th at a meeting of the full board it was decided that because Rattenbury had previously sketched designs for an addition that had not been built, the work should be given to him.

Rattenbury would hardly have expected sympathy from these two architects, now members of the board of arbitration, but he was completely unprepared for the damning accusations they made against him in their final report.

Attached to their award,[9] which gave the contractor $19,500 of the $29,000 he had claimed, was a memorandum in which the arbitrators stated that their investigation had been greatly handicapped by the striking irregularities that had prevailed throughout the whole of the contract. In particular they cited the looseness and evident carelessness shown in conducting the work, the lack of proper and effective means of checking the work, the remarkable number of changes, and changes upon changes, made from time to time by the architect, evidencing a want of proper pre-consideration of the drawings, specifications and contract, and involving much unnecessary labour on the part of the contractor. The imperfect plans and skimpy specifications had produced a chaotic condition throughout construction. "The want of proper precaution in ordering extra work, the informal, rapid and casual way in issuing instruction without due care in keeping records of same . . . has produced a great deal of misunderstanding."

That much would have been enough to drive Rattenbury into a rage for without mincing words the arbitrators had charged him with incompetence both as a designer and as a supervising architect. But the arbitrators continued. Calling it a reprehensible practice, they condemned Rattenbury for interfering with the proper functions of the contractor by ordering and buying materials in his own name. ". . . some hundreds of dollars have been paid out on the architect's orders for goods purchased by himself, the invoices for which we have not been able to see, but from evidence given by various witnesses all the goods charged to and paid for by the Government have not been used in the building . . ."

The arbitrators provided specific examples. Marble specified for use in the banqueting room had been ordered by the architect and paid for by the government, but did not appear in the completed building. And they had also discovered that "while ten English grates have been paid for, only nine have been used, and in lieu of the missing grate, a very much cheaper American grate has been used."

And, the arbitrators suggested, Rattenbury had ordered goods in his own name so that he, rather than the contractor, would receive the kick-backs, euphemistically called commissions, which dealers customarily paid to contractors who placed large orders.

Ratz' fury was evident in the blistering letter he wrote to the Chief Commissioner after having read the award. The memorandum attached to the award was a

... personal and malicious attack upon myself in which the Arbitrators ... have exhausted every source of invective and innuendo at their command to destroy my character as a professional man, both as to my ability, my trustworthyness, and my probity.

The whole of the charges made against me, are gratuitous on their part, and they have been made, *without letting me have the slightest knowledge that they proposed to make such charges and without affording me the slightest opportunity of meeting them.*

I emphatically deny the charges made, and on my part, claim, that they are slanders, maliciously and knowingly made by the Arbitrators, for the purpose of discrediting me, in the eyes of the Government and the people of British Columbia.

It was bad enough that the arbitrators had made the charges, but what was worse was that when the award was tabled in the Legislature, the charges would become public. "The whole will appear when called for in the House, as a verdict against me, arrived at under oath, by impartial and unprejudiced Arbitrators," Rattenbury wrote. Even if the charges were disproved his reputation would be injured beyond recovery and his professional career would be ended.

Hooper and Maxwell Muir had used their "temporary position" as arbitrators to "wreak their private malice upon me," Rattenbury said and he suggested that the government not accept the award until the charges against him had been deleted.[10]

It seems as if the Chief Commissioner, as anxious to avoid a public disclosure of the charges as was Rattenbury, agreed to this proposal, but on January 20, 1904 a petition from Hooper and Maxwell Muir asking for an investigation into all matters relating to the construction of Government House was presented to the Legislature. A select committee was appointed and two weeks later a very public hearing began.

Rattenbury was in a very awkward position. That the building had cost almost double the original estimate was not surprising. Rattenbury himself maintained that it was impossible to erect a building of an artistic nature without making changes and additions as the work progressed. And on Moss Street, just a few minutes' walk away from the site of Cary Castle, lived the new Lieutenant-Governor, Sir Henri de Joly Lotbiniere, a cultured French-Canadian gentleman, who took a most proprietory interest in the house being built for him. Sir Henri had definite ideas about the class of residence suitable for a Lieutenant-Governor and Ratz had been only too happy to oblige him, agreeing among other things to substitute oak panelling for the simple plaster finish planned for the dining room.[11]

But much more serious were the charges that Rattenbury had ordered materials in his own name so that he could pocket the dealers' commissions and also so that he could disguise the fact that materials ordered for Cary Castle and paid for by the government, had been redirected. In their memorandum Hooper and Maxwell Muir had simply stated that some of the marble and an English grate did not appear in the completed building. But anyone who had visited Ratz' home knew that a very unusual grate, easily recognizable as a mate to those at Cary Castle, graced the fireplace in his dining room and that the kitchen of his home contained such an extravagant amount of marble that it remained as cool as a mausoleum, no matter how warm the day or how hot the stove — sheets of marble over an inch thick lined the walls from floor to ceiling, marble covered the counter tops, slabs of marble served as shelves in the pantry, even the back hall leading to the servants' entrance was rich with finely polished marble.

With his accounts in their usual jumbled state, Ratz knew it would be difficult, if not well nigh impossible, to provide the evidence necessary to clear his name. When he learned that Hooper and Maxwell Muir had petitioned the Legislature requesting an investigation, he decided to counter-attack and he engaged Lyman Poore Duff to carry his colours into battle. Duff, for whom Rattenbury had designed a home on Rockland Avenue, was the city's best legal mind. Born in Ontario in 1865, Duff had been appointed Queen's Counsel at the age of thirty-four and in 1904, shortly after having acted as Rattenbury's counsel at the select committee hearings, he would be named a judge of the British Columbia Supreme Court.

Duff informed the arbitrators that his client intended to use any statements they might make to the committee as the basis for launching a legal action charging them with slander. Upon receiving this news Maxwell Muir and Dalton, the Vancouver architect who had served as the third member of the board of arbitration, faded discreetly into the background, refusing to testify and leaving only Thomas Hooper to defend the charges they had made against Rattenbury.[12]

Hooper, anxious to avoid making statements that might be action-
able but at the same time determined to make the charges against
Rattenbury stick, was irritable and unco-operative on the stand. He
took serious objection to being sworn, claiming that the memorandum attached to the award was privileged and that he should not
now be called to defend his statements as if he were in court.

He objected to the presence of lawyers — he was being bulldozed,
Hooper angrily maintained.

Deputy Attorney-General McLean, who was appearing for the
Department of Lands and Works and for whom Rattenbury had also
designed a house, got very little information out of Hooper. Hooper,
who had made it clear that he was giving evidence under protest,
stated that it was absurd for McLean to expect him to remember
every little detail of all the plans, accounts and invoices he had
studied. And later when McLean tried to get clarification of some of
Hooper's cautious and roundabout statements, Hooper responded
that he must be very dense if he didn't already understand the
answers he had given.

When it was his turn to quiz the witness, Duff began by questioning Hooper's own professional integrity. What about the stained
glass for the Methodist Church, Duff asked, referring to a building
Hooper had designed shortly after his arrival in Victoria. Had
Hooper ordered the stained glass himself? Yes, Hooper said, but
only after receiving the consent of the contractor. And what about
the stonework for the same church, Duff asked. Wasn't it true that
Hooper had given that work to his brother? Yes, Hooper bristled,
but there was no parallel between his case and Rattenbury's because
he had always acted with the consent of the contractor while Rattenbury had not.

Did he have a poor opinion of Mr. Rattenbury as an architect,
Duff wondered and Hooper answered, No, as an architect Rattenbury was all right but he was a poor businessman for his client.

Do you think it proper, Duff asked, for contractors to purchase
goods at a ten per cent discount but charge a client the full invoice
price?

Yes, Hooper replied, he thought that was proper.

Well, Duff said, Mr. Rattenbury thought it was not!

He didn't care what Rattenbury thought, Hooper retorted.

Did he now think or had he ever suggested that Rattenbury had
benefited himself improperly through the work on Government

House, Duff queried. "I know nothing about that," Hooper hedged. "I don't know if he did or not."

But it soon became clear that the rumours that Rattenbury had misused government funds had originated with Hooper. Gamble, an engineer with the Department of Lands and Works, had an interesting story to tell. "The question of the marble was brought up," he testified, "and in discussing it with Mr. Hooper that gentleman said something about Mr. Rattenbury having it in his own house. I then said, 'You mean in plain words that Mr. Rattenbury is a thief?' and he agreed with me by nodding his head."

Compared to the cantankerous Thomas Hooper, Rattenbury appeared coolly logical and patiently reasonable on the stand. There might be "a few clerical errors" in his accounts, Ratz admitted but there were positively no architectural errors in the building. He had made some minor alterations and a few little changes had been suggested by the Lieutenant-Governor, but he had always consulted with the Chief Commissioner before proceeding with these changes, Rattenbury assured the committee. He had ordered goods in his own name but he had always made it clear that he was acting in his professional capacity naming the building for which they were intended when placing the order and he had always deducted any commissions paid by dealers before submitting the bills to the government. In fact he had on one occasion written a stinging letter to an English firm upbraiding them for having credited him with a commission amounting to $140. He had deducted that amount from the invoice he sent to the government, Ratz said, and as a result was still out the $140 since the company had not yet sent the money.

Rattenbury had a ready answer to the question of the missing grate. The ten English grates that had been ordered were suitable only for burning coal. A larger grate was needed for the smoking room if the gentlemen were to enjoy a crackling wood fire and so an exchange had been made for a larger American grate. He had then decided to use the smaller grate in his own home and by mistake the supplier had billed the government. But, Rattenbury insisted, he had ordered the dealer to correct the mistake as soon as he had noticed it.

As for the missing marble, he agreed that marble delivered to Cary Castle had been sent elsewhere. A case of marble had arrived at Government House but when he had opened it, Ratz said, he had discovered that it was marble he had ordered for his own home.

He had $500,000 worth of buildings going on under his supervision and it was quite possible for some things to be sent to the wrong site.

Although Rattenbury's answers to the charges made against him had sounded reasonable, the committee members were not satisfied. They had read the memorandum, they had heard the evidence of Hooper, Rattenbury and officials from the Department of Lands and Works, but as yet no one had produced any documents to support his version of the facts. The hearing had gone on for two weeks, much longer than they had expected and now the legislature was due to prorogue. They toyed with the idea of continuing their investigation but in the end they decided to present their findings to the legislature before the end of the session. Their dissatisfaction was evident in the wording of their report, which, while it cleared Rattenbury of the charges made against him, carefully left some room for doubt by hinting that their decision might have been different had they been allowed more time to investigate.

... the Committee is convinced that Mr. F. M. Rattenbury, as Supervising Architect, thoroughly protected the interests of the Province, and that in all matters brought to its notice his conduct throughout has been honourable and satisfactory.

Your Committee further beg to report that, owing to the premature ending of its labours, it feels it is not justified on commenting further on the evidence produced.[13]

The Committee's verdict could be taken to mean not proven rather than not guilty but for Rattenbury it was vindication enough. People would take the charges against him only as seriously as they took his chief accuser, Thomas Hooper, and soon a story would be abroad that seemed to suggest that Hooper himself was not above a little petty larceny at public expense.

For his services as an arbitrator, Hooper had billed the government $1,400. But an inquiry by the Attorney-General uncovered the fact that of the fifty-six separate sessions he claimed to have attended, twenty-three had been afternoon meetings, separated from the morning sessions only by lunch. Hooper, it turned out, had billed the government $545 more than the amount to which he was entitled by the terms of the Arbitration Act. He may have made an honest mistake, simply misinterpreting the terms of the Act. But nevertheless his padded expense account did tend to make him seem rather ridiculous especially since he had appeared so morally indignant and professionally outraged at Ratz' alleged wrongdoing.

Rattenbury had emerged from the Government House hearings virtually unscathed — but it had been a very near thing. Although Hooper's charges had no discernible effect on his reputation or career, Rattenbury's dislike of the other architect remained intense. Still harbouring a grudge two years later, he proved that he was quite prepared to appear small-minded and petty if that was the price of showing his contempt for Hooper. For five years Rattenbury had acted in a casual way as the Jubilee Hospital's consulting architect. In addition to the doctor's residence he had done a number of minor jobs for the hospital board without charging his normal fees counting the gratitude he received and the increased status he enjoyed payment enough. In May 1905 the board asked Hooper to prepare plans for a children's ward — a not unreasonable decision since Rattenbury was planning an extended trip to England at the time. An infuriated Rattenbury immediately placed before the board a bill for $348 for past services rendered — an action correctly interpreted by one board member who stated that he was convinced that Rattenbury would not have said a word if any other than "that certain architect" had been employed.

Hooper's charges of incompetence and dishonesty could not have come at a worse time, for during the years 1903 and 1904 the most important non-governmental client Rattenbury had yet to attract was trading on both his reputation for architectural brilliance and his good name in the community to wring significant concessions out of the City of Victoria. If either his professional ability or his personal honesty had remained in doubt he might well have lost the opportunity to design the building which many see as his best architectural work — the Empress Hotel.

6

Sir Thomas Shaughnessy and the Empress Hotel
to the last tittle and jot

"No," said C.P.R. president Sir Thomas Shaughnessy, "the company has no intention of building a tourist hotel in Victoria."

A story had appeared in an eastern newspaper stating that construction would begin at an early date. But that story was nothing but a rumour, Sir Thomas said, the company was not even contemplating such a move.

The members of the Board of Trade's hotel committee set up to discover what plans the C.P.R. had in store for the city, were stunned. After all, two events had occurred earlier that same year that seemed to indicate that the company would take a lively interest in Victoria's future.

In January 1901 the C.P.R. had purchased the Canadian Pacific Navigation Company and its fourteen somewhat elderly vessels. The C.P.R. intended to update the fleet, Victorians were assured, and particular attention would be paid to the Victoria-Vancouver run.

Then in February it had been announced that after a very keen competition with some of the leading architects in New York, Montreal and Toronto, Victoria's most celebrated architect, Francis Mawson Rattenbury, had been selected to prepare plans for the enlargement of the C.P.R. hotel in Vancouver.

In choosing Rattenbury as their western division architect, the C.P.R. couldn't have done better. In fact the wonder is that they bothered to hold a competition at all. He was practiced in that company symbol, the château style of architecture. He enjoyed an unparalleled reputation in the west for his design of the Legislative Buildings. And, perhaps most importantly, he brought a certain missionary zeal to the promotion of his projects — a quality that would become invaluable later on — for despite Sir Thomas' denials, it seems likely that at an early date the company had decided to build an hotel, but had decided to delay any official announcement until they had winkled the best possible concessions out of the City of Victoria.

Built fifteen years before in Vancouver and the Rockies, the C.P.R.'s western hotels had already proved to the company just how lucrative the tourist trade could be. Although it had already been extended once before in 1892, the Hotel Vancouver had become badly overcrowded and distinctly humble compared with the C.P.R.'s eastern hotels. Following Rattenbury's plans an entire new wing would be added. And as for the existing building, "The idea is," Ratz said, "to rebuild everything except the present dining room." The completed hotel would contain some 250 bedrooms, fitted with all the latest and most approved conveniences. The entire project would cost between $400,000 and $500,000, Ratz predicted and winning a few more points for the C.P.R. in Vancouver he repeated the company's promise that "the work shall as far as possible be placed in the hands of local firms."

"When reconstructed, the Hotel Vancouver will have few rivals in Canada," he enthused. "The Windsor in Montreal will be somewhat larger; the Frontenac at Quebec will be about the same size — and these are the only ones that are really in the same class."[1]

Also in need of improvement were the company's hotels in the Rockies. The C.P.R. had discovered "a number of very scenic picturesque effects" in the vicinity of Field and tiny Mount Stephen House wouldn't begin to be able to accommodate all the tourists who would pour off the trains once the company had cut roads through to the various points of attraction such as the large glacier and the waterfall 1,200 feet high. Under Rattenbury's direction the little Swiss chalet was transformed into a large, but suitably rustic, hotel of fifty rooms, a huge rambling shingled building which combined chalet, château and tudor styles and stood just a few paces away from the tracks dwarfing the little log railway station.

The owners of Victoria's Hotel Dallas, encouraged by the C.P.R.'s promise to improve the passenger service between Vancouver and Victoria and impressed by the company's obvious confidence in the future of the hotel industry in Vancouver, decided to take a leaf from the C.P.R.'s book by commissioning Rattenbury to remodel their hotel on the waterfront near the city's Outer Wharves. After being closed for some months undergoing a most complete refitting and furnishing from top to bottom, the Hotel Dallas re-opened in May 1902. With its magnificent view of the Straits and Olympics, its seventy "tastefully arranged bedrooms, its capacious balconies, its public rooms fitted up in the highest style of the art" and its kitchens which had become "culinary apartments," the Dallas could expect to remain one of the most attractive and favourite resorts on the Pacific Coast. It was after all Victoria's only seaside hotel, and as far as Mr. and Mrs. Patterson, the Dallas' proprietors could tell, it was re-opening for business under very favourable conditions. What they didn't know, was that after he had indulged in an appropriate period of flirtatious hesitation Sir Thomas Shaughnessy was quite prepared to let himself be seduced by the persistent wooing of the Board of Trade's hotel committee.

In June 1902 a month after the Dallas re-opened Shaughnessy arrived in Victoria on his annual cross-country tour of inspection. Welcoming this opportunity to press their suit in person, the members of the committee accompanied by Mayor Hayward, "waited on" Sir Thomas and pointed out all the advantages Victoria offered as the location for a first class tourist hotel. As a site they suggested the gardens of James Douglas' former residence. Close by the Parliament Buildings and enjoying an historical association with the "Father of British Columbia," the gardens represented Victoria's most prominent and prestigious site.

The committee noted that at first Sir Thomas appeared to be averse to the proposal but ultimately he admitted to having been impressed by their arguments.

"It may be taken for a matter of almost absolute certainty," the Board of Trade assured City Council, "that the new C.P.R. hotel will be erected on the property of the Douglas estate . . . an ideal site for such a building."[2]

"It is a matter of common knowledge," the *Colonist* reported, "that the C.P.R. has had a bond on the Douglas property for some time."

Everyone agreed that the Douglas estate was an excellent site. "While handy to the city, and commanding a splendid view of the harbour and its environs, it is close to all points of interest — the Parliament Buildings, Beacon Hill park, the Beach drives, etc." The C.P.R. could do no better. Or then again maybe it could. It was not beyond the bounds of probability, an unidentified informant told the *Colonist*, that the C.P.R. might prefer to build on the reclaimed land behind the newly built Causeway.

Until 1901 the city had been divided by James Bay, a narrow protected inlet which dwindled into a tidal mud flat extending well inland and separating the James Bay residential area and the legislative precinct from the downtown business district and the harbour. In 1859 a bridge had been built across the inlet connecting Government Street with Birdcage Walk and shortening the journey between the two parts of town. Over the years the mud flats had become a stinking tidal garbage dump, rank with rotting seaweed, the occasional dead horse, the effluvia from the Pendray Soap Factory and anything else passing citizens happened to throw into the water. In 1901 the City held a plebiscite asking voters to approve the expenditure of their tax dollars to replace the rickety old bridge with a causeway which would cut the mud flats off from the sea and allow them to be filled in. Appalled by the *Colonist*'s description of the mud flats as an unsightly cesspool and the bridge as a tottering structure and alarmed when the provincial medical health officer termed the flats an absolute menace to health, the voters approved the by-law, little guessing that the reclaimed land would become the most desirable and the most valuable piece of real estate in the city.

After several months passed with no further word from Sir Thomas, a more influential hotel committee was formed comprised of representatives from the Board of Trade, the Tourist Association and City Council. This committee, charged with preparing definite proposals to put before Shaughnessy on his next visit to the city, came up with three alternative suggestions. If the C.P.R. agreed to build on Douglas' garden the City, with ratepayer approval, would exempt the company from taxation for a period of twenty-five years and in addition would, at its own expense, lay out the reclaimed James Bay flats as pleasure grounds and gardens. If the company decided instead to purchase and enlarge the existing Driard Hotel the same exemptions would apply. Then, almost as an afterthought, the committee added a third proposal. If the company should happen to prefer to build on the reclaimed land behind the Causeway, a site which was after all according to the Mayor, practically valueless, then the city would make the C.P.R. a gift of the land, free of cost.

The committee put the sweetened pot on the back of the stove until May 1903 when Shaughnessy once again paid his annual visit to the city. Arriving at the appointed hour, the committee met with Sir Thomas in the parlour of the Driard and received a most distressing piece of news.

"Now, I understand you gentlemen want to talk to me about a hotel," Sir Thomas said, getting right to the point. "I want to say that our company is very much adverse to going any further into the hotel business."[3]

But, the committee protested, a tourist hotel in the city would prove to be a very profitable venture.

"Well, as I have said before," Sir Thomas reminded the despondent committee, "we do not want to go into the hotel business. In addition to it locking up a great amount of capital ... it entails a good deal of permanent expense, and the success of it otherwise rests upon our being able to secure an efficient manager and staff which is often extremely difficult. Consequently such an undertaking is a continual source of trouble."

"At the same time," Sir Thomas continued and the committee's spirits began to rise, "provided I was prepared to recommend to our company the erection of such a hotel, what co-operation could we expect on the part of the citizens?"

What the C.P.R. could expect, the committee assured Shaughnessy, was the acceptance of one of the proposals that had been worked out over the last few months and they carefully explained the advantages of each. After studying the three alternatives, Shaughnessy suggested a fourth.

"If the city will supply the site," he said, "and exempt us from taxation and give us free water for 20 years, we will build a hotel to cost not less than $300,000."

Elated, the members of the committee thanked Shaughnessy for making a distinct offer. But the Mayor did have one reservation. If the City donated the site it might be difficult to win voter approval for a tax exemption lasting twenty years, he warned.

"Well, that is my proposition," Shaughnessy said, "if you care to accept it all right, but if not, you can make one, but bear in mind that the company is not anxious to go into the hotel business."

The committee scurried to City Hall to get a copy of the plans of the James Bay flats, the piece of city owned land they felt most likely to meet with Sir Thomas' approval and taking the plans to Rattenbury, they asked him to sketch in the ground floor of an hotel to prove to Shaughnessy that they were offering him a suitable site.

The following evening, armed with Rattenbury's sketches which showed much more than they had asked for, they called on Shaughnessy and showing him the plans, asked if the four and a half acres they proposed to give the company would be satisfactory to him. Indeed, the land did seem to satisfy Sir Thomas. In fact only one thing concerned him. The plan sketched by Rattenbury was for a five storey hotel of 150 bedrooms. That, said Sir Thomas, would not be large enough! He preferred one of not less than 250 rooms.

"If we build a hotel it must be a good one and adequate to our needs," Shaughnessy informed the members of the committee who didn't stop to think that this was a rather odd thing for Sir Thomas to say since, for the last two years, he had consistently maintained that it was not in the company's best interest to build any hotel in the city at all.

Even stranger was the illustration run by the *Colonist* the following day when the paper broke the story of Shaughnessy's distinct offer. Identified as a sketch "made some time ago" by Rattenbury, it showed a truly monumental Inner Harbour. On the right were the Parliament Buildings, and beside them on the site of Douglas' garden was a building identified as a college. On the left was the already built Post Office and beside that the Carnegie Library. And there, in the middle, atop the reclaimed mud flats, sat the C.P.R. tourist hotel, the magnificent centrepiece, the pivotal point around which Rattenbury's whole grand Inner Harbour scheme revolved.

Surprisingly the sketch raised nary an eyebrow although it had obviously been drawn at least two months earlier, at a time when the committee still considered the Douglas gardens to be the chosen site. After a year of argument and discussion, it had been decided on April 3, 1903 to site the Carnegie Library on Yates Street. But Rattenbury's sketch clearly showed the library at the corner of Government and Humboldt Streets. He had sketched the Inner Harbour plan showing the tourist hotel sitting elegantly on the mud flats two months before the committee had first suggested the site to the C.P.R.

Perhaps Rattenbury had, at the committee's request, sketched plans for each of the three sites proposed to Shaughnessy. Or perhaps the prominent Victorians who served on the committee and City Council had promised the reclaimed land to the company well in advance of any official announcement and had been carefully preparing voters for the city's final offer to the C.P.R. But more likely, like the ordinary citizens who later approved the by-law granting concessions to the company, they too had been manipulated by the

C.P.R. with Rattenbury, Shaughnessy and Captain Troup, manager of the company's coastal steamers, pulling the strings.

Despite the C.P.R. president's apparent disinterest, it seems highly probable that the company had decided to build an hotel at the time they acquired the Canadian Pacific Navigation Company's fleet in 1901. Shaughnessy, had he not recommended the construction of a tourist hotel in Victoria, would have been reversing a company policy which had proved to be highly successful since 1886 when the first tourist hotels in the Rockies had been built.

The C.P.R. had already invested over $700,000 in its coastal fleet, when in February 1902, Captain Troup announced that the company had commissioned the construction of a ship designed to be the fastest and most luxurious vessel in service on the coast and intended for use on the Vancouver-Victoria run. From the beginning Troup had had no doubts that Victoria had the potential of becoming a tourist mecca, attracting the extremely wealthy class of people who were then travelling about the continent in search of the warm climate, the scenic drives and the picturesque waterfront that the city offered. All that Victoria lacked was the truly first class accommodation to which such people were accustomed. With its vast resources and its experience in running grand hotels in Montreal and Quebec City, the C.P.R. was certainly capable of correcting that deficiency.

Rattenbury would have been content with neither a reconstructed Driard Hotel nor a new structure on the Douglas gardens. An architect who could never be accused of thinking small, he had envisioned not just a château-style hotel but a whole harbourscape, a picturesque waterfront ringed with impressive structures, and dominated by buildings he had designed. Sited on the reclaimed land the hotel rising imposingly above the causeway would grasp the attention of passengers lining the rails of steamers sailing into the harbour. The first building seen after rounding Laurel Point, it would become etched on a visitor's memory as the building which, above all others, he identified with Victoria.[4] Such a concept would have appealed to Shaughnessy as much as it did to Rattenbury and there can be little doubt that they decided together that only this spectacular site would do. Of course to have admitted such a thing at the outset would have meant that the C.P.R. might have had to be content with only a gift of the land. By coyly feigning indifference to the very idea of an hotel, the C.P.R. could expect to be showered with civic favours. Victoria was desperately eager to be made a C.P.R. town.

Sir Titus Salt's mill at Saltaire designed by Lockwood and Mawson in 1850.
BRADFORD METROPOLITAN LIBRARIES

Bradford Town Hall designed by Lockwood and Mawson and officially opened in 1873. BRADFORD METRO-POLITAN LIBRARIES

Cleckheaton Town Hall designed by Rattenbury in 1887 and exhibited by the Royal Academy in 1891.
D. REKSTEN

Rattenbury's sketch for the B.C. Parliament Buildings. PABC

Autumn 1893. In a field near the site, stonemasons square blocks of granite for the Buildings' east wall. PABC

Since the government could hardly be left homeless for five years while construction progressed, the new buildings were sited between and around the old Birdcages. PABC

Official opening ceremonies February 10, 1898. The only dignitary conspicuous by his absence was the architect. L. MCCANN AND MARY BURTON

The completed buildings after the removal of the Birdcages. The photographer, perhaps Rattenbury himself, has taken care to capture the view shown on the architect's competition sketch. L. MCCANN AND MARY BURTON

Florence Eleanor Nunn on her wedding day, June 18, 1898. PABC

The *Ora* lining up the Five Finger Rapids. She shot the rapids, Rattenbury reported, without so much as removing even a scrap of paint from her bottom. PABC

Florrie christened the *Nora* and then climbed aboard her for the trip to Dawson. PABC

Pat Burns' Calgary home designed by Rattenbury in 1899. GLENBOW-ALBERTA INSTITUTE

Cary Castle, B.C.'s Government House. A well-loved oddity it was destroyed by fire in 1899. PABC

The kitchen of Rattenbury's home, lined from floor to ceiling with marble. L. CARROLL

Completed in 1903, Rattenbury's Cary Castle was reminiscent of the old but on a grander scale. A Board of Arbitration found that "striking irregularities" had prevailed throughout the course of the contract. PABC

A special English grate, easily recognizable as a mate to those at Cary Castle, graced the fireplace of Rattenbury's dining room. L. MCCANN AND MARY BURTON

"Iechineel," Rattenbury's home on the beach at Oak Bay c. 1900. A country cottage of rough stone and dark stained shingles, it was very much in keeping with Oak Bay's rural character. PABC

The Rattenbury designed Rockland Avenue home of Lyman Poore Duff. PABC

Rattenbury's "addition" to Mount Stephen House. The first gable on the far left is the original hotel. PABC

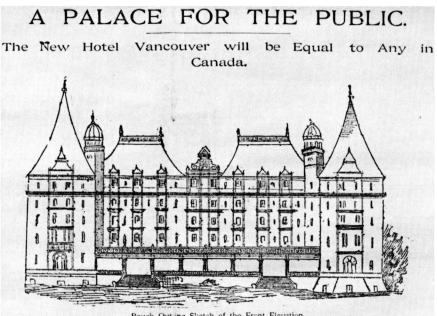

A PALACE FOR THE PUBLIC.

The New Hotel Vancouver will be Equal to Any in Canada.

Rough Outline Sketch of the Front Elevation.

Rattenbury's preliminary sketch for the reconstruction of the Hotel Vancouver.
VANCOUVER PROVINCE, FEBRUARY 19, 1901

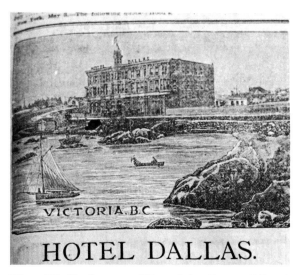

VICTORIA, B.C.

HOTEL DALLAS.

The "Dallas" near Victoria's Outer Wharf, remodelled by Rattenbury in 1902 and bankrupted a few years later by the success of the Empress.
DAILY COLONIST, MAY 4, 1902

SKETCH FOR PROPOSED C. P. R. HOTEL, JAMES BAY CAUSEWAY.

Rattenbury's sketch of the Inner Harbour with the Empress sitting grandly atop the reclaimed mud flats. The Parliament Buildings are on the right and the proposed Carnegie Library is on the left. DAILY COLONIST, MAY 23, 1903

Rattenbury's Empress rising grandly above the Causeway. A banner proclaims that th
was supplied by the Melrose Company Ltd. but doesn't mention that Ratz was one
pany's directors. PABC

The Oak Bay Hotel designed by Rattenbury for his friend John Virtue in 1904.

The Nelson courthouse designed in 1906.

Rattenbury found the continuing urge to improve his home well nigh irresistible and by 1912 the beachside cottage had become a waterfront mansion. PABC

The Victoria High School, designed by Rattenbury in 1901 and described as a "barn-like structure" by school trustee Dr. Hall. PABC

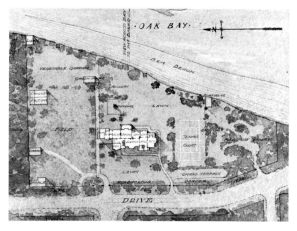

Rattenbury's plans for the grounds of "Iechineel."
L. MCCANN AND MARY BURTON

Prince Rupert c. 1910. The city, Charles Melville Hayes declared, was foreordained to be a western metropolis. The large frame building in the centre of the picture is the Grand Trunk Pacific's first hotel designed by Rattenbury in 1906. PABC

"Take the case of Quebec," Alderman Rickaby intoned. "Ten years ago that city was practically dead, but today it is one of the finest and most prosperous cities in the Dominion. The whole character of the city has been changed by the influence of the C.P.R. hotel there. Tourists and visitors are attracted from all portions of the globe and the fine service furnished, coupled with the historic interest in the environment has caused the fame of Quebec to be known everywhere. The car service is as good as any in the Dominion, and the streets are beautifully paved and clean. Not only the C.P.R., but every other hotel in the city is crowded and business is in the very best shape."[5]

So excited were Victorians, so grateful were they that the C.P.R. had been persuaded into bestowing such great benefits on their city, that it was almost impossible to find anyone who opposed the by-law granting concessions to the company. The ballots, counted on September 16, 1903 showed that while only eighty-five voters had any serious reservations, 1,810 had heartily supported the by-law. The C.P.R. would be given the reclaimed land but the city had driven a hard bargain regarding the other concessions and the company would be provided with free water and tax exempt status for only fifteen years — five years less than the twenty they had originally demanded. However the city did guarantee to complete the land fill, to build good roads and sidewalks around the property, and to prevent the construction of any "bad" buildings near the site.

Sir Thomas announced that he was pleased with the results of the vote and promised Victorians that construction would begin at an early date. By December 1903 Rattenbury's plans were ready.

The company would build a substantial seven storey building, "a picturesque castle effect of the French Renaissance school of architecture ... suggestive of the much-admired Château Frontenac." For skeptical Victorians who pictured so large a stone building sinking majestically out of sight down and down through many layers of fill, Ratz added the assurance that an eminent experienced engineer would be employed to solve the problems of the hotel's foundation. While the foundation was being laid, Rattenbury said, he would prepare the detailed working drawings so that construction could proceed without delay. With its many elaborate features, the hotel itself would become a tourist attraction. Its "Old English style" entrance hall which would be furnished and designed without regard to cost, its large glass roofed palm garden decorated Chinese style in red and gold, its massive dining room which would be nobly and elaborately decorated and would feature "nothing quaint," its oval shaped ladies' salon decorated in the "Marie Antoinette style," and its oak panelled reading room and library with Inglenook fireplaces would lure visitors to the city and charm them into a long stay. To Victorians it all sounded quite exotic and should there be any final doubters, C.P.R. president Sir Thomas Shaughnessy promised that the company would turn the old mud flats into "the beauty spot of Canada." A promise not to be taken lightly according to Rattenbury who said that Sir Thomas intended to fulfill his commitments to the city "to the last tittle and jot."

But to make a beauty spot out of a mud flat took longer than Ratz or the C.P.R. had predicted. An hotel of the size of the one designed by Rattenbury could not be properly centred on the causeway using only the land the company had received from the city and rather than see the hotel squeezed over to the right the C.P.R. had decided to delay construction while they quietly purchased land along Humboldt Street. By June 1904 they had managed to buy out all the property owners except one. He owned a key lot at the southeast corner of Government and Humboldt Streets and he refused to sell. Dismayed at the prospect of one recalcitrant landowner delaying the construction of the long awaited tourist hotel, the City Council decided to expedite the negotiations by adopting the simple course of expropriating the property. Now the C.P.R. was ready to proceed — provided of course the voters would agree to extend the company's tax exempt status to the newly-acquired land along Humboldt Street. Once again ratepayers went to the polls and once again they overwhelmingly approved the granting of concessions to the C.P.R. But the ballots, counted on July 7, 1904, showed that this time the turnout had been much lower. Interest in the much-vaunted tourist hotel was flagging.

By the time construction was finally underway in August 1905, the C.P.R. hotel which had caused such excitement had become a subject viewed with distinct ennui by all those who weren't still grumbling about the delays. It was time for him to pique public interest, Ratz decided.

For years the building had been known simply as the "C.P.R. hotel" or the "tourist hotel." Now, although the company may well have already decided that only the "Empress" would do, evoking as it did the great days of the British Raj when Queen Victoria had been named Empress of India and more practically identifying the hotel with the same company that ran the Empress line of sleek steamers sailing between the west coast and the Orient, Rattenbury suggested that it might be a good idea to hold a public competition to select a name for the hotel and he mused aloud to a handy reporter from the *Colonist* about possible choices.[6]

The question of a name for the hotel was one that "bristles with difficulties," Rattenbury said dangling the carrot in front of the donkey.

There are so many considerations to be borne in mind. [It must be a name both dignified and attractive and it should also have some historical associations.]

"The Hotel Van Horne" is good, but it has been snapped up by Winnipeg. "The Douglas Arms" would have the desired heraldic advantage, but otherwise is the sort of name adopted by places of lesser consequence.

It would be a good idea to get His Majesty King Edward to plant an oak for us, having it shipped out for replanting and name the hotel "The Royal Oak" but that again has its objections, and through constant use has become hackneyed and lost something of its dignity.

"The San Juan de Fuca" has been suggested, but is rather too much of a mouthful, besides having other euphonic objections.

Another suggestion had been "The Camosun" and while Rattenbury admitted that the name did have local colour he felt the reference was obscure and little known and would hardly serve the purpose.

The decision would have to be made soon, Ratz warned, for the hotel would be completed by the following summer.

If all Victoria wasn't talking about the C.P.R. hotel now, it certainly wasn't Rattenbury's fault.

But by November 1906, fourteen months after Rattenbury's optimistic prediction, the hotel had still not opened its doors and the Tourist Association, doubting that it would be ready to receive guests by the following summer, wondered where the visitors attracted by their 135,000 judiciously circulated pamphlets would stay.

"It is high time something be done," Rattenbury said with some disgust, placing the blame for the delay firmly on the city. The agreement between the C.P.R. and the city clearly stated that preparing the grounds for landscaping was a civic responsibility, but as yet the land was still seven feet lower than the necessary level.

The company planned to lay out tennis lawns, pleasure grounds and rockeries, Rattenbury said, "but it is useless to talk of all that until there is some sign of the first preliminary measures being taken by the city to fulfill their part of the contract. Then will be time enough to talk about the completion of ours."[7]

Had he been produced from a company mold, Rattenbury could not have been a more fitting representative of the C.P.R.'s interests on the west coast. And, in his turn, he had exerted a powerful influence over the company's public image. In the space of a few years he had designed an almost new Hotel Vancouver, he had been charged with the interior decoration of the company's luxurious steamer, the *Princess Victoria*, he had designed and supervised the construction of the Empress Hotel. As well as his addition to Mount Stephen House at Field, he had been asked to prepare plans for the enlargement of the Banff Springs Hotel. Soon tourists, journeying from Calgary to Vancouver Island, would travel the entire route stopping off in Rattenbury-designed hotels and sailing to the island on a Rattenbury-decorated ship.

It was astounding news then when Rattenbury announced that he had severed his connection with the C.P.R. He had become impatient with the interference of the C.P.R.'s head architect, Walter S. Painter, in the design of the Empress Hotel. A few months earlier, he had succeeded in defeating Painter's suggestion that the lounge and dining room be moved from the first to the second floor. But Painter could not resist the temptation to meddle with Rattenbury's design. Now, he argued that the smoking room should become a ladies' parlour; the manager's office should be moved to provide a view of the gardens; and a servants' staircase should be added to the exterior so that staff could travel from the upper floors to their basement dining room without having to pass through the kitchen.

Rattenbury was furious. The staircase addition, he deemed "a Hideous excrescence." And as for the ladies' parlour, the original design had included just such a room, but Hayter Reed, the company's Superintendent of Hotels, had objected to it, arguing that "the tendency these days is not to be cut off." Rattenbury had changed the plans accordingly. And now Reed and Painter wanted it back.

"I can see no reason, or at the very best a very inadequate reason, for the sweeping changes suggested by Mr. Painter," he seethed.

On October 30, 1906 he informed the C.P.R., "It is with great regret that I retire from the direction of the completion of the Hotel."

The company accepted his resignation with alacrity, a decision based not only on a desire to support Painter but also because of a growing unease about Rattenbury's loyalty based on his involvement with a competing railway line, the Grand Trunk Pacific.

In November 1902, Charles Melville Hays, second vice-president and general manager of Canada's oldest railroad, the Grand Trunk, had announced that his company intended to built a transcontinental railway with a terminus on the North Pacific Coast. Operating under a separate charter, the Grand Trunk Pacific would inject new life into the moribund parent company by giving it access to the west coast and the lucrative Oriental trade.

Like Van Horne and Shaughnessy, the two men most responsible for the success of the C.P.R., Hays was an American, born in Rock Island, Illinois in 1856. After spending more than twenty-five years in the employ of American railroad companies, Hays, whose forceful personality and innovative ideas had saved several lines from bankruptcy, had accepted the position offered to him by the Grand Trunk and had immediately begun planning the transcontinental rail line which would undo the monopoly the C.P.R. had enjoyed for almost twenty years.

Whatever the C.P.R. did well, Hays decided, the Grand Trunk Pacific would do better. The new line would be of the most modern and up-to-date character, he promised. Bridges would be built of steel rather than wood. The tracks would be carefully laid out to avoid steep grades and sharp curves and ample station facilities would be built to handle passengers and freight. Benefiting from technological advances, the Grand Trunk Pacific would offer passengers the safest and most comfortable ride available on any railroad on the continent.

But as Hays made clear, he had plans for more than just a railroad. "Having reached the Pacific Coast," he said, "the company will undertake to establish a line of steamships to run to China, Japan and the Orient."[8] Ships, Hays might have added, which would offer direct competition to the C.P.R.'s Empress fleet and which would have the advantage of sailing out of a port five hundred miles closer to the docks of Hong Kong and Yokohama.

The Grand Trunk Pacific had selected as its western terminus a location suggested to the C.P.R. by Sanford Fleming in 1877. Taking a much more northerly course than that finally selected by the C.P.R., the tracks would pass through central British Columbia following the Nechako, Endako and Bulkley rivers emerging on the Pacific at the mouth of the Skeena, where the terminal city would be built on a lonely lump of rock and muskeg known as Kaien Island. Kaien, which meant "foam which floats upon water," was hardly a name that rang with promise and in 1905 Hays had announced that a nation-wide competition would be held to select a more appropriate one. For a prize of $250, contestants were asked to come up with a name which had some British Columbian significance and contained fewer than ten letters and no more than three syllables. The contest had the desired effect keeping the G.T.P. in the public eye and attracting 12,000 entrants, some of whom may have been rather distressed when they learned that the prize had gone to the niece of Manitoba's Lieutenant-Governor, Miss Eleanor Macdonald, who had ignored most of the rules, but in suggesting Prince Rupert had apparently come up with a name which sounded just the right note of noble adventure and profitable investment — although just what B.C. connections were enjoyed by the Governor of the "Company of Adventurers of England trading into Hudson's Bay," only the Grand Trunk Pacific knew.

Hays foresaw a day when Prince Rupert would become the Venice of the north, a glittering and elegant city of wide boulevards and magnificent buildings. And it seems that from the beginning Rattenbury had shared his dream. On November 6, 1906 just four weeks before he resigned from the C.P.R., Rattenbury had announced that he had completed plans for a G.T.P. hotel to be erected in Prince Rupert. A handsome frame structure costing between $40,000 and $50,000, it was only the beginning, meant to be used only temporarily until the day when the rail line was nearing completion and a truly grand hotel would be built.

And in 1903, Ratz had purchased eleven thousand carefully selected acres in the Nechako Valley — a full five years before the G.T.P. publicly announced that the tracks would be definitely located through the area. Ratz was certainly blessed with enviable prescience. Or, perhaps more likely, he had received some friendly advice from G.T.P. personnel.

In 1899 he had designed a home on Rockland Avenue for Ernest Victor Bodwell. One of the most prominent lawyers in the province, Bodwell had been appointed by the G.T.P. to act as their agent in the rather indirect purchase, through an American investor Peter Larsen, of ten thousand acres of crown land on Kaien Island and the mainland. Bodwell was certainly in a position to make more than an educated guess about the route the railroad would take through British Columbia and he may well have advised Rattenbury that land along the Nechako River would prove to be a very sound investment.

As well as offering him a chance to dabble in land speculation, Rattenbury's involvement with the G.T.P. would also present him with, what was for an architect, a once in a lifetime opportunity to let loose his imagination and exercise his talents on a spectacularly grand scale. But that was in the future, when the line was nearing completion, and in the meantime Rattenbury would have to endure some hard times and some particularly bitter disappointments.

7

His Reputation Begins to Dull
somewhat disappointed

"A good New Year to you," William Oliver, a lawyer who would later become the first Reeve of Oak Bay, wrote to a friend on January 4, 1906. "We missed you at the national annual sacrament. The usual archangels were there — Pike Holland Hamfields McGregor Irvine Rattenbury Newton. Irvine broke one of my wifes best drawing room chairs, and Rattenbury's dress coat which was bought for the occasion was hanging in rags as he left. It was a very successful celebration and as my wife and family are still in the old country no one was disturbed. I was surprised to find so much spirit of abandon still lurking in lads from 38 to 55."[1]

The year the lads had greeted with such abandon proved to be a most satisfactory one for Rattenbury. In January, he toured northern Alberta with David Ker of the Victoria based Brackman-Ker milling company. Ker, who had travelled to the area to select sites for his company's wheat elevators, and Rattenbury, who remained alert to whatever possibilities for sound investment might present themselves, had been so overcome by the booming city of Edmonton that within twenty-four hours of their arrival they purchased a lot on Jasper Avenue. The sale was a high water mark in the price of realty on Jasper Avenue, the *Edmonton Daily Bulletin* reported, adding that the deal was one of the quickest that had been consumated in Edmonton for some time.

Rattenbury's share of the $30,000 required to buy the property was proof not only of a healthy bank account but also of an unbridled confidence in the success of the Grand Trunk Pacific. Edmonton was already growing apace. Its population, estimated at fourteen thousand people, was increasing at thirty per cent a year as settlers flocked to the city and the surrounding rich farmland from Eastern Canada, the United States and Europe. One transcontinental rail line, the C.N.R., had reached Edmonton the year before but as yet, Rattenbury was convinced, the city was only on the brink of the fantastic growth and development which would follow once the G.T.P. arrived on the scene.

Exhilarated by the thought that he had been one of the first to recognize the potential of the city, Rattenbury became an energetic Edmonton booster. Returning to Victoria in February he painted a glowing picture of "Sunny Alberta." For Edmonton in particular he predicted a splendid future.

"Do you know that you can get coal in Edmonton at the present time for a dollar and a half a ton?" he asked a *Times* reporter. "Think of that, and what we are paying for it on the coast here,* and remembering that the fields are scarcely opened up, and you may perhaps obtain some idea of its possibilities." And not only that, but the surrounding countryside was "very pretty" and the climate "excellent."[2]

While in Edmonton, Rattenbury had purchased another piece of property and the sense of relief he experienced at finally having the deed to Mary Tod Island in his pocket had added to the cheerful optimism that had been so evident on his return to Victoria. The tiny island of about five acres which lay just a few hundred yards off the beach in front of Rattenbury's home and John Virtue's Oak Bay Hotel, which Rattenbury had designed in 1904,[3] had come into the possession of one St. Clair Blackett who resided in Edmonton. For several years Ratz and Virtue had shared the nagging worry that someone might build a house, or even worse a fish packing plant, on the island spoiling the uncluttered view they both enjoyed. But happily, Ratz had induced Blackett to sell and the following summer the gorse and broom which he had planted in his greenhouse in preparation for just this event would make the "rather bleak bit of rock a thing of beauty and an object of attraction."[4]

Other Oak Bay concerns were to occupy a great deal of Rattenbury's attention that year. In 1862 when Victoria was incorporated as a city, little thought had been given to including Oak Bay within the civic boundaries. Lying along the southeast shore of the island, three miles from the centre of the city, Oak Bay was considered to be remote and with its 2,500 acres divided among only five landowners, sparsely settled. The Hudson's Bay Company's 1,000 acre Uplands Farm sprawled over the high ground to the north. South

* $8.00 a ton.

of the Company land was John Tod's 400 acre farm and, except for smaller holdings farmed by the Ross and McNeil families, the rest of Oak Bay was part of J. D. Pemberton's vast estate. In the 1880's following John Tod's death, small parcels of his land were sold and a few houses began to appear scattered along Cadboro Bay Road, the narrow country lane which ran from Tod's farmhouse down to the city. But it was not until the 1890's that Oak Bay came to be regarded as a desirable place to live by more than a handful of people.

Victoria housewives, especially those who lived near the harbour or the business district, had come to dread the hot summer months, when the noise of the city rumbled and clattered through windows thrown open to catch the breeze and the sooty smoke from ships and waterfront industries combined with the dust from unpaved streets to settle in a grimy film over furniture and draperies. Oak Bay with its rural peace, its clear air and its sheltered beaches became home to a growing number of summer people as families deserted the city and spent the season in wooden-floored tents and little cottages strung along the beach.

Witnessing this annual exodus, Beaumont Boggs calculated that fortunes might be made by capitalizing on Oak Bay's appeal. Boggs and a group of fellow Victoria realtors pooled their resources to buy a large tract of land on the shores of the bay. Some of the land they intended to subdivide and sell under contracts carefully drawn to insure the erection of only the finest class of residence. A few acres along the waterfront they set aside as the site of a handsome hotel, with lawn-tennis and pleasure grounds attached, and Boggs threw himself into the promotion of the scheme.

It is certainly fair to say that no more picturesque location could be found. The land itself, interspersed with moss-grown rocks and oak trees, is at once a delightful pleasure resort; while the sandy pebbled beach furnishes a recreation ground for children. The water itself is warm and furnishes splendid bathing; while from the jutting banks of rocks, stretching out here and there, the fisherman seldom returns empty handed. The bay is simply superb, with its placid waters naturally protected by the islands to be seen in every direction, and here the troller will find plenty of salmon or the huntsman water fowl; while in the woods, a quarter of a mile back from the shores the pheasant and grouse are numerous.[5]

And all this, Boggs enthused, was to be found an easy drive from Victoria. Before they had committed themselves to buying the land, the members of Boggs' syndicate had reached an agreement with the Electric Railway Company to extend its Fort Street line out to the water's edge and soon Oak Bay's countryside became easily accessible as well as highly desirable.

Built in 1891, the hotel, designed by architects Teague and Muir and christened the Mount Baker, proved to be an instant success. Managed by John Virtue, who had been lured away from the C.P.R.'s Hotel Vancouver, it became famous on three continents as a popular stopping off place for English residents of the Orient who passed through Victoria on their way to and from the Old Country. And so great were Virtue's innkeeping abilities that it became fashionable for Victorians to hold banquets and balls at the Mount Baker in spite of the fact that these festivities had to end at an un-fashionably early hour so that the celebrants could catch the last streetcar home.

Not wanting to rely solely on the hotel's patrons for customers, the streetcar company developed a sportsfield at the end of the Oak Bay line with space provided for soccer and rugby games as well as track and field competitions. And after the Victoria Golf Club laid out its course on part of the Pemberton estate, Oak Bay could boast of offering the best there was in the way of elegant indoor entertainment and vigorous outdoor recreation.

Gradually people came to think of Oak Bay as more than just a summer resort. In 1899 Rattenbury began building his home on five waterfront acres along the beach from the Mount Baker Hotel. And among those who joined him as early residents were two men who were to become his friends and who would share his interest in the political life of Oak Bay, William Oliver and James Herrick McGregor.

William Oliver had come to Oak Bay to be near the golf course. A lawyer and one-time partner of Lyman Duff, he glowed with the good humour of a man who, despite his prominence in the legal community, refused to take himself altogether seriously.

James Herrick McGregor was a partner in one of the province's largest firms of land surveyors. A cheerful outgoing man who shared with Rattenbury an early and abiding affection for the automobile and who revelled in the hectic races staged by fellow enthusiasts, he also enjoyed solitude and the opportunity to let his mind wander over a wide range of topics. He was an actor, a poet and a philosopher — equally at home spouting Robert Burns' poetry with an exuberance which led people to believe he had been born in Scotland rather than Montreal, regaling the patrons of the Boomerang Saloon with tall stories of his travels throughout the province or composing poetry and essays which combined "pearls of wisdom, bits of philosophy, religion and humour."[6]

By 1906 over one hundred families resided in Oak Bay and to many of them it had become apparent that living in an essentially rural unorganized community had certain drawbacks. To travel on the narrow, rutted roads meant being choked by summer dust or mired in winter mud. Wandering cows grazed through gardens trampling flowers that had managed to survive despite the competition from thistles and other weeds blown from farmers' fields. With no sewage system, Oak Bay's open roadside ditches had developed a distinctive aroma which became particularly disagreeable when combined with the stench from the large piggeries which operated on part of the former Tod farm.

Rattenbury, Oliver, McGregor and other permanent residents including Sam Maclure, who had built his house on the waterfront between the hotel and Rattenbury's home, formed the Oak Bay Improvements Association and after an unsuccessful attempt to convince Victoria to extend its boundaries to include Oak Bay, they petitioned the Provincial Secretary for the right to form a separate municipality. And on July 2, 1906 the Letters Patent were signed creating the "Corporation of the District of Oak Bay." At a meeting of the Improvements Association chaired by McGregor and held "to discuss some unanimous acting with the object of preventing, if possible, the expense and annoyance of an election," William Oliver was appointed Reeve and Rattenbury agreed to serve as one of four Councillors.

One issue which loomed large for Oak Bay's first council was the matter of the municipal seal. At the first council meeting held on July 14, Rattenbury was given full power to act and in due course he produced the design which over the years many people have found somewhat puzzling — for unlike other civic crests, which tend to run to lions, unicorns and matronly angels, the seal of B.C.'s most English municipality carries the likeness of an American mountain. Rattenbury simply gazed out of his window and sketched what he saw — Mount Baker towering above the waters of the straits with a sailboat gently heeled over in the foreground.

But more than local politics was keeping Rattenbury busy in 1906. An architect who had seldom lacked domestic commissions he found that since the completion of Cary Castle his services were even more in demand and during that summer and fall he designed homes for several prominent Victorians, including County Court Judge Peter Secord Lampman. And in addition the provincial government asked him to design two new courthouses, one for Vancouver and the other for Nelson. The Vancouver courthouse, expected to cost $150,000 and described as being classic in design, would "take second place only to the parliament buildings among the large public structures in British Columbia." The Nelson courthouse would not be as massive as that at Vancouver, Rattenbury's plans calling for "a more elaborate form of architecture, beauty instead of imposing grandeur being sought."

By the end of 1906 Rattenbury's influence was felt throughout the province — from Victoria where the Parliament Buildings and Empress Hotel gave a monumental importance to the Inner Harbour, to Vancouver where the C.P.R. hotel and the courthouse defined the heart of the city, to Prince Rupert where the G.T.P. hotel would soon stand as a symbol of the railway's intention to create a magnificent metropolis, and to Nelson and Rossland and other Interior towns where his buildings had become landmarks signifying permanence and confidence in the future. In the fourteen years that had passed since his arrival in British Columbia, his architectural reputation had never been higher. Throughout those years he had managed to win, by one method or another, almost every important commission that he had chosen to pursue. Now he was invariably described by the press as the well-known architect or the celebrated architect. His artistic abilities appeared to be unchallengeable, his position so secure that his continued success was unquestionable. But then quite suddenly and without warning everything changed.

It all began in December 1906, when the C.P.R. surprised him by accepting his resignation. Then on January 3, 1907 he was sent reeling by a very pointed and equally public attack on his ability as an architect.

The Victoria High School, which he had designed six years earlier, had become severely overcrowded and School Trustee Jay had spoken to him about preparing plans and estimates for an addition. Rattenbury had graciously offered to prepare the plans free of charge and had probably thought no more about it. But when Jay suggested, at the School Board's first meeting of the new year, that Rattenbury be asked to prepare the plans, he found himself set upon by one of his fellow board members, Dr. Ernest Hall.

Born in 1861 in Milton, Ontario, into one of the area's oldest families, Ernest Hall had been graduated from the Royal College of Physicians in Edinburgh and for the last eighteen years had practiced his profession in British Columbia. Dr. Hall was nothing if not outspoken. He objected to having the plans prepared by Rattenbury, he fumed.

"The barn-like structure known as the Victoria High School is a specimen of that gentleman's work," Dr. Hall stormed as the other board members fought to retain their composure, "and I don't want any more of his work on the school."

Several trustees disagreed with Dr. Hall. The building was at least serviceable, they opined, and they voted in favour of asking Rattenbury to prepare the drawings and estimates for the addition.

Dr. Hall's remarks might have received little attention and been soon forgotten if Ratz had not been so sensitive to criticism. Quivering with rage, he penned a vitriolic condemnation of Dr. Hall — a long rambling letter in which the height of his passion was matched only by the length of his sentences.

For Dr. Ernest Hall's private opinion as to the merits of any architectural work of mine I have the same contempt as I have for Dr. Hall himself, but I do not propose to allow Dr. Ernest Hall to prostitute his official position as school trustee to the purpose of attacking my professional ability . . .

Some years ago, Ratz recalled, Dr. Hall had written an abusive letter to the *Times* criticizing the design of the High School but he had published it anonymously which, Ratz continued, was characteristic.

Now, acting as a school trustee and posing as an authority, he repeats his abuse — practically saying that he does not consider I have the ability to build an extension to a school. It is too much, I suppose, to expect Dr. Ernest Hall to know what fair criticism is or what is or is not decent and honourable as between professional men.

... the man who could voluntarily get up before the Women's Council as he did lately and deliver an abominable lecture, which I think he entitled "Lifting the Lid Off Hell" in which ... he made atrocious statements reflecting grossly on the men of Victoria, which statements are without any question absolutely untrue and for which he ought to be kicked individually and collectively by every man in Victoria — must have gall enough for anything.

Dr. Hall, credited with being the first to advocate the instruction of both sexes on the subject of venereal diseases, sex problems, etc., would at the slightest provocation rise to his feet and deliver a version of his all purpose lecture entitled "The Relation of Intemperance to Public Life and the Relation of Social Disease to Society." But, although Dr. Hall enjoyed the respect of the most able and successful physicians in the province, Rattenbury was convinced that only self-promotion had prompted his lecture to the women's group.

These statements certainly obtained and were intended to obtain for Dr. Ernest Hall a considerable amount of cheap advertising. Any quack can, however, obtain similar advertising but he generally has to pay for it, whilst Dr. Hall obtained his for nothing.

Such a man, however ignorant he is, may and generally has the cheek, to think that he can offensively criticize anybody or anything. But he certainly, then, cannot reasonably object to others criticizing him. He cannot object to my saying that I consider him a pretty mean specimen of a man, and by no means a credit to his profession. For my own part, I would think, were I to entrust myself to his medical care, I should either be qualified for New Westminster [site of the provincial asylum for the insane] or was desirous of quickly terminating my existence.[7]

It was a particularly nasty, petty exchange and it did not bode well for the following year. And it probably prompted Rattenbury to announce, three weeks later, that he had decided to enter a federal competition being held to select the design for a building to house the Supreme Court in Ottawa. Throughout his career Rattenbury seemed able to find a friendly reporter waiting at his elbow whenever he needed one and this simple announcement was treated as a momentous piece of news.

The competition is open to the world, and will be participated in by the best architects of England, the United States and Canada. That Victoria should be able to boast an architect capable of taking part in the competition with such men is a matter of no small credit to the city.

97

Even should Mr. Rattenbury be unsuccessful in obtaining first place, the fact that Victoria should be represented in the competition at all will serve to bring the city before the attention of the people of the East, while, should his plans be accepted — and Mr. Rattenbury's friends are sure that for the designing of public buildings there are few in America who can surpass him — this advertisement would be one of the best that it would be possible to secure for this city.[8]

So much for Dr. Hall's architectural opinions.

It could be a risky business, this announcing that a bird was in the bush before it was to hand, but luckily for Ratz when the federal government decided to award first prize to E. S. Maxwell of Montreal, the newspapers remained discreetly silent.

It had proved to be so successful an exercise in reputation building that he didn't hesitate to use it again when in August 1907 he was invited to enter another contest — one that he was sure he would win.

For the past two years, since Saskatchewan had entered Confederation and Regina had been selected as the provincial capital, Premier Walter Scott had been puzzling over how best to select an architect to design the province's legislative buildings.

On the morning of September 5, 1906 Scott who was visiting the west coast had met with Rattenbury in Victoria. They had discussed Scott's plans to erect new government buildings and Rattenbury had warned the premier of the dangers of holding a competition. It would be much safer, Ratz had said, to give the work to an architect with an established reputation, namely himself. Scott had hedged. If he decided against holding a competition it might be best to give the commission to a local architect he had said. But Rattenbury was not to be put off that easily. That same afternoon he had written a lengthy letter to the premier in which he had adopted the same tone of disarming helpfulness that he had used six years earlier when he had written to the Chief Commissioner of Lands and Works asking to be retained as architect of B.C.'s Government House.*

* And it should be noted completely reversing his expressed opinions regarding the Carnegie Library.

98

re PARLIAMENT BUILDINGS

Hon Walter Scott
                                    SASKATCHEWAN

Dear Sir

In our conversation of this morning, as to the best method to adopt to ensure the new Parliament Buildings being a success.

You rightly pointed out, how desirable it would be, that the Architect entrusted with this work, should be on the ground, so that he could study the building on the site, and also the materials to be used

A weak point in a Competition would be, that it would only be in rare cases that an Architect in practice could arrange to leave his practice and establish himself in the locality,

In case the great honor of designing your new Parliament Buildings were entrusted to me, I am so situated at the present time, owing to the various large buildings that I am now erecting all being close to completion at the same time.

That I could and would be delighted to come and live in Saskatchewan and study the conditions on the ground, and make the Plans and Models of the building there, and in consultation with you and your Ministers.

I am sure that we could erect Buildings that would utilize the site to obtain a magnificent result, and that the Parliament Buildings both in arrangement and in Design would be worthy of the great future of the Province.

It would be a source of great pride and pleasure to me to be associated in the erection of a Building having such great possibilities to attain a beautiful result

And I would be most happy to make you Sketch Designs on the ground as before suggested, and if I did not achieve as successful a solution of the problem, as you thought possible,

I would not make any charge whatever, and you would be left open to then have a Competition if you deemed it advisable,

I think however that from the experience that I have had in similar works and the Study and labor that I would give to this work, that I need not fear that such action would be found necessary,

I have the honor to be

Yours obediently

F. M. Rattenbury

Architect.[9]

Scott found that his presence was urgently required in Regina and he did not respond to Rattenbury's offer for almost two months.

"While my personal view is pretty strongly in favour of putting the work directly in the hands of an architect of acknowledged standing," Scott had written, "I found that the competition method, especially in regard to a public building, appealed to some of my colleagues with force."[10]

They had decided to hold a limited competition in which Rattenbury and four or five other architects would be invited to enter.

"I shall be most happy to submit Designs in Competition for your proposed Parliament Buildings," Rattenbury had answered "and shall do my best to win."[11]

The following year when he and architects from Regina, Montreal, Toronto, New York and London, England were officially invited to enter the competition, Rattenbury lost no time in informing the Victoria newspapers, and as with the federal competition the resulting article bolstered an architectural reputation that had begun to show some signs of sagging. "F. M. Rattenbury Asked for Designs for Saskatchewan Capital," the *Colonist* headlined the story suggesting to the casual reader that he had already won the contract.

Rattenbury himself may have been lulled into believing that the competition was a mere formality. All contestants had agreed to two assessors or judges — Percy Nobbs, a professor of architecture at McGill University, and Bertram Goodhue, an architect from New York City. But then Scott had written to the competitors asking them if they had any objection to his joining the panel as a third judge. Rattenbury, for one, had no objections. The previous year Scott had written that he had been in favour of giving the contract to an architect of acknowledged standing and Ratz was confident that Scott had been referring to him. He would be most gratified if Scott could see his way clear to act with the other assessors, he wrote to the premier.

"I think it would be a very wise step. For conscientious as Architectural Assessors may be, they are often inclined to lay undue weight on a clever piece of drawing, with the result that whilst the building may be original, it is often not pleasing, and not what you would have desired."[12]

During the previous month, September of 1907, Scott, an angular gaunt faced man whose health was far from robust, had suffered a serious illness and perhaps a recurrence of that illness led him to reconsider his decision to serve as one of the judges. A third assessor was appointed, but he was Frank Day, retiring president of the American Institute of Architects. And Rattenbury was feeling distinctly ungracious when, on November 15, 1907, he received a telegram from Scott asking if he would agree to an extension of fourteen days as requested by some of the competitors.

"My plans completed, so extension of no use to me," Ratz wired back.

The winner was announced on December 21, 1907 and although Ratz would admit to being only somewhat disappointed, it must have been a crushing blow to learn that the winner was E. S. Maxwell, the same architect to whom he had lost the federal competition.

8

Reeve of Oak Bay
to save the golf links

Over the next few years Rattenbury designed no buildings of any consequence — unless he chose to remain unusually quiet about them. With no important commissions tying him down he took the opportunity to indulge his passion for travel. As well as criss-crossing the country several times when he was employed by the C.P.R., he had, since his arrival in British Columbia in 1892, returned to England at least twice — in 1898 to interest investors in the Lake Bennett and Klondike Navigation Company and in 1905 when he had visited London and New York to study the improved modern system of hotel construction.

Not by any means an aimless sightseer, wherever he went he remained alert, actively seeking out new ideas and quick to see how those ideas could be applied to Victoria.

"Two things especially forced themselves on my mind," Rattenbury had reported in 1905 when he returned from his trip to London and New York. "One was that since the motor car as an institution has come to stay, it is obvious that with even the finest system of roads . . . motor travelling is and will continue to be objectionable to everybody, except the occupants of the motor, by reason of the dreadful dust they raise."

While in London he had observed an experimental road paving program with great interest. "What they are doing," he had said, "is to lay on top of the ordinary macadam a layer about six inches thick of a composition made of broken rock, gravel, asphalt and, I understand, some patented mixture." The hoped for result was, he continued, "a pavement at once elastic, practically dustless, fairly noiseless and durable.

"This operation must commend itself to us in Victoria since something of the same nature will certainly require to be done here in the near future."

Something else that had struck him, Rattenbury had said, sounding very much like an architect trying to talk himself into a commission, was the design and the popularity of the modern exhibition buildings to be found in many American cities. Since the city was considering a proposal to build a winter garden, he had been careful to study similar buildings on his travels and had found them to be "palaces of delight for the public."

"Coney Island, for instance, burnt and rebuilt in a palatial manner, remains as a permanent place of amusement and fairyland of light and beauty, and not for the original rough population of Coney Island is this metamorphosis achieved, but for the joy and delectation of New York's working thousands generally. The buildings are practically palaces and are as cheering and attractive as it is possible to make them."[1]

For Rattenbury travel was therapeutic — not because he found it relaxing but because it stimulated and excited him. A man with a fiery temper and burning energy he was only really content when his life was a whirl of feverish activity. When he had no artistic battles to fight, when he had no new ideas or no promising investments to promote, he slipped easily into a state of grim depression. Despondent over the loss of the Regina competition, he decided early in 1908 to take an extended European holiday. Three years before he had been forced to cancel his intended visit to the Continent because of the excessive July heat across the channel. Now he left Victoria in March and taking advantage of the milder spring weather he spent a full three months abroad. He visited Paris and motored around Southern France and then continued south to Florence, Rome, Naples and Pompeii, then turning north he visited Venice and toured the Italian lake district making a special side trip to Lucerne, a city which he felt was in many ways similar to Victoria.

He returned to Victoria in June in what was for him a happy state of impatience and enthusiasm. He had been impressed by what he had seen and he was quick to share the lessons he had learned. And he was driven by a sense of urgency. Victoria's officialdom must follow his advice now — before it was too late.

He was convinced that Victoria's economic future depended on its success as a tourist city. In a tourist city it was especially important, he said, to confine industry to specified areas.

"There has been a piece of beautifying carried out on the causeway," he said referring to the Empress Hotel and its grounds, "and nothing in the way of factories along the James Bay waterfront should be allowed to mar that. The smoke from tall chimneys in that section would be driven over various residential parts, and should not be allowed."

He felt strongly that the height of buildings should be controlled. Lucerne, he said, was strictly a tourist city and everything was made to conform to the idea that it was such.

"A great hotel there of about 6 or 7 stories in height had sought to build 3 or 4 stories higher, but the authorities stepped in and disallowed it, as it would mar the beauty of the place. There was no question raised there as to the power of the municipality to control the situation."

There should also be some civic control over the design of buildings, he argued. In London the city had "an architect of the highest standing in the profession, who exercised, under authority from the council the right to pass on all buildings put up. There the front of a hotel was altered by him because it did not comply with the general scheme of the surroundings as he saw it."[2]

Ratz had always been sensitive to the need to preserve trees. Eleven years earlier, in 1897, he had been aghast when overzealous landscaping had led to the felling of trees around the Parliament Buildings. ". . . it makes me heartsick to see each tree as it falls to the ground," he had written.

"It is so rarely that an architect is fortunate enough to have the opportunity of erecting a large building amongst the delicate tracery of woodland scenery. And the peeps of high masses of stone masonry through the trees gives so distinctive a charm so different to what one would ordinarily see, that words fail to express my grief at seeing that charm disappear. . . . The old axiom is a good one, to think twenty times before you cut down any tree."[3]

He had been pleasantly surprised to learn that in Lucerne the civic authorities agreed with him. There the course of a street had been altered to save a tree. "Imagine a Victoria council doing that," he exclaimed.

He had also come to recognize the importance of setting aside land for parks and playgrounds in rapidly developing cities. In Chicago, he said, determined efforts were now being made to institute a system of parks. "The land is being repurchased at enormous cost, whereas with proper precautions years ago it might have been reserved without an outlay."

He cited Vancouver as an example of a city which had rapidly reached metropolitan proportions only to feel the effects of this grave oversight.

"Already people there who have been almost feverishly engaged in building and expanding in a material way, realize that they have no open spaces in the centre of their city and are agitating to have the provincial government convey the old court house square, now of enormous value, to them for that purpose."

Ratz felt that the government "should insist that all townsite plans should pass a board or bureau, whose duty it would be first, to reserve these open spaces and second, see that the deadly straight street with its deadly rows of uniform buildings, should be prevented, and instead some artistic taste brought to bear in the treatment of streets and buildings."[4]

Rattenbury's ideas must have sounded wildly radical to the members of Victoria's city council. Progress was synonymous with development and might not development be slowed if controls were exercised? And if a man owned a piece of property didn't he have the right to build whatever he wanted on it whether it was a factory or a housing subdivision laid out in the economical grid system? And wasn't Victoria's future as a tourist city guaranteed now that the Empress had finally opened its doors and become the subject of the C.P.R.'s world-wide promotional campaigns?

If they had paused to consider the source of these new ideas they might have reacted differently. Rattenbury was after all something of a land speculator himself and as an architect he had consistently defended his right to exercise full artistic control. He would not have pleaded for governmental control of development unless he felt it was absolutely necessary.

The City of Victoria ignored him. Over the years industries along the waterfront expanded. A paint factory was established on Laurel Point and huge oil storage tanks were sited across the harbour from the Empress Hotel. With no design controls, architects adopted the stark unadorned new styles which might look well in other cities but seemed to be strangely at odds with the city's quaint character and old world charm which the tourist brochures continued to describe with such conviction.

Almost seventy years would pass until it would suddenly occur to Victorians that Rattenbury had been right. Only then, when the flow of tourists had dwindled to a trickle, would businessmen-politicians begin to see the necessity of controlling the design of new construction. And only then would a program be launched to reclaim the industry-scarred land around the Inner Harbour.

But Rattenbury did see his theories put into practice — in his home municipality of Oak Bay and especially in that part of Oak Bay known as the Uplands. The Uplands, although it lay within the municipal boundary, was set up as a distinct entity, subject to by-laws which did not apply to the rest of Oak Bay and from the beginning the exclusive subdivision built on more than four hundred acres which had been part of the old Uplands Farm, benefited from long range planning and strict controls. Laid out by landscape architect Frederick Law Olmstead, Jr., whose father was credited with being America's first landscape architect and town planner, roads in the Uplands flowed gracefully, winding and curving as they followed the natural rise and fall of the land. Only residential buildings were allowed and those buildings were required to meet rigid quality standards, not the least of which regulated design. Houses could be built in whatever style the owner preferred, but they must be unobtrusive, blending with the landscape in keeping with the character of a garden community. The Uplands Company didn't have to look far for an architect whose ideas dovetailed with their own and, as the early development of the Uplands proved, their decision to appoint Rattenbury as their advisory architect was a wise one.

But Rattenbury's influence was felt not just in the Uplands, but throughout the whole municipality. From 1906-1908 he served as a member of Oak Bay council and at his urging a special committee, which became known as the Beauty Committee, was set up "to keep watch and ward over the decorative effect produced by trees planted on boulevards and sidewalks." As the *Times* noted, "The protection of the trees in the municipality of Oak Bay is a perennial question much as it is in the City of Victoria, only that the Oak Bay council seems more anxious to protect than are the aldermen of the city."

In January 1913 Rattenbury announced that he had yielded to the expressed wishes of a host of friends, and had consented to stand for the Reeveship. He was running to save the golf links, he said. The continued existence of Oak Bay's magnificent waterfront golf course was threatened by rising municipal taxation. At that time only land was assessed for tax purposes and if some members of Oak Bay Council had their way the golf course's hundred acres would be assessed at the same rate as land used for housing. The owners of the land, the Gonzales Point Land Company, were bound by an agreement, made at the time of purchase, which fixed the rental charged to the golf club at a maximum of $3,000. If the assessment were to go beyond the amount of rents collected, the Gonzales Point Land Company would subdivide the property. Ratz had decided to run to prevent the subdivision of the golf course but once involved in the campaign he made it clear that it was not the only issue that concerned him.

For Victoria 1912 had been a boom year and the optimism that had prompted the city's growth had had its effect on Oak Bay. Victoria realtors had predicted that the population of the city would soon reach 100,000 and for a time it had looked as if they might be right. In the Fairfield district the swampy fields where children had skated the winter before had become the site of solid Edwardian middle-class houses. On Douglas Street the Hudson's Bay Company had begun construction of the city's largest, most up to date department store. Plans had been announced for a ten-storey skyscraper on Johnson Street. And the first of Victoria's famed cluster lights, known as "Morley's Folly" after the mayor who had campaigned for their installation, had appeared on downtown streets.

In Oak Bay a new municipal hall had opened at the corner of Hampshire and Oak Bay Avenue. Property in the Uplands had been offered for sale and the McNeil farm and part of the Pemberton holdings had been subdivided into small residential lots.

Rattenbury, who carried with him a mental picture of Saltaire, the community designed by Lockwood and Mawson, as an example of what could be accomplished if thoughtful planning preceeded growth, hoped that Oak Bay could avoid the unhappy results of rapid urbanization he had seen in other cities. His platform, as defined in an open letter to the electors, established what has become a tradition in Oak Bay for since his day few municipal elections have been fought in which the preservation of the urban environment has not been the central issue.

I think that the Oak Bay district is one of the most lovely residential areas that I have ever seen, and it is my desire to retain this beauty as far as possible, and the hope that I can help to do so is my only reason for being a candidate at the coming election for Reeve.

One of the leading thoroughfares to Oak Bay is Oak Bay Avenue. There seems to be a tendency at present to erect along this avenue very ugly and cheap looking shacks rented as stores. I think this is ill-advised and will depreciate the values of the property, not only in the avenue itself but in Oak Bay generally. I am of the opinion that regulations should be passed to prevent this, for with very little extra expense these buildings could be made attractive in appearance, and this should be insisted upon.

The beautiful beach drive through the golf links and along Shoal Bay has been the favorite walk and drive in Victoria for years, and there are few drives in the world more beautiful and with such rich and glorious scenery.

To force the links into the ordinary, though perhaps lucrative, building subdivision, — destroying this lovely drive — would be a calamity to Oak Bay and to Victoria, and every effort should be made to avoid this occurring.

Rattenbury was determined to make his appeal as broadly based as possible. "We do not have very many working men in Oak Bay," he wrote, "but I certainly think that in all municipal works, preference should be given to the ratepayers and inhabitants of Oak Bay." And there was one particular municipal work uppermost in his mind. "I think the time has come to build permanent roads," he said. "The old macadam roads will no longer sustain the heavy traffic of today, and any money spent on them seems to be absolutely wasted."

But more than anything else he was concerned about the effects of rapid, unplanned growth which, he was convinced, would erode the residential quality of Oak Bay.

The subdividing of property into comparatively small lots is proceeding so quickly that it is easy to foresee the time when the youngsters will have nowhere to play but in the streets. Open spaces where they can play games should, and must, be obtained immediately.

In regard to taxation, the leading principle to be followed should be that as far as possible all those who pay taxes should receive an adequate return. I personally think that in a residential district it is a question whether the exemption of taxation of all buildings is in accordance with this principle. To my mind it would appear that the taxation of gardens for the support of buildings providing fire protection, police, lighting and schools for the buildings means that inevitably gardens will disappear and close building ensue.[5]

Rattenbury and the slate of aldermanic candidates who supported his views received the backing of a group of prominent Oak Bay residents, which included such men as William Oliver, the ex-Reeve, and John J. Shallcross, a wealthy insurance agent and importer whose Maclure-designed house was set in a five acre Oak Bay estate. Oliver, Shallcross and the other members of the group campaigned for their chosen candidates by placing in the *Times* and *Colonist* large advertisements which seemed to suggest that it was not considered gentlemanly to ask a candidate just where he stood on any particular issue.

We have not asked these gentlemen to pledge themselves to any special policy nor have we asked them to express an opinion on municipal affairs.

We support them simply because we consider them reliable businessmen who may be trusted to manage the affairs of the municipality in a competent and fairminded manner. As such we ask you to vote for them.[6]

If Rattenbury had committed a minor gaucherie by publicly stating his policies, he at least forced the hand of his opponent William Henderson. Henderson, who had the honour of being Oak Bay's first elected reeve, was a seventy-six-year-old architect who had for many years been employed by the federal government. He was running, he said, at the urgent request of a large and influential body of ratepayers.

"I am entirely dissatisfied with the manner in which the affairs of the municipality have been conducted during the past year," he said, taking aim at Oliver, who had served as Reeve in 1912 and whose devotion to the game of golf bordered on conflict of interest. While many property owners had seen their assessments tripled, the golf course continued to be assessed at a very low rate. He didn't want to see the golf course driven out of business, Henderson said, but it was only fair that that property assume a more reasonable share of the tax burden.[7]

The keenest election in years was held on January 18, 1913, the intense interest resulting in one of the largest turnouts in Oak Bay's history. J. Herrick McGregor and the other candidates who had allied themselves with Rattenbury won handily. But Rattenbury himself squeaked in with a majority of only twenty-four votes. Nevertheless he soon proved that despite his slim majority he intended to put his ideas into practice, when in the first months of his reeveship he arranged for the purchase of three and a half acres of land along Willows beach. Children needed open spaces, he had said.

It may well be that given the opportunity he would have initiated bylaws regulating lot size and controlling the design of buildings, but early in his term in office Victoria's speculative bubble burst and the shock waves were felt throughout Oak Bay. Lots went unsold and as development pressure eased, the incentive to institute controls was lost. With the golf course no longer threatened, a change in the method of assessment became an unpalatable prospect, particularly as it became apparent that some Oak Bay residents would be unable to pay their current taxes. And the area's roads continued to be a problem as municipal bonds, meant to finance Rattenbury's extensive road paving program, went unsold.

Rattenbury could hardly have chosen a less auspicious time to serve as Reeve and by the end of 1913 he must have felt discouraged and somewhat dejected. But the realization that he had been able to accomplish so little was only a minor disappointment compared to what the next few years would bring.

9

A Bankrupt Railroad and a Failing Marriage

In 1898, Chief Commissioner of Lands and Works, George Martin, was reputed to have said of the Parliament Buildings, "Never, in 500 years, will the government have enough employees to fill this vast building." But by 1911 the work of the government had expanded to fill every available nook and cranny. Rather than hold a competition, the government decided to ask Rattenbury to design the additions which would nearly double the size of the original buildings. From the time he submitted the first designs, which the government rejected, until he testified at the hearings which seemed to wind up most large government contracts, the east and west wings and the south wing, housing the glass-domed provincial library, would keep Rattenbury busy on and off for the next five years. But they were far from being important enough to occupy his full attention, for although he would have been enraged had any other architect been employed on the Parliament Buildings, his work for the government ranked only second to the commission he had been given by the Grand Trunk Pacific Railway.

By 1911 construction of the line was far from complete, in fact three years would pass before the first transcontinental train steamed into Prince Rupert. But while progress seemed slow the ultimate success of the railroad remained unquestioned, mainly due to the skills of Charles Melville Hays, an aggressive and imaginative promoter.

Prince Rupert had a special place in Hays' affections. Only he could have looked fondly on the bare rocks, the water-logged ground and the raw tree stumps that marked the townsite in 1906 and declare that Prince Rupert was foreordained to be a western metropolis. Expert surveyors were at work planning the streets and parks, the G.T.P. reported in that same year, and American landscape architects would be employed to ensure that Prince Rupert became "the most perfectly laid out and most beautiful city in the Dominion . . . the Washington of Canada."

So convincing was Hays that in May 1909, when the first town lots were auctioned in Vancouver, very spirited bidding from 1,500 eager purchasers pushed prices up to as much as $8,000 for a single lot.

G.T.P. literature promoted the growing town with glowing pride and rosy optimism.

To this new port will come the ships of the Seven Seas. Ships of the East, laden with silk and rice will soon be riding at anchor in this splendid harbor, to sail away laden with lumber; . . . ships from the shore of far-off continents, trading through the new and picturesque port of Prince Rupert . . .[1]

New it certainly was, and some may have found it picturesque in a rough frontier sort of way — but with an annual rainfall of almost one hundred inches it was, above all else, muddy. And by 1909 the 3,000 residents found it advisable to take to the intricate system of boardwalks if they wished to avoid being mired in the ooze. But to Charles Melville Hays the streets were lined with gold. His optimism never wavered.

The town was incorporated the following year, and Hays to avoid heavy municipal taxation and to gain other concessions for the G.T.P., agreed to build a large modern hotel. The work of designing that hotel he gave to Rattenbury.

Ratz later said that it was not until 1911 that he had been appointed architect for the Grand Trunk Pacific. But it seems that at a much earlier date, perhaps at the time he designed the original frame hotel for Prince Rupert, Hays had given him to understand that he would receive this commission. On his grand European tour of 1908, Rattenbury had "visited every hotel of standing possible in the hope of gaining future knowledge in that line of architecture to be used by him in the future." Since he was at that time no longer working for the C.P.R., it seems likely that Rattenbury was intending to apply this knowledge to the G.T.P. hotels and the buildings he designed for the rail line certainly evidenced a great deal of thought and careful consideration.

As designed by Rattenbury the G.T.P. hotel at Prince Rupert would be part of a great transportation complex. At the water's edge would be a long covered dock dominated by two sixty foot high cupola-topped towers. Passengers disembarking from a G.T.P. steamer would be enveloped in luxury the moment they stepped ashore. Just behind the steamship terminal, where the tracks of the Grand Trunk Pacific hugged the shore, would be a deluxe railway station carefully designed to impress passengers alighting from G.T.P. trains with its splendor. And whether a tourist arrived by boat or train he would find himself at the doorstep of the most imposing château style hotel ever designed for the west. Located on a slight rise above the steamship terminal and railway station, the hotel, with its 450 bedrooms and its dining room capable of seating 265 people, was expected to cost as much as two million dollars to construct. Twice as tall as the Empress, it would reign supreme over a garden city of formal parks, wide tree-lined boulevards and gently curving residential by-ways envisioned by the landscape architects.

But it was not only for Prince Rupert that Rattenbury was asked to design hotels. Keeping a watchful eye on the C.P.R., Hays must have noted with interest that the Banff Springs Hotel was becoming almost too popular. During the summer of 1910 the hotel had often been booked to capacity and an overflow of four hundred people had been bedded down in sleeping cars near the Banff station. The following season had been even more hectic with 22,000 persons registering at the hotel during the summer of 1911.

Taking the Yellowhead Pass through the Rockies, the Grand Trunk Pacific passed through spectacularly beautiful country. As eager to capitalize on the scenery as the C.P.R. had been, the G.T.P. commissioned Rattenbury to design a string of resort hotels sited to take advantage of the best the mountains had to offer. Three locations were selected; at Jasper by the shores of Lac Beauvert; at Miette, where hot springs offered the same therapeutic benefits that drew tourists to Banff; and at the base of Mount Robson, the tallest peak in the Canadian Rockies.

The Mount Robson hotel conceived by Rattenbury was the most sensitively designed of all the mountain hotels. Compared to fortress-like structures such as the Banff Springs Hotel, the Mount Robson appeared light and airy, almost delicate. Six wings decorated with Dutch gables radiated out from a château style centre block and the irregular roofline, broken by slender randomly spaced towers, echoed the peaks and valleys of the surrounding mountains. Set in formally landscaped gardens with circular drives and curving walkways, Rattenbury's Hotel Mount Robson would epitomize Edwardian elegance.

As well as planning a promotional campaign appealing to tourists, the G.T.P. intended to entice settlers aboard their trains by extolling the virtues of the rich farmlands the line would open for colonization. And, as it happened, much of that land belonged to Rattenbury. In 1908, a few days after the G.T.P. had stated that the line would definitely be constructed through the area, Rattenbury had announced that he had sold his Nechako Valley holdings to Trafford Huteson, an Englishman recently arrived in Seattle, who in turn intended to promote the sale of parcels of the land to bona fide farmers. The $100,000 Ratz claimed to have received for his 11,000 acres must have gone a long way to financing his travels. But he had, by no means, sold all of his land. He still retained some 50,000 acres in the Bulkley Valley and through his company, Rattenbury Lands Ltd., he intended to oversee the colonization of this land himself. He was an empire builder, he bragged to his friends.

He could foresee a day in the not too distant future when his influence would be felt from the Rockies to the Coast. All G.T.P. buildings would have been designed by him — from the most rustic mountain railway station to the magnificent hotel at Prince Rupert. Settlers pouring off G.T.P. trains would collect their baggage at a Rattenbury-designed station and then spread over the countryside to begin farming thousands of acres on which Rattenbury would hold the mortgage. The $100,000 he had collected in 1908 would be a paltry sum compared to the money he could expect to make once the railroad was completed. When that day came his land holdings would bring him great personal wealth and the Grand Trunk Pacific hotels would become monuments to his genius, the buildings that would mark the high point of a brilliant architectural career.

But then disaster struck, a disaster from which Ratz and the Grand Trunk Pacific never really recovered. In the spring of 1912 Hays travelled to England to promote the company and to gain the approval of its British shareholders for his latest plans which included a contract with a Pittsburgh syndicate for the export of coal via the Grand Trunk Pacific and Prince Rupert. Returning from England with all his visionary plans in his head and the signed contracts in his pocket, Hays went down with the *Titanic*.

He was replaced by E. J. Chamberlain, a more cautious man who shared neither Hays' determined optimism nor his enthusiasm for the potential of Prince Rupert.

If Hays' death was a major blow to the G.T.P. the coup de grâce came two years later. The tracks had finally been completed and the first train rolled into Prince Rupert on April 8, 1914. Regular service was scheduled to start in September and the company had launched an extensive advertising campaign designed to appeal to both tourists and settlers.

Trains of the Grand Trunk Pacific will traverse some of the finest scenery to be found on the American continent, across wild and fertile fields, by the banks of mighty rivers of the North, through deep dark canyons where in midsummer from beneath the north windows of west-bound trains will come the sweet fragrance of wild roses while from the south windows the traveller can look out on a glittering glacier whose cloud shroud trails to the margin of the mountains — this is the trail the railroad follows on its shortcut across Canada.[2]

Just how many settlers might have been attracted to the fertile fields, or how many romantic tourists lured aboard the Grand Trunk Pacific by the promise of wild roses and glittering glaciers, will never be known for on August 4, 1914 Britain declared war on Germany and the Grand Trunk Pacific was finished before it had even begun.

Since few tourists could be expected during the war years, work on the G.T.P.'s mountain hotels was postponed indefinitely. And, although the railway did make a desultory start on the hotel at Prince Rupert, digging the foundation and ordering some building materials, it, like the resort hotels was never built for by the time the war finally ended the Grand Trunk Pacific was bankrupt.

The hoped-for colonists did not materialize. What settlers there were left the land to serve in the army or work in factories. "All the money I earned in building the Parliament Buildings, the Empress Hotel and numbers of other buildings, I invested in buying lands,"[3] Ratz said. And now, rather than a profitable investment those lands had become a burden, tens of thousands of undeveloped acres on which he would have to pay taxes and from which he could expect no return. He hung on to his land holdings, not through any sense of optimism but simply because there were no buyers and other than forfeit the land to the Crown there was nothing else for him to do.

He had been engrossed in his architectural work for the Grand Trunk Pacific for at least three years, doodling rough sketches on odd bits of paper, experimenting with designs and finally preparing presentation drawings. Now he rolled up all his plans and sketches and put them away in his attic where they remained out of sight but no doubt very much on his mind. His grand architectural dream had become a nightmare that would haunt him for the rest of his life.

In 1911 he had served as President of the Architectural Association, but now he let his membership lapse and although he was later credited with designing several buildings in Victoria during the twenties, he never again entered actively into the practice of architecture.

Ratz had invested everything — his reputation, his hopes and his money in the railroad's future. The failure of the Grand Trunk Pacific was a professional and personal disaster. He would never again exhibit quite the same brash, energetic confidence, but he did survive the blow — only because he seems to have anticipated it.

Rattenbury, perhaps more than anyone else, would have realized early what Hays' death could mean to the success of the G.T.P. He was enough of a promoter himself to know that opportunities must be seized by men of vision who revelled in the taking of risks. Caution and faint hearts did not build empires in central British Columbia or anywhere else. When Hays was replaced as G.T.P. president, Ratz may have begun to feel less sure of the ultimate success of the rail line. There is one small hint that he may have sensed that the Parliament Buildings, rather than the string of elegant and sensitively designed railway hotels, would come to be the body of work on which his architectural reputation would depend.

The cornerstone for the foundation of the Provincial Library was laid on September 28, 1912, five months after Hays' death. To the original plans he had submitted the year before, Rattenbury had made several changes and one rather significant addition. Set in niches, high on the Library's exterior walls were statues — not of the thirty-five English monarchs that had adorned Henry Francis Lockwood's Bradford Town Hall, but of the men who had shaped the history of British Columbia, such men as Captains Cook and Vancouver, Dr. John Helmcken and Sir Matthew Baillie Begbie. Lockwood, an architect whose talent Rattenbury greatly admired, had designed many buildings, but Bradford's Town Hall was regarded by many as his magnum opus, the one building felt to mark the pinnacle of his career. And so it may be that the Library's statues, gazing grandly out over the city from their high niches, were intended by Rattenbury to be a symbolic postscript to an architectural talent that would now never be fully realized. Some twenty years before he had designed a building, probably based on an original Lockwood design, and now that building would remain his master work, his most significant contribution to the architectural heritage of British Columbia.

Rattenbury's interpretation of Hays' death as a warning, an omen foreshadowing the demise of the railroad, was due at least in part to the fact that his personal life was so joyless that he was predisposed toward pessimism. In 1912 he was forty-five, his red hair thinning and touched with grey, middle-aged but still vigorous and handsome. Slender and straight, a dominating forceful man whose sensitive aesthetic eyes belied his irascibility and impatience. He enjoyed good health, he was prosperous and successful. He should have been happy and content. But instead he was resentful and despondent, for before him stretched years of marriage to a woman for whom he had developed an intense dislike.

From the start Florrie had seemed an odd choice for a man of Rattenbury's stature in the community. Ratz was capable of controlling his passions and acting in a calculating and logical way when the situation demanded it. A man with a healthy sense of his own worth, the major factor in his life was his towering ambition and he might have been expected to choose as a wife the daughter of one of the city's monied families, a woman who enjoyed some connection to Victoria's aristocracy. But Florrie brought her husband neither wealth nor position. Her father, Captain George Elphinstone Nunn, had served with the British Army in India for several years before news of the Fraser River gold rush attracted him to British Columbia's west coast. In 1862 he had sailed into Victoria's harbour with his wife, older children and parrot in tow to find that while the gold excitement had abated, the free port of Victoria was thriving. He signed on as an officer on one of the coastal vessels sailing between Victoria and San Francisco, leaving his wife in Victoria to raise their growing brood of children. Some fifteen years later, when she learned of Captain Nunn's death in San Francisco, Florrie's mother, apparently having had quite enough of the joys of single parenthood, packed her bags and left town moving to Portland,

Oregon to live with one of her older daughters who had married rather well. Her younger children, Charles born in 1874 and Florrie some three years earlier, she left with friends in Victoria. Charles was raised on a farm in Saanich and Florrie was left in the care of Eleanor Howard who had been widowed, as she put it, by the appearance in Victoria of her husband's first wife and who supported herself by running a genteel boarding house on Rae Street near the city's business district.[4] Florrie had no money, no family and to the city's elite her origins were distinctly humble. Rattenbury had not improved his position or his prospects by marrying her.

But neither was Florrie the type of woman who inspired men to reckless, headlong, pursuit. She was stocky and rather plain, a short little woman with a large nose and stubborn jaw. Her pale blue eyes were her most prominent feature, but even her friends admitted that they were perhaps too prominent — frog-like, they described them. A shy retiring girl, gifted with a patient serenity, Florrie was recognized by many people as the kindest, sweetest person they had ever met. And perhaps that's the way Ratz felt about her too for his relationship with her seems to have been marked by growing familiarity rather than fiery passion.

When he first arrived in Victoria in 1893 marriage had been far from his mind. An architect caught up in the largest and most complex commission of his career, he had little time for social calls, but it happened that the one man whose company Ratz did seek out lived at the Rae Street house. An Irishman who had resigned his commission in the Royal Engineers to settle in the Yale district and to engage in mining and in raising imported blooded cattle, Forbes G. Vernon had been elected to the provincial legislature in 1874. He had served several terms as Chief Commissioner of Lands and Works and, although he would resign to become the province's agent-general in London in 1894, he still held that important cabinet post during the time the decision to build new legislative buildings had been reached and Rattenbury had been selected as their architect.

Vernon, who found the old Birdcages as cramped and inconvenient as did many other members of the government, directed much of the work of his department from Mrs. Howard's boarding house and Rattenbury was a frequent visitor, meeting with Vernon to discuss working drawings, estimates for the buildings' foundation and the time-table for the first phase of construction.

If, as seems likely, Ratz had met Florrie shortly after his arrival in Victoria his courtship of the girl was quite unchivalrously unhurried. They were married on June 18, 1898 in a quiet evening ceremony at Christ Church Cathedral. After their return from the Klondike from what must have been for Florrie a romantic adventure despite its hardships, they took up residence in "Hochelaga," the elegant Rockland Avenue home Ratz had rented from A. J. C. Gellately, the manager of the Victoria branch of the Bank of Montreal. And there on January 14, 1899 their first child, a son, was born.

The boy, christened Francis Burgoyne Rattenbury, was born with clubfeet, so badly deformed that it seemed unlikely that he would ever be able to walk. Florrie had reacted with predictable maternal concern, smothering him with attention, and later, when he was older, taking him many times to San Francisco where she hoped more sophisticated medical attention might straighten his twisted feet.

Frank was in awe of his father, soberly repeating Ratz' most outlandish boasts to anyone who would listen. On one occasion Ratz, an avid motorist, had purchased a sleek, black electric car. His father said it was a black pearl, Frank informed his friends, and black pearls were the most expensive.

Their second child, a daughter, born on May 11, 1904 and named Mary after Rattenbury's mother, grew into a lovely girl, tall with her father's erect carriage and his sensitive eyes. But Mary was a nervous, highly strung child who developed an emotionally rooted speech impediment as she sensed the tensions and growing hostility that existed between her parents.

At first Ratz and Florrie had seemed happy enough. He had designed for them a picturesque home of rough stone and dark stained shingles on the beach in Oak Bay and there Florrie had been content. The city's fashionable Rockland Avenue had not been her milieu for she lacked the confidence or practised grace that might have allowed her to ease herself gradually into Victoria's social scene. Wealthy matrons did not overlook the fact that she was the adopted daughter of a boarding house keeper or that her brother Charles was nothing more than a waiter at the Globe Restaurant. But in Oak Bay Florrie could avoid the stigma of not being accepted. At the time Rattenbury built their house there were few other permanent residents along the beach. There were summer people, like the Helmckens, who deserted the city as the warm weather came and for two or three months of every year lived in their little cottages dotted along the waterfront of Oak Bay. With these people, relaxed by beach-side casualness, Florrie could feel comfortable and each year she and Ratz entertained at a summer garden party at which Florrie, who treasured the flowers in her seaside garden and who took more pride in a clever floral arrangement than in the grand table on which it was placed, could feel secure under the oaks heavy with hanging flower baskets as her guests were easily distracted with games of tennis and croquet.

Ratz surrounded Florrie with the accoutrements of wealth and position; exquisite jewels of such high quality that they achieved a fame of their own; expensive, finely crafted furniture; and as many as six servants — a cook, gardeners, a chauffeur, maids and a governess for the children. But despite it all Florrie remained a simple soul, kind, motherly, increasingly stout and, above all else, dull. Rattenbury moved easily among the lawyers, politicians and businessmen who were forming Victoria's new aristocracy and he may have resented the fact that Florrie could not do the same. And Florrie had become more prim than the most proper society matron. She avoided their nearest neighbours because she was convinced that Mrs. Bowker Senior, born Mary Tod, had been part Indian. She had an unbending code of what she considered correct deportment for her children's playmates. On one occasion Frank's friend, Tom Floyd, had been sailing high on the garden swing when he had called out to a boy who had come dangerously close, "Watch out or I'll bloody your nose." To his amazement Tom had been promptly banished by Florrie who had been incensed by his bad language.

For a time Ratz and Florrie had been able to conceal the growing antipathy they felt for each other. Kyrle Symons, headmaster of Frank's school, seems to have noticed nothing amiss in January of 1912 when he and his wife accepted an invitation to have tea with the Rattenburys. In fact if anything impressed Symons as being out of the ordinary it was Rattenbury's casual generosity. To attend "Symons' School" in those days amounted to having private tutoring. The school with a total enrollment of only six boys was conducted in Symons' rented home on Esquimalt Road. Proud of his school's academic program, Symons had to admit that the rocky sloping lot on which the house stood did not encourage the kind of games one usually associated with the playing fields of Eton. One day as he stood on the verandah of his house Symons had watched the boys at play.

"One of them," he told Rattenbury, "was on all fours and being led along by the others with a rope around his neck — stopping at intervals to crop a bit of grass. They were all farmers and he was a cow being taken out to pasture."

"Look here, Symons," Rattenbury said, "go round and find some level ground, build a house for yourself and a school on it. I'll pay for it and you can repay me in so many years."[5]

Symons, aware that Rattenbury had a reputation for being close, had been surprised by this offer but taking him at his word he ran up a bill for over $5,000 which Ratz apparently paid without complaint.[6]

Gradually the animosity between Ratz and Florrie had grown until finally they had stopped speaking to one another, communicating only through Mary who carried messages between the two. Ratz' room became a separate apartment in which he dined in solitude while the rest of the family sat around the dining room table below. He became a hermit in his own house avoiding Florrie and "Grannie" Howard who had moved into their home after giving up her Rae Street boarding house and whose perpetually clacking knitting needles and staunch loyalty to Florrie Ratz found particularly irritating. Never an abstemious man, he was known as a jolly good fellow, a rowdy participant in the not-so-gentlemanly revels which took place at Victoria's Union Club. But now his drinking habits changed. Each night, alone in his room, he steadily consumed the better part of a bottle of whisky as he brooded over the shambles his personal life had become and worried about the future of the Grand Trunk Pacific, the grand scheme in which he had invested so much money and so much hope.

In the winter of 1913 as his term as Reeve of Oak Bay neared its end, he decided to shake himself out of his depression by taking a trip, an around-the-world cruise with the only person of whom he was genuinely fond, his daughter Mary. For a time Mary had attended St. Margaret's School where, having been gifted with her father's artistic ability, she had won many drawing prizes but as the estrangement between her parents had deepened, Mary's "nerves" had become worse and she had dropped out of school to be taught at home by a private tutor. Now, Ratz instructed her teacher to concentrate on history and geography so that Mary would be better able to appreciate the many countries they would visit and Mary began to look forward to the unexpected treat of an extended holiday with her father. She knew that he doted on her, "spoiled her rotten" her friends said, and she responded with feelings of deep affection for him. Alone with her father, away from the domestic strife at home, she could expect to be relaxed and happy, fussed over and catered to, and she would also have a chance to visit her brother Frank who was at school in England.

Frank had been sent to Wyllie's School at Hampstead Heath outside London. Wyllie's offered "special tuition . . . for boys to whom Preparatory or Public Schools may not be suitable." His son was being trained for the diplomatic corps, Rattenbury said.

By July of 1914 Mary's wardrobe had been chosen, their tickets bought and their schedule finalized when Mary suddenly changed her mind. She loved both her mother and "Grannie" Howard. To go away with her father, whose dislike of the two women was unconcealed, Mary suddenly saw as treacherous disloyalty and she decided to remain at home.

Ratz, sorely disappointed and no doubt blaming Florrie for Mary's change of heart, set out alone. He arrived in England in August and Frank travelled up to London to meet him. The two were together dining in a London hotel when the orchestra leader interrupted the dinner music to announce that Britain had declared war on Germany and to break into a stirring rendition of "God Save the King."

Accompanied by Frank, Rattenbury returned home to Victoria, to a town that was very different from the one he had left. The Willows race track had been transformed into an army camp; the temporary billet of over a thousand volunteers who waited to be shipped overseas. Uniformed men were everywhere; digging trenches at Clover Point and the Willows, polishing their marching skills along city streets, taking part in patriotic rallies and on one wild night, when news of the *Lusitania*'s sinking sparked anti-German rioting, patrolling downtown streets and mounting guard outside the grounds of Government House.

Frank recalls that Rattenbury tried to enlist but that he was turned down because, at forty-six, he was considered too old. James Herrick McGregor, two years his junior, was more successful. In September 1914 McGregor resigned from the presidency of the Union Club and from his seat on Oak Bay council[7] and enlisted in the 50th Gordon Highlanders. Seven months later, serving in France as a captain and paymaster of the 16th Canadian Scottish battalion, he was shot down as he "strolled along with a cane under his arm, seemingly unaware that a war was being fought around him."[8]

There was no getting away from the war and the effect it had on Victoria. It seemed as if almost every day the *Colonist* carried the sad news received by a Victoria family that a son or brother was wounded or missing in action. Throughout the city houses stood empty, their owners somewhere in France. "For Rent" signs became permanent fixtures on the office blocks built during the boom years before 1913. As businesses folded and men were thrown out of work, some families were reduced to such desperate straits that in Oak Bay municipal employees were put to work growing potatoes and beans in vacant lots and in Willows Park to feed them.

Although they may not have actually gone hungry, the city's architects were faced with some lean years. Even a man as sought after as Sam Maclure found that there was little work to do and closing his business office, he worked out of his home on Beach Drive. Rattenbury, thanks to the work he had been given by the provincial government fared better than most. His additions to the Parliament Buildings which cost over two million dollars netted him tens of thousands in commission — more than enough to see him through the war years. But nevertheless those were years of debilitating inactivity for Ratz. When the war everyone had thought would last for only a few months finally ended, he was past fifty and the years of enforced idleness had taken their toll. He had become fleshy, his features blurred and coarsened by the whisky upon which he was becoming increasingly dependent. In 1919 when the Grand Trunk Pacific declared bankruptcy and was taken over by the Canadian National Railway any faint hope he may have had that his hotels might yet be built was dashed. The western terminus of the C.N.R. was Vancouver and instead of a bustling city at the western end of a transcontinental rail line, Prince Rupert became an almost forgotten town at the end of a not very profitable branch line. And in the twenties when the C.N.R. built a resort hotel at Jasper, it was a cautiously modest shingled building, quite unlike anything Rattenbury had designed for the Grand Trunk Pacific during the headily optimistic pre-war years. Now he knew for a certainty that he would be remembered for the Parliament Buildings and he also knew that it was common gossip in Victoria that he had stolen their design. The irony of it all added to his grim despondency. He became increasingly bad tempered. The children of the neighbourhood called him "Old Ratz" and, agreeing that he was not a nice man, did their best to keep out of his way. His mood had darkened when he heard that William Oliver had dropped dead of an apparent heart attack while holidaying at his summer home on Cowichan Lake. Oliver had been a friend. And now he was dead at fifty-three — exactly the same age as Rattenbury.

In 1920 as Victoria began to stir with post-war prosperity Rattenbury chose not to re-open his architectural office. He was weary of his architectural practice and soured on life. He seemed content to live off the commission he had received for the additions to the Parliament Buildings while he tried to promote the sale of his land holdings in the Bulkley Valley. But then, in 1921, the Victoria Chamber of Commerce approached him with an idea that soon re-kindled his interest in architecture on the grand scale and brought back some of his old vitality.

In 1912 the Chamber of Commerce had backed a by-law which would have increased municipal taxation to pay for a civic swimming pool and although at the time Victoria was enjoying widespread prosperity the voters had soundly defeated the referendum. In 1921 the Chamber re-introduced the idea and sensing that the taxpayers' former reluctance may have been due at least in part to the crude design which had been used to promote the scheme, they turned to Rattenbury knowing that if they could pique his interest he would produce plans for an exciting building and would also promote the scheme aggressively and skilfully.

For years, ever since he had been so impressed by the palaces of delight for the public he had seen at Coney Island, Ratz had hoped to see something of the sort built in Victoria. The opportunity to design such a building was perhaps the only thing that could have brought him back to his drafting table. He produced sketches of a building which must have stunned even the Chamber of Commerce with its magnificence. The Chamber had asked for a swimming pool. Rattenbury gave them an Amusement Centre. Covering an area of over 100,000 square feet, the building contained not one but three heated sea-water swimming pools. Towers at each corner would fly bright and festive banners and the whole complex, which would include ballrooms, picture galleries and shops, would be topped by a greenhouse roof of glass and steel. By day sunshine would sparkle on the water of the pools and play on the leaves of the lush tropical garden planned for the wide promenade above the pools. By night, the centre would become an exotic fantasy world. Coloured lights on the floors of the pools would glisten in a glorious rainbow effect through the water and a fountain of water shooting forty feet into the air would be specially lit to give it the appearance of a living stream of fire. The building would become a magical garden, a wonder palace.

Reluctant to seek taxpayer support too soon, the Chamber began to cautiously test the waters by canvassing other businessmen and Rattenbury in the meantime asked another architect, Percy Leonard James, if he would be interested in doing the actual work of producing working drawings and supervising construction should the Amusement Centre he had designed ever be built.

Designing the Amusement Centre and the prospect of promoting it to the voters, had made of Rattenbury a new man. Almost. Still gnawing away at him were the bitter feelings of disappointment and regret he had experienced over the last few years. While this current project had stimulated and excited him, he lacked the energy or the desire to re-open his architectural practice. James, an architect in active practice who had had experience in the construction of swimming pools in England before settling in Victoria in 1909, readily agreed to do the more detailed, time consuming work in return for a share of the commission. Over the next two years, while the Chamber dithered about the advisability of launching a full scale campaign to win support for a new money by-law, the two, Rattenbury and James, decided to extend their unofficial partnership to include other buildings as well. Clients, attracted to Rattenbury by his still prominent name got little more than that. Ratz would make the original contact and produce the first rough sketches, but all the rest of the work was left to James. The finished product might owe more to James than Rattenbury but Rattenbury's name appeared on the drawings and an owner could say that his home had been designed by the architect of the Parliament Buildings and Government House, a boast considered by some to be well worth paying for.

By 1923 the Chamber of Commerce had reluctantly admitted defeat. No matter how grand the scheme, or how prominent the architect, a new swimming pool by-law had little chance of passing. Then Victoria's "old friend," the Canadian Pacific Railway, came up with a suggestion that bowled the Chamber over with its generosity. The concessions the company had enjoyed for fifteen years, since the completion of the Empress Hotel in 1908, had expired. Now, the C.P.R. said, they were prepared to build an Amusement Centre, costing not less than $200,000 provided that the city leased them the site for one dollar a year; exempted the building from taxation for twenty years; provided free water for the swimming pool for twenty years; and froze the current taxes paid by the Empress for the same period.

In return for a $200,000 Amusement Centre which would be open to the public at popular prices and the profits of which would be kept by the C.P.R., the company would receive new concessions amounting to some $750,000. But as the special Amusement Centre committee set up by the Chamber pointed out to Victoria taxpayers, it wouldn't actually cost the city anything.

As the Committee got into high gear Rattenbury's sketches appeared everywhere; on thousands of handbills printed by local newspapers, on the screens of Victoria's motion picture cinemas, in shop windows all over town. And Rattenbury appeared everywhere — speaking to the Music Society, the Rotarians, the Alpine Garden Society — extolling the virtues of his Amusement Centre.

The referendum, held on December 29, 1923, passed with an overwhelming majority of 2,909 to 352. That evening a celebratory banquet was held in the Empress Hotel and Rattenbury was the man of the hour, fêted for his contribution as architect and pro-moter.

After the dinner, flushed with success and buoyant with praise he drifted into the Empress' lounge to enjoy an after dinner cigar with his admirers and there he met Alma Pakenham and his life was never the same again.

10

Alma
Which Mrs. Rattenbury?

Alma Victoria Clarke Dolling Pakenham was beautiful. She had a lovely oval face, deep hauntingly sad eyes and full lips which easily settled into a pout, at once fashionable and sensuous. A modern woman, quite uninhibited by any lingering code of Victorian morality, she was a flapper, gay and adventurous, a woman who drank cocktails and smoked cigarettes in public. She wore the shapeless clothes dictated by fashion and her hair was bobbed, cropped almost to her ears. But on Alma, the clothes, despite their boyish cut, revealed the soft round figure of a woman and her dark blonde hair escaping the bonds of her headband curled playfully around her face. She was funloving, warm, generous and kind. But she was also a creature ruled by her emotions, a person totally lacking in empathy, unable to understand how anyone could take offense to, or be hurt by, anything she did.

She had learned early that the world revolved around her. Born in 1895 or 1896, she was the daughter of Walter and Elizabeth Clarke of Kamloops, B.C., a community of some 1,500 which had grown up around the C.P.R. station and served as a supply centre for the ranching district. Walter William Clarke was co-owner of the *Kamloops Standard*, a weekly newspaper that he somehow managed to publish every Thursday, despite the fact that he had the triple task of managing the paper's business affairs, writing the news, and then printing it on the press in his home on Victoria Street. Alma's mother, herself an able musician, had been quick to recognize in her daughter the glimmerings of a precocious musical talent, a talent that she, as a teacher of piano and violin, felt a special responsibility to develop and nurture. It was not long before she became convinced that Alma was nothing less than a child prodigy and Alma learned early to enjoy and to need the approval and praise that a good performance could win for her. But Alma did not become a withdrawn, lonely child-genius. She was born with an out-going, bouncy vivacity that overcame the long, solitary hours of prac-tice. Her teacher at St. Ann's School remembered her as a well-adjusted child, "brilliantly clever . . . a vivid little thing full of happi-ness and music, with a special attraction of her own."[1]

By 1902 Clarke had given up Kamloops and the *Standard* to become a travelling journalist and for the next twelve years the family moved so often that only fleeting glimpses of Alma remain. In 1902 they were in Toronto where, Raymond Massey recalls, Alma was enrolled in his class at Havergal School.[2] The following year the family was in Victoria and as a result of her mother's care-ful coaching Alma was making a name for herself in the city's musi-cal circles, the ladies quite taken with the little girl with the blonde curls, "a tiny little thing whose feet could barely reach the pedals."[3]

Alma would later blame her lack of emotional control on the strain of these early performances. But with the strain came applause and acceptance. She was pampered and spoiled, patted on the head and told that she was pretty and clever and talented and she learned that tantrums could be excused as artistic temperament and that she had a special sparkle that made people want to make a fuss of her and to make allowances for her.

Before long the family was on the move again, returning to To-ronto, where, when she was seventeen or eighteen, Alma gave the performance which she would remember as the highlight of her public career. At a concert given by the Toronto Symphony Orches-tra she played two different concertos — one on the piano, the other on the violin.

Then it was back to the west coast, to Vancouver where her father had taken a job with a local newspaper, the *Sun*. And it was in Vancouver that Alma met and married her first husband, Caledon Robert Radclyffe Dolling. Dolling was a younger son, educated at Tonbridge School in preparation for Sandhurst and the Indian Army but poor eyesight had ended his hopes of a military career and he had left England for British Columbia lured west by the C.P.R.'s breathless accounts of the province's booming economy and un-paralleled opportunities.

Arriving in Vancouver in 1910, a year that saw the city's popula-tion growing at the rate of 1,000 a month, Dolling had opened a real estate agency in partnership with Robert Stark and the following year was advertising himself as a specialist in Port Mann and New Westminster properties.

He and Alma were married in the spring of 1914. In August, three days after the declaration of war, Dolling offered his services, and his eyesight having improved relative to the worsening situation, he was given a commission and sent to Prince Rupert as second in command of the garrison there. Alma travelled north with him and the young couple immediately gained the friendship of everyone in the station. Dolling organized boxing and football matches and Alma's brilliant piano playing was particularly appreciated.[4] Some months later Dolling was gazetted to the 2nd Battalion Welsh Fusiliers and sent to France. And Alma followed him to England taking a job at Whitehall so that she could be with him when he was sent to London on leave.

In February 1916 he was wounded and received the Military Cross. He was wounded again in April and invalided back to England but he had returned to his regiment by July, in time to fight in the battle of the Somme. And then Alma received word that on the night of August 20, 1916, 2nd Lieutenant and Temporary Captain Caledon Dolling had been blown apart by a shell during the battle of Mametz Wood.

"You have the whole regiment's sympathy," his commanding officer wrote. "They are all fond of him and relied on him and trusted his leadership. . . . He was such a man and had no fear and loved his work . . . I have lost a brilliant company commander and a friend."[5]

Alma left her job at Whitehall and joined a women's ambulance corps hoping that she would be sent to France where she intended to search for her husband's grave. Instead she found herself in Salonika working as a field ambulance orderly and it was later said of her that she displayed remarkable aptitude in her work, so much so that she received a decoration from the French government.[6]

With the end of hostilities Alma returned to London and there she met her second husband, Thomas Compton Pakenham, nephew of the renowned Admiral Pakenham, and a hero in his own right having won a Military Cross for his exploits as an officer in the Coldstream Guards. The problem of Pakenham's five-year-old marriage to Phyllis Price was overcome by a divorce in which it seems likely Alma was named co-respondent. She and Pakenham were married in 1921 and almost immediately afterwards left England for New

York where Pakenham had been offered a position at an American university. Their son Christopher was born on July 8, 1921 but their marriage proved to be a disaster. By 1923 Alma's mother, distressed by the letters she was receiving from her daughter, travelled to the east and brought Alma and Christopher back to Vancouver with her. Alma took up her music once again and she was so well remembered that soon she was being invited to give concerts in Vancouver and Victoria. The night that the banquet to celebrate the success of the Amusement Centre by-law was held she had been in the lounge of the Empress, relaxing after having played at an evening recital.

"I had been playing in Victoria," Alma wrote to a friend, "and on returning to the hotel I sat yarning for a while with K. in the lounge. From the banqueting hall came the sounds of revelry and singing. Those men whoever they were did put some real enthusiasm into 'For he's a jolly good fellow'. You know how raucous this can sound. This was quite different. So much so that we guessed that every word was meant.

"K. suggested that we should try to get a peep into the room, which we did, and to K.'s amazement he found that the honoured guest, the man who had inspired this outburst, was an acquaintance.

"Soon after we had gone back to our places in the lounge the banquet ended, and some of the men strolled in to finish cigars and pipes. K. introduced me to his acquaintance, and so it was that I first met my Ratz.

"The memory of that singing had gone to my head, and though I had resolved, as you know, never to marry again, but to devote myself to my music, that song seemed to make all the difference. . . . Well, my dear, if I don't love him, I simply don't know what love is."[7]

Of course it had been more than the heartfelt song that had interested Alma. Alma, who had never met Ratz before, could not know how drastically his appearance had altered, could not guess that he was barely recognizable as the same man who had served ten years earlier as the Reeve of Oak Bay. She saw only the tall elegantly dressed man who stood before her, flushed with success and exuding confidence as he accepted the praise and gratitude of the city's most prominent citizens. He had designed the very hotel in which they met and from almost any window she could look out and see the outline of his Parliament Buildings, still unmatched as the best known and most important architectural work in the city and the province. Alma was impressed.

Soon afterwards, they met again, at a dance given by the Bullens to celebrate the completion of their Rockland area home. In December, 1923, Rattenbury described the encounter in a letter to his family in England. "... at a dance in a lovely big house — a young married wife about 26 — the belle of the dance and a marvellous musician — knocked me out by suddenly saying, 'Do you know you have a lovely face?'

"'Great Scot,' said I. 'Have I? I am going right home to have a look at it. I've never thought it worth looking at yet.'

"'I'm not joking,' she said. 'You have almost the kindest face I ever saw.'"

Just how or when they agreed to meet again is unknown, but early in 1924, Alma moved to Victoria, settling for a time with an aunt who lived on Dallas Road until a house was found for her in James Bay near Beacon Hill Park. She would support herself and her small son by giving piano lessons, Alma bravely declared. And the ladies of the community welcomed her with open arms — unaware that her little house on Niagara Street had become the place of discreet meetings between Alma and the still married Rattenbury.

Mrs. Maclure who with her architect husband Sam was the leader of the city's artistic and musical community had been quick to make Alma feel at home. She invited Alma and her little boy to afternoon tea and the Maclure daughters, who counted their mother a strict disciplinarian, wondered at her patience as they watched Christopher, or "Toffy" as Alma called him, dismember their parlour. First Toffy began with the cushions, removing them one by one until they made a satisfying heap in the middle of the floor. Then he started on the ornaments, placing them precariously on top of the cushions.

"Mummy doesn't want you to do that, Toffy," Alma protested ineffectually, remaining seated in her chair and Toffy, ignoring her continued. Mrs. Maclure held her tongue until Toffy climbed upon a cushionless chair and reached for the pictures hanging on the wall.

"Don't let him get at the pictures," Mrs. Maclure warned with angry finality. "They might fall and hurt him"[8]

But Alma and Toffy were forgiven this breach of etiquette and invited to return for Mrs. Maclure, like many others, found that

131

Alma, who as a girl had shown such promise and as a woman had experienced such tragedy, was not an easy person to deny.

A few weeks later Mrs. Maclure heard that Alma had not been well and feeling sorry for her she began taking soups and hampers of food to the Niagara Street house. At least the poor girl wouldn't have to worry about cooking, Mrs. Maclure thought. Then one day she received a call from a friend, a singer who happened to live across the street from Alma. Shortly after Mrs. Maclure's last visits, the woman reported, she had seen Alma and Rattenbury leaving the house. They had strolled to Beacon Hill Park and there had picnicked happily on the contents of Mrs. Maclure's thoughtfully prepared hamper.

Mrs. Maclure was furious. She telephoned Alma and confronted her with the story. Alma denied nothing.

"People have been saying things about you," Mrs. Maclure told Alma, "and now I can see that they were right."[9]

Alma didn't care. Those same people would be begging to come to her house one day, she retorted and it was obviously what she believed. In the past people had always been forgiving and understanding. She had always been fussed and spoiled, always able to get her own way. Why should anything be different now, especially since Rattenbury's position in the community seemed unassailable.

And Ratz must have felt the same way. Florrie had been all but ignored by Victorian society. A stout little woman who kept to herself pottering about in her garden, she was never invited to the winter dinner parties or summer picnics at which Victoria's wealthy residents met to listen to good music, to gossip about the latest scandal, to play energetic games of tennis and sedate games of croquet, and to discuss the merits of investing in developing industries. But Ratz was a frequent guest. On the piano, he was a gifted amateur. On the tennis courts, he played with the skill that comes of hating to lose. He was a member of the Yacht Club and when he wasn't sailing he was sketching boats. Yawls and ketches with the wind in their sails appeared on the presentation drawings of every building he designed which happened to be sited by a body of water. He was a smart businessman who carefully set aside part of his income for safe investments including shares in an Alberta brewery and in a local painting and decorating firm.

He knew that people had wondered over the years why he had married Florrie and he was sure that while a divorce might cause tongues to wag, his decision to leave his wife would be understood and accepted. At first he had tried, quietly and privately, to convince Florrie to consent to a divorce while he kept his affair with Alma hidden. But now that Mrs. Maclure had uncovered their secret and there was no longer any need for discretion, he became blatant. He acquired a prominent box in the theatre and clad in a newly purchased opera cape swept in with Alma on his arm, flaunting their relationship.

He seemed set on inviting censure and Sam Maclure who had known Rattenbury for almost thirty years was at a loss to explain his behaviour.

"The man's bewitched," he said shaking his head.[10]

And there were those who went further, who could not believe that feminine charms alone accounted for Alma's sorcery. They said she was addicted to drugs and hinted that Rattenbury had become a changed man under their influence.

Probably no one will every know for a certainty if this was the case. Alma may well have developed a drug dependency during the years she spent with the ambulance corps during the war. In battlefield hospitals both morphia and cocaine were used as anaesthetics and while morphia was known to be addictive, the properties of cocaine were not clearly understood. But cocaine was known to increase vitality and the capacity to work and since it was generally regarded as a harmless drug, Alma may have begun to use it to keep her going for long hours of unaccustomed hardship and labour. And cocaine was also known to produce exhilaration and lasting euphoria, both commodities in short supply amid the ugliness and stench of war. Other Victoria girls, serving as nurses or drivers during the war, had returned home with an addiction to morphia or a dependency on cocaine, but most surrounded by the soothing presence of family and friends in peaceful post-war Victoria had overcome their drug habit. Perhaps Alma had not — for Alma certainly had an addictive personality. Self-denial was alien to her. One drink, more often than not, led to two or three more. She was a chain smoker who found it difficult to finish a meal without pausing between courses to smoke a cigarette. Rattenbury's children, Frank and Mary, who were twenty and twenty-five at the time *l'affaire Rattenbury* became the talk of Victoria, remain convinced and take some comfort from their conviction that "dope" played a role in their father's entrapment and they may be right. Cocaine may have brought back his youthful virility and may have induced in him a state of excitement and euphoria that encouraged his recklessly indiscreet behaviour.

But Rattenbury's behaviour can be easily understood without accepting the rumours that Alma had seduced him by introducing him to stimulating drugs. When they met he was fifty-six years old and beginning to feel his age. For twenty-six years he had been married to a woman for whom he now felt only an intense dislike. For the last ten years he had been weighed down by the conviction that his artistic career was at an end. Coincidentally, with his meeting Alma, he had been given the opportunity to design the Amusement Centre, or Crystal Garden as it had come to be known, the building which would become the social heart of the city, winning the affections of Victorians as no other building ever could and in the campaign to win approval of the voters for its construction he had proved himself to be an hypnotically persuasive promoter. That alone could have brought back some of his driving energy. And how his manly pride must have been aroused by the discovery that a beautiful woman, a gay, giddy, vivacious and talented young woman, thirty years his junior, was in love with him.

Common sense might have suggested to him that he keep Alma as a mistress preserving his reputation by maintaining a façade of respectability. But his passion for her was so great that he was past discretion, past caring, or so he thought, about Victoria's opinion of him. Florrie — stubborn, dull, matronly Florrie — was the obstacle to his happiness. He must rid himself of her.

But Florrie remained adamant. She would not divorce him. And so Ratz embarked on a course of action that would result in his complete ostracism by even his oldest friends and associates. As everyone said, it wasn't so much what he did, as the way that he did it.

He decided to harass the seemingly immovable Florrie. He moved out of the house, the house called "Iechineel" which meant, Ratz had once said, "a place where a good thing happened," and sent moving vans to remove the better pieces of furniture. But as the movers carried one piece out the front door, Florrie with the help of her Chinese servant, Wee, moved another into the maid's room, the one room in the house for which only Florrie had the key. Between them they managed to squirrel away the most valuable pieces of furniture and Florrie took particular pleasure in noting that part of their hoard included Rattenbury's stock of imported champagne.[11]

Ratz retaliated by laying siege to the house, ordering the light and heat turned off and Florrie, fortified by the food hampers she now received from Mrs. Maclure, took him to court filing a successful injunction against him on July 28, 1924 for a declaration of the plaintiff's right to reside in the house of her husband.

Disgusted by this turn of events, Rattenbury left Victoria for two months, taking, it was rumoured, a Mediterranean cruise with Alma. On his return, in a desperate attempt to finally be free of the woman, he devised a particularly mean scheme. He began bringing Alma to the house entertaining her in the parlour and forcing Florrie to retire to one of the upstairs rooms, where she took to her bed, the throbbing indignation and resentment she felt affecting her heart that she had already strained by years of overweight.

One night Florrie was lying in her bed, listening with a combination of anger and fear to Alma gaily playing the piano and to the sound of her own wildly beating heart. Mary, concerned at seeing her mother so agitated, had gone downstairs and asked her father and Alma to please be quiet as her mother was upset and unable to sleep. Alma responded by playing a thumpingly loud rendition of the funeral march, its heavy chords resounding through the house and filling the room in which Florrie lay.

Perhaps the events of that night finally convinced Florrie that she would not know a moment's peace until she agreed to a divorce for soon after she and Mary moved out of "Iechineel" into a house on Fort Street and she resignedly began divorce proceedings against her husband.

But although the divorce was granted on January 28, 1925 Rattenbury would discover that until her death he would never be quite free of Florrie. In addition to an alimony payment of $225 a month he had agreed to provide her with a house of her own. Real estate agent Chartres Pemberton took Florrie about town showing her several sites on which her house might be built. But none of them would do, for as Pemberton discovered there was one rather special criterion which the site would have to meet. The place where she built must have a good view of her husband's house. "She was very definite about that," Pemberton remembered. She finally selected a lot just off Oak Bay Avenue at the top of Prospect Place. And there she sat, in her little Maclure-designed bungalow, a silent watchful presence on the rocky hill above "Iechineel."

Rattenbury and Alma were married that spring. "I have a wonderfully happy home," he reported in June, "bright and joyous and full of fun all the time." He was looking forward to "years of happiness and interest instead of the loneliness," but he was also coming to realize just how much his scandalous personal conduct would affect his professional life.

In May 1925 architect Percy Leonard James, perhaps emboldened by the general disfavour with which Rattenbury had come to be viewed, wrote to Ratz claiming that he had done the lion's share of the work on the Crystal Garden and demanding a greater share of the commission. Rattenbury's reply had been nothing less than insulting. Except for minor details the completed building had been constructed according to his original design, he informed James. James could have turned down the work, he continued, in which case he would have hired a draughtsman to do the job. He had really done James a favour. ". . . you were not only satisfied with the terms—but very pleased to get the work—."[13]

What had begun as a business disagreement became a personal feud. Now James not only wanted a greater share of the commission but he also felt that all of the credit for the building's design should go to him and he found no shortage of people who would champion him in a dispute with Rattenbury. "Stick to your guns," they told him, relishing the prospects of seeing Rattenbury put in his place.

Rattenbury took his case to the press. The Crystal Garden had been "designed and sketched out by me," he wrote in a letter to the editor and any statements to the contrary were very erroneous.[14] Then he called on Basil Gardom, the C.P.R.'s Superintendent of Construction, sure that the company would support his claim of being sole architect of the Crystal, since they had hired him as architect in the first place. But Gardom had been only too happy to stand by James. "Rattenbury came to my room like a lion," he reported to James, "but left in quite a decent frame of mind and I am sure the truth of what I told him was brought home to him . . ."[15]

Rattenbury now realized that as well as a social outcast he had become, almost overnight, a professional pariah. It seems that for a time he and Alma left Victoria, Ratz to avoid further humiliation and both of them hoping that their absence would cause the scandal to die down. It may be that they were married during this extended trip, for on their return in the spring of 1927 Alma was calling herself Mrs. Rattenbury and was anxious to be re-admitted to the city's cultural community. She telephoned Mrs. Maclure. "Mrs. Rattenbury speaking," she introduced herself. "Which Mrs. Rattenbury?" Mrs. Maclure demanded and upon being told, informed her caller that she knew only one Mrs. Rattenbury — the Mrs. Rattenbury of Prospect Place.[16]

Ratz fared no better. He continued to be avoided on the street, cold shouldered in the Union Club and shunned by former clients and business associates. A man who was short tempered, blunt and almost unscrupulously ambitious, he had never been an easy person to like but he had been accepted because he was wealthy and, while he had concealed many of his professional failures, his successes had been well-publicized and were undeniably brilliant. He had been seen as an important man, a genius many people said. He had relied on his reputation as an architect and as a prominent citizen to attract commissions but now his name had become an undesirable commodity and his reputation as an architect counted for nothing. Now people found just how very easy it was to despise him. To divorce and re-marry was bad enough but to have left his wife for Alma who was seen as an immoral woman, "a man-eating tigress," was quite beyond the pale.

The birth of their son John on December 27, 1928 did nothing to soothe the community's outraged morals. And Alma, as she pushed the baby carriage along Oak Bay streets, would find that her friendly smile and warm hello would not receive so much as an answering nod from people who had once welcomed her into their homes. Alma's relatives and a few of her friends remained loyal but Rattenbury's ostracism by his former associates was complete as people who had once never given Florrie a second thought now saw her as the victim of a "harlot's" attempt to improve her social position.

On October 13, 1929 Florrie died and Alma in an act of quite incredible insensitivity called on Mary to offer her sympathy. Alma may have felt genuinely sorry for Mary. In anything that did not relate directly to her own happiness she could be kind, open-hearted and disarmingly generous. More than one visitor to her home had been rather disconcerted when their admiration of some object would be answered by Alma's urging them to take it. "If you like it, it's yours," she would say, admitting later that it might not make much sense but that was her disposition. She sincerely believed that she would never knowingly hurt anyone, apparently the victim of a most convenient mental block when it came to other men's wives. She would have found it hard to believe that Mary would harbour any negative feelings toward her and she may have felt that they would fall into each other's arms, let by-gones be by-gones, and become friends.

But self-interest rather than sympathy may have prompted her visit. With Florrie dead, Mary might welcome the offer of friendship. If Mary was prepared to forgive and forget, if she was prepared to accept Alma as her father's wife now that her mother was dead . . . the community as a whole might gradually follow suit.

Whatever the case she had seriously misjudged the depth of Mary's feelings. Still harbouring feelings of bitter hatred and resentment some fifty years later, she was on that day in no mood to forgive and she refused to talk to Alma, saying afterwards that Alma had been "high on dope" at the time of her visit.[17]

Mary's angry dismissal of Alma was the final wedge between Rattenbury and his daughter. Realizing that there could never be a reconciliation and without it he and Alma would remain *persona non grata*, he decided to leave Victoria. But not before he changed his will. In a new will, dated December 18, 1929 he disinherited both Mary and his son Frank. His entire estate would go to Alma, Christopher and John. Only Ratz knew just how empty a gesture it was.[18]

Soon afterwards, they left Victoria for good. Only Frank appeared at the dock to see them off. It was an humiliating departure and particularly so if Frank's recollections are correct. "Alma was in a stupor," he reported, adding darkly, "booze, I suppose, or something else."[19]

Part II

ALMA: England 1930-35

11

Bournemouth
Oh poor Ratz. What has happened?

Nothing more was heard of them until September of 1930 when a small item appeared in the local newspapers. Mr. and Mrs. Francis Mawson Rattenbury, it was reported, had visited Okehampton for the purpose of having their son John baptized in the parish church.

It would seem that Rattenbury, having acted on his decision to leave Victoria, had begun to feel rootless and strangely anonymous away from the symbols of his success and the reminders of the man he had once been. For Okehampton was not just any town. It is in that ancient village in the gently rolling hills of west Devon that the first records of the Rattenbury family appear. During the seventeenth century the family had risen to a position of considerable importance in the town, the most prominent member being one John Rattenbury who was remembered as "one of the principal burgesses ... having been town clark and steward of the borough for above thirty years and four tymes mayor, a great preserver of the Records and priviledges belonging to the town." For many years mayors of Okehampton had proudly worn "a little silver seale, having Okehampton town arms engraved thereon, tyed with a black ribbon" which John Rattenbury had presented to the mayor in 1654.[1]

But if Rattenbury had hoped that this pilgrimage to Okehampton would lead him to discover a proud sense of his family's history and to help him recapture feelings of personal importance, he must have been disappointed for Okehampton had become a depressing backwater, "an ugly, dirty and stupid town" and the little silver seal which his ancestor had presented to the town so many years before, had been lost.

Another hint that Ratz was finding it difficult to put his old life in Victoria behind him was his decision to settle in Bournemouth. If he had searched the wide world over he could not have found a place more like Victoria. Both cities look south over the sea. The gulls, the cliffs, the pine scented, ozone-laden air were the same. Even the people were the same — for Bournemouth, a young city by English standards, had become a retirement centre to which well-to-do colonials flocked to enjoy a life of ease. And Bournemouth must have been Rattenbury's choice for it would not have been Alma's. Alma would have opted for London with its theatres and shops and its promise of parties and concerts. Still in her thirties she was energetic and talented with lingering musical ambitions. But she was also compliant. She had an easy unquestioning willingness to take whatever fate placed in her path whether it was another woman's husband or premature retirement. And so they settled in Villa Madeira, a cottage on Manor Road a few paces away from the East Cliff and there amid constant reminders of Victoria Ratz discovered too late just how important his former prominence had been to his self esteem.

In Victoria he had been such a well-known figure, a man who had played so significant a role in the developing province, that his home was included on the tourist circuit. He had often listened with amusement and no small amount of pride to the drivers of the tour buses that crawled past "Iechineel" every day in the summer informing their passengers that this is the home of Francis Mawson Rattenbury. And as they rattled off the highlights of his career tourists would crane their necks hoping to catch a glimpse of the renowned architect.

But in Bournemouth he became just another retired colonial with a few interesting stories to tell. No one remembered the brash young man with dark red hair and clipped moustache whose ambition had left an indelible mark on a capital city and whose imaginative schemes might have changed the course of a province's history. Instead they saw only a tired man, a man past sixty and showing his years, a man becoming increasingly deaf, his features puffy and blurred by heavy drinking and an elderly man in the slightly ridiculous position of having encumbered himself with an infant son.

He was certainly no longer the man with whom Alma had pictured herself madly in love. Alma would later recall that since the birth of their son she and Ratz had ceased to have sexual relations. His advancing years in combination with the whisky he drank had, it seems, rendered him impotent. Alma had become little more than a loving companion. She saw to his needs, humoured him, drank with him and tried to jolly him out of his increasing bouts of depression. Other than Dr. O'Donnell, Alma's physician, whose calls to

142

the house were too frequent to be entirely professional, they had few friends or visitors. As Ratz became more solitary and introspective, sinking deeper and deeper into a state of near constant gloom, Alma tried to coax him into a lighter mood by suggesting interesting outings. In September of 1932 she persuaded him to accompany her to visit a phrenologist, who after examining her head, declared that she "was a woman of small brains, with weak will, no grit, no backbone . . . one of those people who when they come under influence, give way to temptation very easily," an unsound woman who must guard against emotional excitement. Oh yes, Alma said, he was quite correct and Rattenbury found that he too had no cause to quarrel with the man's assessment of his wife.[2]

What Ratz needed to cheer him was work — a building to design or a scheme to promote — but although he occasionally managed to pull himself together and design a few speculative apartment blocks, the plans came to nothing. He had never been able to cope with idleness and now to enforced leisure was added a new anxiety; he was very nearly broke. Although Alma still considered him well off, Rattenbury knew better. His land holdings in British Columbia had become almost worthless. Before leaving Victoria he had challenged the government's right to levy heavy taxes on unimproved land. He was not a land speculator, he claimed, he had done everything humanly possible to encourage the colonization of his holdings. He had taken his case all the way to the Supreme Court of Canada, but the Court had upheld the government leaving Rattenbury with not only an enormous tax bill but large legal fees as well. Some of his land had been settled but he held the mortgages and as the real value of the land fell below the face value of the mortgage many farmers had stopped making payments. Casting about for some way of increasing his income, he had hit upon the idea of turning his beachside home in Oak Bay into an inn. "St. George and the Dragon," he had decided to call it and hoped to turn at least a small profit from the venture but his plans had been turned aside by the successful lobbying of irate Oak Bay ratepayers who bombarded the local council with their protests, furious at the thought of an absent Rattenbury proposing a scheme that might destroy the character of the neighbourhood he had once so staunchly defended.

During those years they spent in Bournemouth, living in the same house, if not actually together in the accepted sense of the phrase, Alma seems to have been strangely content. Deeply attached to her children she was a devoted mother who often visited Christopher at his boarding school and eagerly anticipated his visits home during the holidays and who spent hours of every day playing with John before tucking him into his little bed in the corner of her room. Although she no longer gave public concerts, music still played an important part in her life. Under the name of "Lozanne" she had turned to composing popular, dreamily sentimental ballads of good enough quality to win the collaboration of well-known lyricists and to be recorded by vocalists such as Frank Titterton, a tenor who set feminine hearts aflutter. Several times a year she visited her music publishers in London where she was still remembered as many as forty years later as a pianist who was so expert that she could make even a poor composition sound good. But perhaps more than her children and her music Alma's happiness depended on Irene Riggs. Irene, the daughter of a local gravedigger, had spent several years in service before coming to work for Alma as a companion help. Some ten years younger than Alma, she had been flattered by the friendship which grew up between them, touched by Alma's generosity and grateful for the opportunities to accompany Alma on her occasional trips away from Bournemouth. They became more like sisters than mistress and maid and Irene was careful never to abuse her position, never to betray a confidence.

It was Irene who sat with Alma through the long nights when, either as a result of the tensions created by her unfulfilled sexual needs or, as it would be hinted later, as the result of taking cocaine, she exploded in bursts of frenetic energy. These bouts usually began after Alma had consumed more than her customary number of pre-dinner cocktails. With John safely asleep upstairs and Ratz lying more unconscious than asleep in his own room, Alma would begin to pace frantically about the house, wringing her hands, a stream of words pouring from her lips, pausing in her ramblings only to refill her glass. Irene would keep vigil with her during the night, comforting and consoling, until, hours later, Alma exhausted and spent, would allow Irene to lead her to bed.

As the years passed Rattenbury became more and more preoccupied with his dwindling finances. Brooding about the dead end into which he had directed his life, he began to talk about committing suicide. Alma would try to cheer him up, try to brighten his dark moods with gay chatter and friendly attentiveness. But one July night in 1934 her patience wore thin.

Ratz in a particularly black mood that day again stated his intention to end his life.

"Why don't you do it then?" she impatiently demanded.[3]

Ratz with a sudden surge of desperate fury struck her in the face blackening her eye and stormed out of the house apparently bent on hurling himself off the East Cliff. Dr. O'Donnell arrived at midnight, gave Alma a quarter grain of morphia to calm her and in response to her tearful pleadings left with Irene to search for Ratz who wandered into the house sometime later, cooled down, sobered up and somewhat abashed at Alma's hysterical reaction to his suicide threats.

Life at Villa Madeira might have gone on, its routine broken by occasional scenes if Alma had not taken a lover. A warm, openhearted woman she had been deprived of normal sexual relations with her husband for almost six years. For several years she had suffered from smouldering tuberculosis and was prone to the increased sexual desires often afflicting victims of this disease. And yet Alma with an incurious, distracted husband and many opportunities when she travelled to London to visit her music publishers did not seek out a lover. She waited until fate presented a man on her doorstep under the most unlikely circumstances.

On September 23, 1934 the following advertisement appeared in the *Bournemouth Daily Echo* under "Situations Vacant":

> Daily willing lad, 14-18, for housework:
> Scout-trained preferred. Apply between
> 11-12, 8-9, 5 Manor-road. Bournemouth.

One of the applicants was Bert Parsons who remembers being interviewed by a woman with beautiful blonde hair and a gorgeous figure who reminded him of Madeleine Carroll. He was distressed when he learned that driving would be part of his duties, and he had to admit reluctantly that he didn't know how to drive a car.

"We'll soon teach you," Alma smilingly assured him. "The job is yours if you want it."

Bert went to talk it over with his older sister, who advised him not to take the position, concerned that it seemed a bit too good to be true.[4]

There was at least one other applicant and having none of Bert's misgivings he accepted the job. George Percy Stoner was short and stocky with slightly bowed legs. He was far from handsome but he did have an open honest face with a boyishly appealing charm.

145

The son of George and Olive Stoner, he was an only child born while his father served with the Machine Gun Corps during the war. After the war his father had found it necessary to travel about the country in search of work and rather than take the boy along his parents had settled him with his grandmother who lived in the working class suburb of Ensbury Park some three miles from the fashionable cliffside residences of well-to-do Bournemouth.

As a child Stoner had "something the matter with his legs" and did not learn to walk until after his third birthday. His grandmother found him "an extraordinarily good boy" but even she had to admit that he was "very, very backward."

He grew up shy and solitary with no companions of his own age. "He never wanted to go out on the road and play with other children; he always wanted to stay in and mess about with his old bicycle or making things up to try and get electricity." The few friends he had were "rather younger than himself, and he was a champion boy for those boys, because if they were oppressed at all he would help them out."

A weak child subject to fainting fits, he had very little schooling. His father admitted that he "did not seem to be very brilliant in mind at lessons" and was vague about the number of years he had spent at school.

For a time he worked with his father as a carpenter's helper and a few weeks before applying for the position at Villa Madeira he had worked for a local motor firm.

He seemed admirably suited for the job Alma offered him and began work right away counting himself fortunate at finding a position which so well suited his meagre talents. His duties were certainly not onerous. Each day he would drive John to and from school, chauffeur Alma and Irene about town on shopping excursions and then spend the rest of the day doing odd jobs around the house, returning to his grandmother's home for the night.

He was shy, not very bright, totally unsophisticated and at seventeen young enough to be Alma's son, but the mere fact of his daily physical presence about the house was too much for Alma and she seduced him. By November he was installed in the spare bedroom and had become Alma's lover-in-residence. And Alma, sentimental and romantic, convinced herself that she was in love with him.

He became part of the household. Seeing him lounging about the house, smoking a relaxed cigarette in the drawing room or companionably playing cards with Ratz, many callers to the house took him for a visiting relative rather than hired help.

Alma did not see the potential for trouble in their relationship. She had been able to control her unusual friendship with Irene whom she could address as "Darling," trust with intimate confidences and still impatiently reprimand if household chores were not performed satisfactorily. Rather than resenting the fact that she was treated as a friend but still expected to perform as a servant, Irene had become a loyal ally. Alma may have thought the same thing was possible with Stoner and for a while it was.

But Stoner like Alma had fallen in love. And by Christmastime the pressures of his dual relationship with Alma were beginning to tell and his grandmother worriedly noticed that on his visits to her home he appeared pale and withdrawn. A boy who no one could ever remember having been seen with a girl, he was now the lover of an experienced woman whose charms had attracted three husbands. Overwhelmed by new sensations, he was preoccupied with Alma and found it difficult to accept the transition from passionate lover in the bedroom to servant in the parlour.

At first he reacted with boyish simplicity. He must impress Alma, make her understand that his feelings were something to be reckoned with. He took to carrying a dagger about with him, a swaggering imitation of the dashing movie heroes of the day. He also tried melodrama, telling Alma that there was something queer about his brain, for which he had to take a mysterious medicine. This had the desired effect and for a time Alma, both interested and alarmed, quizzed him about it, but then deciding he was really quite normal she let the subject drop.

Stoner was driven wild by the possibility that Alma might lose interest in him. He was jealous of her small attentions to Ratz and reacted passionately to any suggestion that he and Alma should sever their relationship. On several occasions Alma, needing reassurance, had worried aloud to Stoner about the difference in their ages and suggested that it might be better if Stoner found a younger woman. The violence he showed on these occasions both dismayed and pleased her. And she took secret pride in this proof of the depth of his feelings for her. But on at least one occasion she went too far.

The argument had begun in the usual way, Alma suggesting that their affair end. Stoner responded angrily and a noisy altercation raged back and forth between their two bedrooms. Then Stoner dropped a bombshell. He was addicted to drugs he told her. He used them regularly and was going to London the next morning to make a purchase. Alma, who by this time seems to have developed a profound aversion to anything she considered dope, had responded with passion and finally the screaming and shouting had risen to such a pitch that Irene had run into Stoner's bedroom and found them there, Stoner with his hands around Alma's throat seemingly about to strangle her.

Alma should have been worried that his love for her could bring out such violence in a normally quiet, shy boy. But she continued to put it down to play acting, to attempts for effect, sure of her ability to placate him and smooth things over. Given to a certain theatricality in her own behaviour, she remained insensitive to Stoner's true feelings and saw no potential for trouble when she suggested the trip to London which would ultimately precipitate two deaths.

In March of 1935 Alma once again found herself overdrawn at the bank. She knew that if she told Ratz he would be annoyed and lecture her about her extravagance. She considered him mean with money, sure that he was still well-off despite his brooding worry about his finances. Rather than asking him often for small amounts, she had adopted the technique of three or four times a year fabricating some excuse to ask for a large sum which would see her through several months. This time using her chronic chest problems as an excuse she told him that she needed £250 for an operation to be performed in London.

With Stoner driving, she set out on the morning of Wednesday, March 20. Arriving at the Royal Palace Hotel in Kensington that afternoon they signed the register as "Mrs. Rattenbury and brother" and were given rooms across the hall from each other. They stayed on in London until Friday evening and for Stoner those three days became a strangely real fantasy. With no cruel reminders that he was simply a chauffeur, Stoner became a gay man about town, squiring Alma to dinner and the theatre. And Alma made sure he looked the part. Soon after their arrival she led him to Harrod's where under her direction Stoner was outfitted from head to toe. It was Alma's nature to be generous but that day she really outdid herself. At the end of their shopping spree Stoner was the proud new owner of three shirts, three ties, one dozen linen and two silk handkerchiefs, three pairs of socks, two pairs of gloves, two suits of underwear, two pairs of shoes, two suits and three pairs of *crêpe de Chine* pyjamas. In the space of one afternoon she had lavished him with gifts totaling £40 14s. 6d. — an amount that Stoner could not have matched had he worked for nine months and saved every penny he earned.

In London away from Irene and Ratz and Villa Madeira it was easy for them to fool themselves, to pretend they were quite different people in quite different circumstances. Their self-delusion was so great that Alma could quite seriously appear grateful and touched when Stoner presented her with a diamond ring which she had given him the money to buy.

For Alma their sojourn in London was no more than a pleasant and delightful interlude and she could quite easily put the charade behind her when they returned to Bournemouth expecting Stoner to do the same.

They returned to Villa Madeira late Friday night and as usual by this time of day Ratz was feeling extremely mellow, so mellow in fact that he didn't think to inquire about her operation.

Saturday was a restful routine day, Stoner driving Alma and John to watch a cricket match in which Christopher was playing and it seemed as if Stoner might be able to slide easily back into his role as hired help.

But Sunday found Ratz particularly depressed, sunk in what Alma called the blues. Hoping to cheer him up she coaxed him to accompany her and John on an outing to visit their puppies being boarded at a nearby kennel and a resentful Stoner was required to drive while Rattenbury took his place beside his wife.

Sunday was Irene's half day and after she left for the afternoon it was Stoner's job to serve afternoon tea to Alma and Ratz. As usual they took their tea in Alma's bedroom sitting by the French doors which opened onto the tiny balcony overlooking the garden.

Ratz was morbid and gloomy. Money was particularly tight and he was having difficulty financing a block of flats which he had designed and hoped to build. And to make matters worse he had spent the weekend reading a singularly depressing book. It was called *Stay of Execution* and in it Ratz had found Stephen Clarke, a character with whom he could immediately identify.

Stephen is bent on suicide. He has thought it all out coldly and logically. At one time a man of driving ambition and lusty appetites, now, at forty-five he feels worn out and useless, filled with revulsion at the prospects of old age. He is sitting in his Chelsea flat, a revolver in his mouth, his hand on the trigger, when he is interrupted by the arrival of a friend who persuades him to give life another chance, to put off his suicide for a month and think things over. Stephen grudgingly agrees. During his thirty day reprieve he meets Cecily, a young girl who is fascinated by his world weariness and fancies herself in love with him.

Ratz had read on wallowing in depression and despair along with Stephen until he came to page 296. The sharp stab of recognition was so intense that he marked the page and rather pointedly read it to Alma at tea that Sunday afternoon.

Cecily has declared her love for Stephen and begged him to marry her and Stephen tries to convince her that it won't work.

"What sort of person do you think would stand you?" she asked.

"Oh — some elderly frump, who couldn't get anything else. A staid motherly soul, who'd treat me like a child . . ."

"You don't think marriages between young girls and — and men a good deal older than themselves are possible?"

"They're possible all right. For some reason elderly men have a peculiar attraction for young girls. That may be due, nowadays, to the quality of young men of the day; but I don't think it is. It's always been so. And — the old men like to marry young girls; and after a bit it's hell for both."

"Why?"

"Because it's naturally annoying to a young girl to see her husband mouldering while she still feels frisky. To see the bare patch on the back of his head growing bigger and shinier. To have the shock, one day, of coming across most of his teeth grinning at her out of a glass of water. And there are other things, besides."

"What things?"

"Well — if you will have me enter into physiological details — a woman, let's put it, always wants more than a man. And when a man's a good deal older, she wants a good deal more than him. A good deal more than he can give her. It takes all his time for a young man to keep pace with a young girl. And an old man hasn't a chance of doing it. And then — she usually goes somewhere else to make up the deficiency."[5]

Alma was stunned. She had decided long ago that Rattenbury either didn't know or didn't care about her affair with Stoner. He was becoming quite deaf and he consumed enough whisky to guarantee that he slept soundly and in addition his room was on the ground floor. There was a chance that he had simply never heard what was going on upstairs. But if he had known, he had never given any indication that he cared, even when Alma some months before in an attempt to ease her conscience had alluded to her relationship with Stoner by telling Ratz that she intended to live her own life.

Now she knew that at the very least he suspected that Stoner had become her lover and that he not only cared, but cared very deeply. Just how Alma reacted to this news is unknown. But it is certain that the bedroom door usually held ajar was closed that afternoon and that Stoner who had heard snatches of the conversation was convinced that Alma had made love to her husband. Later Stoner's belief that Ratz and Alma had had intercourse would be explained as an hallucination induced by cocaine and Alma herself would recoil from the very suggestion that she might have performed as a wife that afternoon. But it does seem likely that she and Rattenbury had enjoyed some form of marital intimacy. Rattenbury might often talk of suicide but he had never taken any deliberate steps to end his life. Alma may not have been the brightest woman in England but she certainly had enough sense to realize that rather than establishing a further reason for suicide he had been asking for reassurance, begging to be shown that she still considered him a man. Alma did not want Rattenbury to die, hated to see him so depressed but, at the same time, she knew that she would never be able to bring herself to give up Stoner. Faced with this crisis, the most natural thing for her to have done was to quietly close the bedroom door and then kiss and caress her husband, perhaps even arousing some of his long lost passion. Whatever she did or said she appeared downstairs later that afternoon cheerful and unruffled, sure that she had nothing to fear from the revelations Ratz had made that quiet Sunday afternoon. She had managed to pull him out of his despondency and had encouraged him to take a practical approach to his business woes. Why not visit Mr. Jenks, she had said. Jenks, a business acquaintance of Rattenbury's, might be persuaded to provide the capital to get his apartment building scheme off the ground. He lived in a large manor house surrounded by pleasant grounds near Bridport, a quiet little town some two hours' drive from Bournemouth best known as the Port Brede of Hardy's novels. There was no need to travel back and forth in one day, Alma coaxed, they could combine business with pleasure and stay overnight at the manor. Rattenbury agreed and seems to have been somewhat cheered by the prospects of their visit's success.

After tea, with Ratz comfortably ensconced in his armchair, a drink in his hand, Alma called Jenks on the phone and gaily made arrangements for their visit the following day. Stoner overheard the conversation. As soon as she replaced the receiver he grabbed her, thrust what she took to be a revolver in her face and in a rage vowed he would kill her if she went to Bridport. He either knew or guessed that their secret was out and he was convinced that Alma in order to placate Ratz had made love to him that afternoon. He was terrified that he might soon be told by Rattenbury to leave the house. The trip to Bridport, where he was sure that Ratz and Alma would share a room, he saw as the beginning of a new relationship between Alma and her husband.

Alma managed to keep her head. He was a fool, she told him, of course she had not slept with Ratz and there would be no need for them to share a bedroom in such a large house as Mr. Jenks'. Gradually Stoner calmed down and after Alma agreed to two childishly simple promises, that she would never again close the bedroom door when she was alone with Ratz and that if they did go to Bridport she would not expect Stoner to drive, he appeared to have relented and Alma once again felt that she was in control of the situation.

Stoner left with the car to visit his grandmother, and Alma, sure that she had soothed his anger and anxiety, relaxed playing cards with Ratz until 9:30 when she went upstairs to pack.

Irene returned to Villa Madeira some 45 minutes later and as it seemed the rest of the household had retired she went directly to her room, but then feeling hungry, she decided to go back downstairs to the kitchen to make herself something to eat. As she walked along the lower hall she heard the sound of unusually heavy breathing and she stopped, a strange sense of unease which she would later describe as a premonition that something was wrong creeping over her. She listened outside Ratz' bedroom and then carefully opening the door, she reached inside, turned on the light and peered into the room. The bed had not been disturbed. She concluded that he had fallen asleep in the drawing room chair and slumped into an awkward position was beginning to snore. Although she felt relieved the experience had unnerved her and driven the thought of food from her head and she returned to her room without going to the kitchen. A few minutes later as she walked along the landing to the bathroom, she found Stoner dressed in pyjamas, leaning over the railing looking down into the hall below.

152

"What's the matter?" she asked and Stoner replied, "Nothing, I was looking to see if the lights were out."

Moments after she had returned to her room she was joined by Alma who sat on her bed and chatted happily about the planned excursion to Bridport. She had had a bit of a rumpus with Stoner, she said, but now it had blown over. She wasn't sure whether Stoner would be driving them to Bridport, but she was convinced that she would be able to fix it all right.

After Alma's visit Irene settled herself into bed and was on the edge of sleep when she heard the sound of someone rushing down the stairs followed minutes later by Alma screaming hysterically "Irene! Irene!"

Alma had been in bed with Stoner when their whispered conversation had been interrupted by a loud groan from below, a groan that had brought her leaping out of bed and flying barefoot down the stairs. She had found Ratz slumped in his chair and at first she thought he was asleep, but then she saw that his right eye was purple and swollen and his hair was matted with blood. There was blood on the chair, blood in a pool on the carpet. She had snatched up Ratz' unfinished whisky, gulped it down, retched, and fought to keep down a second mouthful. Somewhat steadied she had begun her feeble attempts to make Ratz all right. Picking up his false teeth which had flown out with the force of the blow, she had tried to get them back in his mouth thinking that if only he had his teeth he would be able to talk to her and tell her what had happened. And then suddenly appalled by her actions she had backed away from the chair and screamed for Irene.

She told Irene to phone for the doctor and then together they called for Stoner and between the three of them managed to carry Ratz to his bed. Stoner was dispatched to collect the doctor and while Irene tried to get Ratz undressed, Alma, another drink in her hand hovered over her husband moaning, "Oh poor Ratz. What has happened?"

Dr. O'Donnell arrived at the house just before midnight and found Ratz unconscious, his head bathed in blood, his breathing laboured and his pulse slow and irregular. Ratz' condition was serious and realizing he needed help, O'Donnell telephoned for a local surgeon, Mr. Rooke, and while he waited for Rooke to arrive he turned his attention to Alma who was already in his opinion inclined to be intoxicated. Thinking that perhaps Ratz had fallen and hit his head on the piano or some other heavy piece of furniture, he asked Alma what had happened, but she evaded his question.

"Look at him, look at the blood," she wailed. "Somebody has finished him."

Alma, still relatively sober, hoped that she could fix the blame on an unknown intruder, a mysterious somebody. But as O'Donnell questioned her further a new possibility struck her. Perhaps she could convince the doctor that Rattenbury had taken his own life. He had been reading a book about suicide, she said, here it was on the piano. She thrust the book at O'Donnell urging him to read it, but the doctor impatiently told her to put it away and returned to his patient.

Mr. Rooke arrived shortly after midnight and almost immediately decided to remove Rattenbury to a nursing home. Not only was he badly wounded, but a proper examination was made impossible by Alma who was making a nuisance of herself by her stumbling and clumsy attempts to minister to her husband.

"If you want to kill him you are going the right way to do it," Rooke reprimanded her. "Do let me near him and attend to him."

An ambulance carried Ratz to the Strathallen Nursing Home and there Rooke, after making a careful examination, concluded that his injuries had not been accidental but were the result of three separate blows to the head delivered by a blunt instrument. He called the police.

Constable Bagwell arrived at Villa Madeira at about 2:00 o'clock that morning. He questioned Alma about her husband's injuries and she made the first of a series of statements, each recorded by the police, which would lead her to the Old Bailey..

"At about 9 p.m. I was playing cards with my husband in the drawing room and I went to bed," she told Bagwell. "At 10:30 I heard a yell. I came downstairs and went into the drawing room and saw my husband sitting in the chair. I then sent for Dr. O'Donnell. He was then taken away." Alma was still clinging to the hope that she could place the blame on a stranger to the household.

Shortly afterwards a second policeman arrived at the house. Inspector Mills found Alma very excited and although it was apparent to him that she had been drinking he too questioned her about her husband's injuries. She repeated the same statement she had made to Bagwell only this time it had not been a yell but the sound of someone groaning that had brought her downstairs.

154

Mills pointed to the French doors opening off the drawing room into the garden. "Were these windows open when you came down?" he asked.

Without pausing to think Alma answered, "No, it was shut and locked." And then in one of her last moments of clarity she realized her mistake. If she had said, yes they were standing open, she might still have had a chance of convincing the police that a burglar had come in by these doors, awakened Rattenbury and panicked by discovery had delivered the blows to silence him and then fled before Alma entered the room. Now she realized that the police would certainly suspect someone in the house and as the minutes passed a new thought lodged itself in her whirling brain. She saw herself as the only alternative to Stoner. She must accept the blame.

Inspector Mills had gone to the nursing home leaving Bagwell behind at Villa Madeira, when fortified by several more whiskies, Alma approached the constable and said, according to Bagwell's later testimony, "I know who done it." Bagwell cautioned her and Alma continued, "I did it with a mallet." Why, Bagwell asked. "Ratz has lived too long." Where was the mallet, Bagwell wanted to know and Alma answered, "It is hidden." There came a dim realization of the enormity of the crime to which she was confessing and Alma's resolve weakened. "No, my lover did it," she blurted out and then recoiling from this accusation she tried to buy the constable's silence. "I would like to give you £10," she declared, but then perhaps seeing from Bagwell's reaction that that approach wouldn't work she gave up saying, "No, I won't bribe you."

The next hour was a difficult one for Bagwell. Alma was becoming very drunk. Perhaps to console herself she had put a recording of one of her songs on the record player and as the sentimental strains of "Dark Haired Marie" filled the house a new idea had occurred to her.

> Are you waiting in your garden
> By the deep wide azure sea?
> Are you waiting for your loveship,
> Dark haired Marie?
>
> I shall come to claim you someday,
> In my arms at last you'll be,
> I shall kiss your lips and love you,
> Dark haired Marie[6]

. . . the tenor sang and Alma began to think of romance. In the past her charms applied at the right time had always smoothed things over for her. She need only win Bagwell over and everything would be all right again. She began to relentlessly pursue the constable about the house, fawning over him, trying to kiss him. And Bagwell finding it impossible to discourage her finally stepped outside. Determined to follow him, Alma rushed to the door and would have trailed him into the garden if Irene had not caught hold of her, forced her into a chair and then sat on top of her in a desperate attempt to calm her down. Luckily for Bagwell he encountered a policeman walking his beat and in the company of this constable he felt it was safe to re-enter the house.

At 3:30 a.m. Inspector Mills returned to Villa Madeira and informing Alma that her husband was in critical condition, he cautioned her, warning her that anything she said would be taken down and used as evidence. Alma then made a rambling, disjointed statement in which she accepted full blame for the attack. "I did it," she said. "He gave me the book. He has lived too long. He said, 'Dear, dear.' I will tell you in the morning where the mallet is. Have you told the Coroner yet? I shall make a better job of it next time. Irene does not know. I made a proper muddle of it. I thought I was strong enough."

Some ten minutes later Dr. O'Donnell returned to the house accompanied by Stoner who had spent the last few hours peacefully asleep in the car outside the nursing home waiting for the doctor. O'Donnell was astounded at the scene that greeted him at Villa Madeira. Lights were blazing from every room in the house. Two other constables had joined Mills and Bagwell and Alma was on her feet staggering from one to the other, clinging to them, trying to wrap her arms around them, talking excitedly over the din of the record player. O'Donnell took her upstairs to her room and gave her a half grain of morphia, hoping to quieten her.

As morphia joined the alcohol in her spinning head, Alma suddenly saw a fourth alternative. Ratz had been wounded not by a burglar, not by Stoner and not by herself, but by someone who she knew detested her and who remained incurably bitter about Ratz' second marriage — his eldest son. This sudden inspiration drove Alma from her room and down the stairs to Inspector Mills.

"I know who did it — his son," she said to the Inspector.

156

"How old is he?" Mills asked thinking the only Rattenbury son was six years old tucked in bed upstairs.

"Thirty-two," Alma answered and then for a moment reason returned and seeing it was no use she added, "but he is not here."

Mills and O'Donnell half carried Alma back to her room and she was left to sleep, but not for long.

At 4:30 Detective Inspector Carter arrived at Villa Madeira and after making an inspection of the house and grounds he took up a position in Alma's room. He was there when she awakened from drugged sleep at six o'clock. He ordered coffee for her and while she bathed under the supervision of a police matron, he questioned Stoner. He had gone to bed just after eight o'clock the night before, Stoner said. He had been aroused at 10:30 by Alma's shouting for him to come down. Alma had been screaming and crying. He had asked her "How did this happen?" and Alma had answered that she didn't know. He had never seen a mallet on the premises before and he had heard no sounds of a quarrel before he had been called.

Satisfied with Stoner's version of the events of that night Carter returned to Alma's bedroom. She was dressed and appeared to be rational and able to understand him. Shortly after eight o'clock he charged her with the wounding of her husband. "At about 9 p.m. I was playing cards with my husband," Alma said, "when he dared me to kill him as he wanted to die. I picked up the mallet. He then said, 'You have not guts enough to do it.' I then hit him with the mallet. I hid the mallet outside the house. I would have shot him if I had a gun." Written down by Carter and read and signed by Alma, it was the most damaging statement she had made that night.

Alma was taken to the Bournemouth Police Station where the charge against her was repeated and so there could be no mistake she answered the charge with the words, "That is right. I did it deliberately and would do it again." And it seemed that she had sealed her fate.

In the days following Alma's arrest an edgy truce existed between Irene and Stoner both of whom remained in residence at Villa Madeira. On Tuesday they were together in Rattenbury's car, perhaps going to collect Irene's mother who had agreed to move in with her for the time being. Stoner chose a route which led past his grandmother's house, pointed it out to her and, with the braggadocio of a small boy who has escaped punishment for some minor misdemeanor, proudly informed her that that was where he had borrowed the mallet.

Irene had no reason to doubt him. She had been convinced that Alma could never have delivered the blows to her husband's head. But to be absolutely sure that she was not misinterpreting an empty boast for an admission of guilt, she asked him, "Won't your finger-prints be on the mallet?"

"No," Stoner replied. "I wore gloves."

Irene was in a terrible quandary. Alma was in prison charged with wounding her husband but so far her relationship with Stoner had remained a secret, a secret which Alma had trusted Irene to keep. If the police were to direct their attention to Stoner, all the details of Alma's adultery would become public. Until she saw Alma, Irene decided, she must keep her conversation with Stoner to herself.

The following day, Wednesday, March 27, was Irene's usual evening off. Although not a Catholic, she had visited a priest not so much to ask advice but to confide in someone on whose silence she could rely. When she returned to Villa Madeira, her mother met her at the door and told her that Stoner was very drunk. He had been brought back to the house by a taxi driver who had found him wandering up and down the road and now he wanted to speak to Irene. Stoner, who Irene found to be in a very peculiar state, told her that the following morning he was going to travel to London to visit Alma. He was determined, he said, to give himself up.

Stoner had received a letter from Alma that day and perhaps for the first time understood the seriousness of her situation. In the letter sent from Holloway Prison Alma had written.

I am trying to have the lawyer's letter I received to-day sent to you, darling, so that you can make arrangements to come up with him, or make arrangements yourself with the governor. But I must see you darling. Please write to me. This is the third letter I have written. Hope you receive this. I hardly know how to write now. Let me know how Ratz is getting along. No more now. God bless you. My love be with you always.
                                                    Lozanne

Have you talked with Dr. O'Donnell about how Ratz is? Goodness there is so much I want to know. Please tell Irene to give you a few bobbing pins for my hair. I think they would be allowed.

The next morning Stoner got up early and caught the train to London. While he was gone Dr. O'Donnell arrived at the house. Rattenbury had died that morning without regaining consciousness, he told Irene. Alma would now be charged with murder.

Irene phoned the police and when Stoner stepped off the train from London, Detective Inspector Carter was waiting for him. Charged with the murder of Francis Mawson Rattenbury, Stoner responded simply, "I understand."

12

The Old Bailey

On May 27, 1935 Alma and Stoner were brought to trial in the Old Bailey. The case against them seemed one of classic simplicity. To the Crown the motive for murder was clear: "The relationship between Mrs. Rattenbury and Stoner had ceased to be that of the wife of the employer and the man employed but had become an adulterous intercourse and Mr. Rattenbury stood in the way of their indulgence of this guilty passion."[1]

Alma had first become the object of police suspicions as the result of the statements she had made during the hours after the discovery of Rattenbury's injuries and now, although she had repudiated her confessions saying that she had been drunk and drugged and that she hadn't known what she was saying, her own words recorded by the police remained the strongest evidence against her.

Stoner's situation was quite different. The Crown would produce expert testimony which would prove that the murder weapon had been a heavy wooden mallet belonging to Stoner's grandmother and witnesses would testify that Stoner had borrowed the mallet on the evening of the attack. And Stoner, too, had confessed to the crime. But unlike Alma, he had confessed not to wounding but to murder. The day after Rattenbury's death Stoner had been sitting with Detective Constable Gates in a detention room waiting for his appearance in police court when he had turned conversationally to Gates. "You know Mrs. Rattenbury, don't you?" he asked. Gates had answered that he did and Stoner had continued, "Do you know Mrs. Rattenbury had nothing to do with this?" Gates cautioned him and Stoner had stated simply and matter-of-factly, "When I did the job, I believed he was asleep. I hit him and then came upstairs and told Mrs. Rattenbury. She rushed down then. You see, I watched through the French windows and saw her kiss him goodnight, then leave the room. I waited and crept in through the French window which was unlocked. I think he must have been asleep when I hit him, still it ain't much use saying anything. I don't suppose they will let her out yet. You know there should be a doctor with her when they tell her I am arrested, because she will go out of her mind."

Another telling piece of evidence against Stoner was a letter Alma had written to Irene from Holloway Prison on April 18th.

Darling,
Was glad to see you looking so nice, also your M. and F. I wrote you dozens of letters in my mind last night, and have nothing but an empty box on top this morning. Will you hand to Mrs Greig [wardress] to give me before I go to Court a pair of tweezers, Yvettes' rouge, things to do my nails with, and liquid polish, light colour. I think the perfume in small bottles will last longer, also that gray or fawn pair of slippers (same colour you were wearing), in case the brown suede are not O.K. and I can best in that case change over. The brown shoes with laces would be best. You might tell Mrs Greig how much I appreciate her kindness, which has been most considerate. Oh darling, I hardly know how to write. My mind is frozen. When Manning [her Bournemouth solicitor] advised me to write about nothing but clothes &c., it almost made one smile. I can hardly concentrate on even them. I think my macintosh would help. Also that red woolen dress the skirt needs a hook on or something, and if I haven't a red belt; you might get a wide one. Oh Lord, and tomorrow Good Friday and I dare not think of the children. I even pretend I haven't any here. If one thought for five minutes they'd go mad. I saw nothing in the papers yesterday except what was cut out; I seem to see nothing but the missing parts. Darling, will one ever be happy again? Friday will be like Sunday here. Of all the days in the week Sunday is the worst. I have to control my mind like the devil to not think of little John. Yes, take him out on Sundays, darling. C. [probably her other son Christopher] was awfully pleased to hear from you. I cannot understand my M. not doing anything, can you? Messages of love are not much use to me now, when I wanted her help with Long &c. However, if I feel awfully sad, being separated in such a ghastly way from everything one loves, S's feelings must take some weighing up, but he'll be the same and not allow himself to think. Should think his remorse at what he's brought down on my head, the children's &c. — smashed lives — would drive him a raving lunatic — a frightful responsibility to hold in one persons hands. God deliver me from such a hellish responsibility. I couldn't have courage to bear that pain; my own is enough in a hundred lifetimes as it is. Two times have found my feelings very hard and bitter — Oh, my God, appallingly so — but have managed to drown these feelings and get one's heart

soft again. Darling, God bless you, bless us all and get us out of this nightmare. My love to your M. and F. My love be with you always.

Lozanne

There was little doubt in anyone's mind that the "S" referred to by Alma in her letter was Stoner and the implication was clear, Alma held him responsible for the attack on Rattenbury.

"How do you plead?" Alma was asked and standing in the dock she answered softly, almost inaudibly, "Not guilty." Her confessions, her defence would claim, had been hysterical, irrational ramblings produced by a mind sodden with whisky and confused by morphia.

Although Stoner did not deny the veracity of the statement he had made to Constable Gates, he too answered, "Not guilty," to the charge. He was addicted to cocaine, he would claim. He had been under its influence at the time he had attacked Rattenbury and the drug had rendered him incapable of forming the intent to kill. He was suffering from a disease of the mind and was guilty, but insane.

In England, as in Victoria, interest in the case was intense. Some twelve hours before the trial was due to commence a line of people had begun to form along the pavement outside the entrance to the Old Bailey. The next morning late-comers had gladly parted with a few pounds in exchange for a place in the queue and the chance of being admitted to the spectators' gallery. Most of the curiosity was directed toward Alma and for the press and the public the highlight of the trial came on the third day when Alma was called to the stand to testify in her own defence.

"She walked slowly across the well of the court followed by a wardress," observed a *Daily Mirror* reporter, "and took the oath in a low voice." Mr. T. J. O'Connor, K.C., Alma's counsel, asked her to "help us all by speaking up" and Alma answered his questions clearly and with quite remarkable composure. O'Connor gently led her through the details of her personal history; she had been married to Rattenbury for seven or eight years; she had been married twice before, her first husband had been killed in the war and she had divorced her second; from her second marriage she had a thirteen-year-old son Christopher who was away at school and she had another son who would be six and a half in June, a child of her marriage to Rattenbury.

"Since the birth of that child, did you and Mr. Rattenbury live together as man and wife?" O'Connor asked.

162

"No."

"Did you occupy separate rooms?"

"Yes."

"On what terms were you with your husband?"

"Quite friendly."

"No marital intimacy, but you were friendly?"

"Absolutely."

"Was your married life happy?"

"Like that." Alma gestured with her hands, implying that it was no better and no worse than many other marriages.

"We were told about a quarrel. Were quarrels between you and he frequent or not?"

"Not very frequent."

"Were they severe when they occurred, or were they just trifling quarrels?"

"It all depended on whether Mr. Rattenbury got into a temper or not," Alma said. "Sometimes he did." Then O'Connor led her through an account of the night in July when Rattenbury had blackened her eye. "He was queer, morbid," Alma said, "and there was the usual talk of committing suicide, so I asked him, seeing that he was always frightening me that he was going to commit suicide, why did he not do it for a change?" Rattenbury had lost his temper and hit her, Alma said.

The prosecution alleged that Alma had obtained money from her husband for the sole purpose of financing the "orgy" at the Royal Palace Hotel, while Alma claimed that she had needed the money to balance her overdrawn account and that having concocted a story she and Stoner had had to travel to London, her absence being necessary to support her story that she was having an operation.

"What were the relations between you and your husband as regards money?" O'Connor asked her. "Was he free with money?"

"Very close — well, not very generous."

"Used you to have to say things of which you are ashamed in order to get money from him?"

"All my married life, yes."

"Tell him lies?"

"Yes; it saved rows." O'Connor would return to this subject later. Now he began to quiz Alma about her relations with Stoner.

Stoner had been employed as a chauffeur in September of 1934,

Alma testified. She had become his mistress two months later, before he had come to live at Villa Madeira.

"Just taking it quite generally, from that time until your husband's death did relations take place between you and Stoner regularly?"

"Yes."

"In his room or yours, or in both?"

"Yes."

"One or the other. What attitude did your husband take towards this, if he knew it?"

"None whatsoever."

"Did he know of it?"

"He must have known because he told me to live my own life quite a few years ago."

"As I understand it, there was no occasion on which you told him about Stoner, but your husband knew about it."

"No, I told him that I had taken him at his word and was living my own life."

"Oh, you told him that did you? Can you tell me when that was?"

"No, I would say it was somewhere round about Christmas that I told him." Alma was not being completely honest. She was telling the truth when she stated that she was reasonably sure that Ratz had known about her affair with Stoner, but she had much more recent evidence that this was the case. She could not have heard Ratz reading that particular passage from *Stay of Execution* without being convinced that he knew about her relations with Stoner. But she could not let the jury know that this revelation had been so recent for had they known that Rattenbury had confronted Alma with her infidelity on the afternoon of the attack, the jury would certainly have interpreted it as a motive for murder.

O'Connor turned his attention to the Friday night before the murder, the night Alma and Stoner had returned from London.

Had her husband asked her anything about the operation she was supposed to have had in London, O'Connor wondered.

"No," Alma said, "he was always jolly late at night," and O'Connor established that jolly was a euphemism Alma often used for drunk.

The weekend had been unremarkable, the same as many previous weekends, except that Ratz was particularly depressed.

"Did you say anything to try and cheer him up?" O'Connor asked.

"Yes, I was very nice to him to try and make the 'blues' go. He had the 'blues'." She had persuaded him to come for a drive on Sunday but that hadn't improved his mood and he had remained very depressed. They had had tea together in her room, Alma testified, Stoner had served them, the usual practice when Irene was out. O'Connor questioned her about the door to her room and Alma said she thought that for at least some of the time the door had been closed.

"The normal thing was the door to your room should not have been closed?" O'Connor asked.

"Exactly," Alma said.

O'Connor returned to her husband's mood. He had been reading a book, Alma said, about a person who committed suicide. He said he admired a person who finished himself off before he became old and doddering. He was obviously depressed and gloomy, O'Connor observed. "Now what did you do to cheer him up?" Alma replied that she had suggested many things, among them a trip to London, finally getting him to agree to a trip to Bridport to visit a business friend, Mr. Jenks.

She had telephoned Jenks sometime between 6:30 and 7:00 and while she was telephoning Stoner had come into the room. He had what looked like a revolver in his hand. Stoner was very angry, Alma said. "He said he would kill me if I went to Bridport."

Rattenbury had been in the next room. "Could you go on talking without being overheard by your husband?" O'Connor wondered.

"Yes, practically. One could have, because Mr. Rattenbury did not really take very much notice."

Stoner had accused her of having relations with her husband behind the closed bedroom door, Alma said. She had assured him that she had not. "He was very annoyed at my going to Bridport. We had quite an unpleasant time about it, but afterwards I thought it was all right."

"Did he say why he did not want you to go to Bridport with Mr. Rattenbury?" O'Connor asked.

"He was very jealous of Mr. Rattenbury — unnecessarily so."

Stoner thought, Alma said, that she and her husband would have to share a bedroom at Mr. Jenks' home. She assured him that they would not and she felt that he had believed her and calmed down.

After this scene with Stoner she had gone into the drawing room and chatted with Ratz. "I talked about how nice it was we were going to Bridport the next day, and I still tried to make him 'jolly', you know, and drive away the 'blues'."

She had put John to bed sometime between 7:30 and 7:45, Alma said. Then she had played cards and talked to Ratz who was quite "jolly" by then. At 9:30 she had let the dog, Dinah, out by the French doors and gone upstairs to prepare for bed. She had gone along the upstairs hall to the bathroom and when she returned to her bedroom some five minutes later Dinah was there.

She had closed her bedroom door, she said, and begun to make preparations for the trip. Shortly after ten o'clock she had visited Irene to tell her about the plans for the next day. Then she had returned to her room and sometime later, she really had no idea how much time had elapsed, Stoner whom she had been expecting had come into her room in his pyjamas and got into bed with her.

She noticed that he was a little queer.

"How long had he been in bed before you noticed what you are just going to describe?"

"Almost right away."

"What was it? Tell your own story Mrs. Rattenbury. I do not want to lead you at all on this."

"Well, he seemed agitated, and I said, 'What is the matter, darling?' and he said he was in trouble, and could not tell me what it was, and I said, 'Oh, you must tell me,' and we went back and forth like that for two or three minutes, and he said no, that I could not bear it. I thought he was in trouble outside, you know — his mother or like that — and then I said I was strong enough to bear anything and he told me that I was not going to Bridport the next day as he had hurt Ratz. It did not penetrate my head what he did say to me at all until I heard Ratz groan, and then my brain became alive and I jumped out of bed."

"Did Stoner say anything about how he had done it?" O'Connor asked.

"He said he had hit him over the head with a mallet."

"Anything more about the mallet?"

"That he had hidden it outside."

She had rushed down to the drawing room, Alma said, and found Ratz sitting in his chair. "I tried to rub his hands; they were cold. I tried to take his pulse, and I shook him to try and make him speak."

"Did you call for help?"

"Not right away. I tried to speak to him, and then I saw this blood, and I went round the table and I trod on his false teeth, and that made me hysterical, and I yelled — I cannot remember, only vaguely. I took a drink of whisky to stop myself being sick."

"Was that the only drink of whisky you had?"

"No, I took one drink of whisky neat, and I was sick, and then I remember pouring out another one. I cannot remember drinking the next one; I tried to become insensible, to block out the picture." And according to Alma's version of events she had been successful for she claimed to remember nothing more about what had taken place that night.

"Mrs. Rattenbury," O'Connor asked, "did you yourself murder your husband?"

"Oh, no."

"Did you take any part whatsoever in planning it?"

"No."

"Did you know a thing about it till Stoner spoke to you in your bed?"

"I would have prevented it if I had known half — a quarter of a minute before, naturally."

O'Connor was finished for the time being and he turned the questioning over to Mr. J. D. Casswell, Stoner's counsel. It was not necessary for Stoner's defence for Casswell to shift the blame to Alma and before he began to question her he assured her that he was not suggesting that she had had anything to do with the attack nor was he implying that she had incited Stoner or that she had had any advance knowledge of Stoner's intentions. What he was going to suggest, and this he did not tell Alma, was that Stoner was a seduced innocent, the victim of the practiced charms of an older woman, who had used the lad unfairly to relieve her loneliness and boredom.

He asked her about her relationship with Stoner. Had she suggested their living together, he wanted to know. No, Alma replied, she thought that the idea had been mutual. Casswell found this hard to believe.

"Mutual? Because you see, he was in a position of a servant was he not?"

"Yes."

"And quite a young man?"

"Yes," Alma replied and the jury must have thought it unlikely that Stoner would have suggested the liaison without a good deal of encouragement.

"Did you think it might have had a deleterious effect on him?"

"No," Alma answered, "I would never have started it if I had."

Had she told Stoner that she and her husband were not living together as man and wife, Casswell asked and Alma responded, "It was obvious to anyone living there; they would know it."

"He would know it?"

"Naturally."

"Did you tell him you were looking for sympathy?" Casswell asked.

"No, most decidedly not," Alma said firmly.

"You were looking for that from someone?"

"No, I certainly was not." Casswell was painting an unattractive picture of her and Alma answered his questions indignantly.

Casswell turned to the subject of drugs, asking Alma if she herself had ever taken drugs. "No, absolutely not," Alma replied and in this she may have been less than truthful, but Casswell unaware of the dark rumours of her drug-taking that circulated in Victoria, lacked the information which might have allowed him to pin her down with a more specific question.

"Are you quite sure of that?" he pressed.

"Absolutely."

"From time to time we have heard that you used to get very excited at times and then get drowsy afterwards?" Casswell said implying that this sounded like the results of drug taking to him.

But Alma had a ready answer, "Well all my life with Mr. Rattenbury was so what we call monotonous that at times I used to take too many cocktails to liven up one's spirits — take them to excess, say, or wine." Stoner did not drink with her, she said, in fact he was upset about her drinking and she stopped taking cocktails after he came. Casswell hardly wanted to discover that Stoner had been a good influence on Alma, he was after all attempting to show that she had been a bad influence on him. He quickly changed the subject, quizzing her about Stoner's claim that he was addicted to drugs.

She had gone to see Dr. O'Donnell in February, Alma said, because she had become very alarmed about Stoner's violent behaviour. Stoner had said he had to go to London that morning to get his drug. "I begged him not to go, but he had to go, and when he went I was so upset — it was dreadful — I telephoned to Dr. O'Donnell to explain everything to him and said could he help this boy."

"Now had you any doubt that that boy at that time had such a craving that he went to London and nothing you said would stop him?" Casswell asked, sure that Alma's answer would support Stoner's defence. But she replied, "To be perfectly candid, I was not certain then, and I am not certain now. I cannot answer that and say yes or no. I do not know." The doctor had reported back to her that Stoner claimed to be addicted to cocaine. "Did you do anything more about it?" Casswell asked her.

"No," Alma said, "because Stoner was better from then onwards, and he said he could not get the drug, and I did not want to agitate him in case he was longing for it, we just went on smoothly, and I never brought the subject up again. He said he had stopped it from then onwards, and, well, everything was all right. I thought he had."

Justice Humphreys was curious about something, something that had not yet been answered to his satisfaction. "Did you know his age when he came to you?" he inquired from the bench and Alma replied that she had thought he was older. Stoner had told her that he was twenty-two. When had she learned that his real age was eighteen, the judge asked. On his birthday, Alma said, on November 19. And Casswell missed an important point in Stoner's defence for Alma was not being entirely honest. She had earlier testified that their affair had begun on the 22nd of November so she had known Stoner's true age when their sexual relationship began.

When Mr. R. P. Croom-Johnson, K.C., began the prosecution's cross-examination he knew that Alma's testimony had damaged the Crown's case against her. True, Alma had admitted that on many occasions she had lied to her husband, that on occasion she drank too much and that she had welcomed a sexual relationship with a boy young enough to be her son. But Croom-Johnson was aware that none of this had seemed so scandalous or reprehensible when Alma spoke about it quietly and openly. Wearing a dress of navy blue silk with a fur cape about her shoulders and speaking in her rich low voice, she had appeared as dignified as it were possible for a woman to do under the circumstances and Croom-Johnson knew that she had impressed the jury.

He questioned her about the state of her husband's finances. Wasn't her husband retired and living largely, if not wholly, on his means, he asked her. And Alma said, yes, but she understood he was very well off. Had the question of money between you and your husband been a matter about which you had differences of opinion in the past, Croom-Johnson wondered. "Oh, yes," Alma said.

"Am I putting it fairly when I suggest that you were in the habit of deceiving your husband in order to get what you regarded as sufficient money for your needs?"

"Absolutely," Alma replied with disconcerting directness.

Did she know that her husband's securities had fallen considerably in value, he asked.

"No. He was always talking like that; so it was the case of the lamb crying wolf; if it was so one would not have believed him."

Alma was distinctly vague about the state of her husband's finances and Croom-Johnson had no better luck when he questioned her about her own. How much money did her husband give her in the course of a year, he inquired. "Oh, I really could not tell you that," Alma replied sounding surprised that anyone could seriously ask her such a question.

"Considerable sums in the course of a year?" Croom-Johnson persisted. And again Alma could not answer.

"Hundreds?"

"I suppose so," Alma helpfully agreed.

Croom-Johnson tried another tack. Out of her household account she had paid the servants' wages. Yes, Alma agreed, all the household expenses and all the clothing for her husband and the children and their schooling. "It was too much; that is why I was always overdrawn."

"About how much a year did he give you?" Croom-Johnson asked. And Alma remembered now that it was about fifty pounds a month but she was always overdrawn and had to ask for more.

"Fifty pounds a month would be about six hundred pounds a year," Croom-Johnson said.

"I see," Alma said with interest as if it was a new piece of information for her. With the additional money she had asked for that would be something over one thousand pounds a year, Croom-Johnson prompted. "Yes, I daresay," Alma answered offhandedly. The prosecution's suggestion that Alma had asked for £250 for the purposes of financing the "orgy" in London, had been badly undermined by Alma's answers which must have proved to the jury that finances were not her forte and that her reason for asking for the money was simply to balance her household accounts.

Croom-Johnson dropped the subject and began to quiz her about her intimacy with Stoner, knowing that he could bring out facts which would shock the jury and might lead them to believe that she was capable of anything.

"You have told us that on Sunday night Stoner came into your bedroom and got into bed with you?"

"Yes."

"Was that something that happened frequently?"

"Oh, always."

"Always? Were you fond of your little boy John?"

"I love both my children."

"Were you fond of John."

"Naturally."

"Did John sleep in the same room?"

"Yes, but in another bed at the other side of the room," Alma said as she caught the drift of Croom-Johnson's questions.

"It is not a very large room?"

"No, but little John was always asleep."

"Are you suggesting to the members of the jury that you, a mother fond of her little boy of six, were permitting this man to come into this bedroom with you, in the same room where your little innocent child was asleep?"

"I did not consider that was dreadful; I did not consider it an intrigue with Stoner," Alma protested weakly. Alma stood convicted of a complete lack of taste. The only thing that could be said in her favour was that John did indeed seem to be a sound sleeper. In no witness's version of the events of the night of March 24th, when the house was full of policemen wandering in and out of the bedroom, is there any mention of John who seems to have slept through the whole thing.

Croom-Johnson next turned to Alma's alleged loss of memory. She remembered calling for Irene, Alma said. She remembered pouring herself a glass of whisky and being sick. But after that nothing. "Are you telling the members of the jury that from the time practically that you were sick and poured yourself a glass of whisky your memory does not serve you at all?" he challenged her.

She remembered, she said, placing a towel around her husband's head. She remembered rubbing his cold hands, she remembered trying to get his false teeth back in so that he could talk to her and tell her what had happened. And that was all, except for little John's face at the door the next day when she was being taken away.

"Do you recollect Dr. O'Donnell coming?"

"I cannot," Alma said and although Alma admitted that the doctor was a person whose presence should have soothed her rather than excited her, she insisted that she had tried to remember but it was all a complete blank. Strangely, Croom-Johnson did not refer to a statement she had given on the 28th of March in which she said she remembered both Dr. O'Donnell and Mr. Rooke arriving, Mr. Rooke telling her to keep out of the way, and later Dr. O'Donnell returning to the house and giving her something to make her sleep. Apparently Alma's loss of memory was most conveniently retrogressive.

In spite of repeated attempts by Croom-Johnson to trap her into an admission that she remembered more than she had previously testified, she remained consistent. She remembered none of the policemen, none of the statements attributed to her. Shown her signature in the notebook in which Carter had recorded her statement, she shook her head, she couldn't remember, "It's all double-dutch to me."

In his re-examination of the witness, O'Connor, Alma's counsel returned to the subject of Alma's confessions. In previous testimony a parade of police witnesses had clung to the official version of events. Yes, they had admitted, Alma had been drinking but she had not been drunk, at least not incapably drunk. Inspector Carter had assured the jury that when he had taken a statement from Alma on the morning after the attack she had appeared normal and had spoken clearly and deliberately. In Alma's favour was the testimony of Dr. O'Donnell who had stated that in his opinion Alma had been very intoxicated and had not been in a fit condition to make any statements. But Dr. O'Donnell was one witness who had not impressed the jury favourably. He had admitted that in response to Alma's entreaties he had asked Stoner what drugs, if any, he was in the habit of using and upon being told by Stoner that he was addicted to cocaine he had simply advised him that cocaine was a dangerous drug and left it at that. He had made no attempt to discover how much of the substance Stoner used or where he purchased it. His inaction in the face of what he admitted could be a serious medical problem cast a pall of doubt over his competency and his reliability as a witness.

That Alma had said she had delivered the blows that killed Rattenbury could not be denied. Whether or not she had been mentally competent when she confessed to the crime remained in doubt. O'Connor knew that even if they accepted his assertion that Alma had been hopelessly drunk when she had said "I did it" the jurors would ask themselves why she would confess to such an act without being guilty of at least complicity. Now he hoped to provide the answer — Alma had confessed to protect Stoner.

"When Stoner told you this story, what did you desire to do as regards to Stoner?" he asked.

"I thought he was frightened at what he had done because he had hurt Mr. Rattenbury. I think he just sort of thought he had hurt him bad enough to stop him going to Bridport, and when I said, 'I will go and see him', then he said, 'No you must not.' He said, 'The sight will upset you' and I thought all I had to do was to fix Ratz up and that would make him all right."

"When you saw your husband, did you make any decision as to what you were going to do regarding Stoner?"

"No, he was worse than what I anticipated." Alma was missing the point. The answer O'Connor wanted was that she had decided to protect Stoner, for only this explanation would satisfy the jury that her drunken confessions had not been prompted by guilt.

"Did you decide to do anything as regards Stoner?" he asked again, but still Alma did not see what he was getting at. "No, my mind went — awful, dreadful," she said.

O'Connor adopted a new tactic, attempting to prove that the statements Alma had made were in themselves full of irrational sentences. Yes, Alma said, she had played cards with her husband that night, the first part of her confession was true.

" 'He dared me to kill him as he wanted to die'." O'Connor read. "Had he ever dared you to kill him?" and Alma answered that Ratz had often mentioned suicide. "Did he dare you to kill him?" O'Connor persisted. "No, not to my knowledge," Alma said, "except that he had talked of suicide and the gas oven and things like that; that would be a dare. That is why I had that quarrel that night. I was getting fed up."

"Very well," O'Connor said and he must have cursed his client's obtuseness for instead of simply declaring her statements to be ridiculous Alma seemed determined to make sense out of them. " 'I picked up the mallet'," he said reading the next sentence in Alma's signed statement. "Do you have mallets lying about in the drawing room?"

"I could not have picked it up; it would have been an impossibility to pick up a mallet that was not there." Alma was finally on the right track.

O'Connor continued reading Alma's statement, "He then said, 'You have not guts enough to do it'. I then hit him with the mallet" and asked, "Did you hear the police sergeant say there was no sign of a struggle on the part of Mr. Rattenbury?"

"Yes," Alma said, she had heard that the blow was struck from behind.

O'Connor turned to other absurdities which had appeared in some of the other statements Alma had made that night. In one she had accused Rattenbury's son. And Alma said that she had known him to be in Canada on the night of the attack. Inspector Mills had testified that Alma had asked him if he had told the coroner about Ratz' injuries. "Did you imagine that these important officials were available at half past three in the morning," O'Connor asked and Alma answered, "No, it is too absurd." Constable Bagwell claimed that Alma had attempted to bribe him. "Has it ever crossed your mind that you might get off on a charge of unlawfully wounding by giving the police ten pounds?" "No," Alma said, "it is all absurd," and O'Connor hoped that the jury would agree with her.

Stoner's defence was not well served by the expert medical witnesses called to the stand by Casswell.

Dr. Lionel Weatherly, who said he had been a medical man for sixty-two years, listed a string of impressive credentials which included past-presidency of the Society of Mental and Nervous Diseases. Dr. Weatherly had examined Stoner ten days after his arrest. He had noted that Stoner's pupils were dilated and did not react to light and such physical symptoms were undoubtedly consistent with the taking of cocaine, he said. And Stoner had described fairly, feasibly and accurately the effects of taking a dose of cocaine and had described an unusual hallucination — the sensation of a rash under the skin, a rash that seemed to move about — that was, in the doctor's opinion a definite symptom of cocaine.

Cocaine might affect the emotions and trigger an insane suspicious jealousy, he said. Addicts experienced very definite delusions of persecution which explained Stoner's carrying a dagger about with him,

Dr. Weatherley testified. According to the doctor, Stoner's belief that Alma and Rattenbury had had intercourse behind the closed bedroom door was entirely an hallucination of hearing.

Stoner's behaviour on the night of the attack, his sudden and violent reaction to the proposed trip to Bridport, his waving a revolver in Alma's face and his threatening to kill her were consistent, the doctor maintained, with his having taken a dose of cocaine that afternoon.

And Mr. Justice Humphreys inquired from the bench, "Are they also consistent with his being very angry and very jealous of his mistress?" To which Dr. Weatherly who was several more years removed from the passions of youth than was Justice Humphreys answered firmly, "I doubt it."

Dr. Weatherly was in his eighties, an elderly gentleman who was enjoying the spotlight. In all his years as a doctor he had treated only three cases of cocaine addiction. And after Crown counsel's careful interrogation, it became clear that in his excitement at having been presented with what appeared to be a classic case of cocaineism he had allowed his judgment to become impaired and had accepted Stoner's story with unprofessional alacrity.

Dr. Robert Gillespie, who followed him to the witness box, was more cautious than Dr. Weatherly had been. It was extremely difficult to tell whether a person was an addict, he said. Rather than physical symptoms, one looked for sudden mood changes, elation coupled with mental and physical activity followed by lethargy and depression. In extreme cases an addict might lose weight and begin to hallucinate. Although he too testified that Stoner's actions had been consistent with the taking of cocaine, Dr. Gillespie admitted that they might just as well have been the result of passionate jealousy.

In defending Stoner, Casswell must have known he was faced with an almost impossible task. The jury, if they were typical of the general public, felt more sympathy for Stoner than they did for Alma. But Alma had taken the stand and although she may have been reluctant to do so, she had thrown the blame on Stoner. She had impressed the jury. Stoner did not testify. His defence depended entirely on Casswell's ability to convince the jury that his client had been driven near madness by cocaine. It was a feeble defence and Casswell must have had little hope of winning an acquittal.

Stoner had described the cocaine he had taken as being brownish in colour with darker flecks and even his staunchest defender, Dr. Weatherly, had been forced to admit that cocaine, even grossly adulterated cocaine, was pure, snowy white. The sensation Stoner had described as a moving rash under the skin was a not unknown symptom of prolonged and intensive cocaine use. Usually described as the feeling that insects were crawling about under the skin, this sensation drove those afflicted to pull and tear at their skin opening running sores all over their bodies in their efforts to remove the cocaine bug. Stoner's description of this hallucination may have been original but no evidence was introduced to show that he had ever exhibited any of these characteristic lesions. And, the jury must have asked themselves, how could Stoner on his salary of £4 a month have supported an expensive habit.

The jurors reached their verdict with little dissension or debate. Recessing for only forty-seven minutes they filed back to their places and Stoner and Alma listened tense and immobile as the Clerk of the Court asked, "Do you find the prisoner, Alma Victoria Rattenbury, guilty or not guilty of murder?"

"Not guilty." Alma heard the verdict with composure giving no outward sign of emotion.

"Do you find the prisoner George Percy Stoner, guilty or not guilty of murder?"

"Guilty," the foreman said, "but we should like to add a rider to that, we recommend him to mercy." Alma staggered and seemed about to collapse. Those sitting near the dock thought they heard a choked "Oh, no!" before she was helped from the dock and supported out of the courtroom by a wardress.

Stoner moved to the centre of the dock and heard the judge deliver formal sentence of death. It was Friday, May 31st.

13

Suicide and Reprieve

At 8:30 on the evening of June 4th William Mitchell was walking along a lonely path near the outskirts of Christchurch, a town lying on the coast a few miles east of Bournemouth. Employed by a local dairyman, he was distracted from his task of rounding up stray heifers by the sight of a woman sitting alone on the riverbank near the arched railway bridge which carried the London to Bournemouth train over the River Avon.

It was unusual to see anyone in this remote spot which could only be reached with some difficulty either by crossing a swampy meadow, clambering up the steep railway embankment and following the tracks across the bridge to the other side, or by walking through several hundred yards of wet marshland thick with reeds and rushes. His curiosity aroused, Mitchell made his way up the embankment to the tracks, intending to cross the bridge to get a better look at the woman who sat quite still and alone smoking a cigarette amid the wild irises and buttercups of the riverbank.

As he approached he saw her stand and shed a short fur coat. His interest turning to astonishment he watched as she strode, her arms swinging purposefully, to the water's edge. She seemed to bend into a crouching position and then topple into the water.

Now really alarmed, Mitchell ran to the spot and wading into the water tried to catch hold of the woman's feet. But she had floated out too far and Mitchell who was unable to swim couldn't reach her. He threw himself up the bank and grabbing the woman's coat swung it out to her.

"Catch hold of this," he yelled but the woman did not respond. Instead she seemed to thrust herself backwards and Mitchell saw with mounting horror that the water around her body was red.

He raced for help. Arriving at the nearest cottage he told its occupant, James Penney, about what he had seen and while Penney hurried to the scene, Mitchell made for the police station on a borrowed bicycle.

By the time the police arrived, Penney had succeeded in getting the woman ashore. She was dead, her left breast lacerated by ugly knife wounds. The police examined her few belongings left behind on the riverbank; a tin of cigarettes, a hat and a fur coat, a fountain pen, a brown paper bag containing an empty dagger sheath and a handbag. Rummaging through her purse hoping for some clue as to her identity, they found a strange assortment of scribbled letters. One dated June 3rd read:

If only I thought it would help Stoner I would stay on, but it has been pointed out to me all too vividly I cannot help him. That is my death sentence.

The other letters were written on June 4th.

I want to make it perfectly clear that no one is responsible for what action I may take regarding my life.

I quite made up my mind at Holloway to finish things should Stoner ... and it would only be a matter of time and opportunity.

Every night and minute is only prolonging the appalling agony of my mind.

Eight o'clock. After so much walking I have got here. Oh, to see the swans and spring flowers.

And how singular I should have chosen the spot Stoner said he nearly jumped out of the train once at.

It was not intentional my coming here. I tossed a coin, like Stoner always did, and it came down Christchurch.

It is beautiful here. What a lovely world we are in. It must be easier to be hanged than to have to do the job oneself, especially in these circumstances of being watched all the while. Pray God nothing stops me tonight.

I tried this morning to throw myself under a train at Oxford Circus. Too many people about. Then a bus. Still too many people about. One must be bold to do a thing like this.

It is beautiful here and I am alone. Thank God for peace at last.[1]

The dead woman was Alma Victoria Rattenbury. They placed her body on a stretcher, carried it across the bridge and over the fields to a waiting ambulance at Stony Lane and then as Alma's body was whisked away to the mortuary at Fair Mile House, the police prepared to begin their investigation into her last five days.

Rattenbury's sketch of the impressive transportation complex and towering château style hotel which the Grand Trunk Pacific planned to build in Prince Rupert. PABC

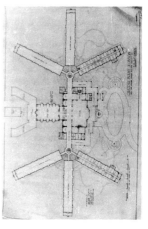

As designed by Rattenbury the G.T.P.'s hotel at Mount Robson would epitomize Edwardian elegance. PABC

Rattenbury c. 1913, Reeve of Oak Bay.   MUNICIPALITY OF OAK BAY

Alma Victoria Clarke Dolling Pakenham taken at about the time she first met Ratz.

Mrs. Florence Eleanor Rattenbury. PABC

Francis Mawson Rattenbury c. 1924. He was barely recognizable as the man who had served as Reeve of Oak Bay. VCA

Alma and Ratz with John on the beach at Bournemouth. DAILY COLONIST, APRIL 25, 1935

"Villa Madeira," 5 Manor Road, Bournemouth. An unlikely setting for murder. D. REKSTEN

George Percy Stoner. He was eighteen, shy, not very bright and totally unsophisticated.

Marked only by a stunted hydrangea, Rattenbury's grave at Wimbourne Road Cemetery, Bournemouth. D. REKSTEN

The public's last glimpse of Alma had been on Friday, May 31st when she had been ushered out of the Old Bailey by the barrister's entrance to avoid the crowds gathered outside the main entrance hoping to catch sight of her.

Dixie Dean, a young photographer with the *Daily Mirror*, guessing she would take this route, pursued her to the door of the taxi waiting to speed her away to a nursing home. Dean, who would have been content with a picture, couldn't believe his good fortune when Alma invited him to accompany her. Together they rode to a nursing home in Cleveland Gardens, Bayswater, where Dixie had another surprise.

Would he wait while she got herself settled and then come up to her room, Alma asked.

Dean readily agreed and later found himself the rather embarrassed witness to Alma's sorrow as she sat propped up in bed holding a picture of Stoner, bewailing the fate of her "darling boy" and asking Dean to photograph her as she lovingly kissed the portrait she held in her hand.[2]

Bordering on hysteria, Alma had been in no state to answer Dean's questions and the next day, Saturday, June 1st she seemed little improved.

On Saturday she had had at least two visitors; Ratz' nephew Keith Jones who had remained loyally concerned throughout the trial and who had arranged for an acquaintance of his, a Dr. Bathurst of Harley Street, to care for her and Irene Riggs who had arrived with an armful of pink roses. To Irene Alma had spoken of her intention to commit suicide and had begun planning her funeral telling Irene she wanted to be buried in a pink coffin wearing a pink nightgown. As Alma might have guessed Irene had become greatly distressed and finally the matron of the nursing home had thought it wise to put an end to their tearful meeting.

Alma spent her moments alone reading newspaper accounts of the trial, re-living her testimony over and over again, worrying over each answer she had given. She thought of no one else but Stoner and the evidence she had given against him. She wrote to him at Pentonville Prison and then read the following day that he had been moved to another prison. Grief stricken, sure that he would not receive her letter, she begged the matron to telephone the prison. But by the time she learned that Stoner was still being held at Pentonville, she had decided that a letter wasn't enough. She had to see him. She begged the doctor and the matron to help her saying, "If I had just one word with him, even if I just had one look at his face again, he would understand. I must see him once again . . . Can't something be done?"[3]

Dr. Bathurst, fearing for her sanity, petitioned the governor of the prison asking that Alma be allowed to see Stoner. He received a "most charming and sympathetic letter" in reply, but it arrived too late. By the time the visit had been arranged Alma was dead.

On the morning of Monday, June 3rd the matron had noticed a change in Alma and feeling the time was ripe she suggested her standard remedy for feminine depression, a full beauty treatment. As she had suspected, it worked wonders. A hairdresser had waved Alma's hair and a manicurist had come to do her hands. Her face had been carefully made up and the matron had been gratified to note that Alma was like a new woman.

That afternoon Alma had written to her Bournemouth solicitor, Lewis Manning, instructing him to spare no expense in an effort to win an appeal or a reprieve for Stoner. Money was no object she assured him, convinced that her notoriety would bring her songs at least a brief burst of popularity.

"Now is the time for the rest of my songs to be published; they'll sell like hot cakes now," she said, showing she had gained a nicely cynical hold on reality.

Dr. Bathurst, who visited Alma daily, had also noticed a definite improvement when he called at the nursing home at 5 o'clock that same afternoon. To him she had seemed to be infinitely better. Whereas before she had been highly nervous and hysterical, that afternoon she had spoken to him quite calmly and seemed to have regained full control of herself. She had not objected when he told her that he wanted her to stay in the nursing home at least a month. She seemed anxious to recover her health and had spoken at length about her future plans which centred obsessively on how best she could help Stoner.

Dr. Bathurst had left that afternoon feeling, for the first time, optimistic about Alma's chances for recovery. He had been astounded when he received an excited telephone call from the matron late that same night telling him that Alma had left the nursing home. Totally mystified, he was sure that something must have happened to make Alma change her plans and as it turned out he was quite right.

In the first days after the trial Alma had spoken wildly of suicide. She had appeared so distraught and hysterical that no one had been hopeful that she would ever regain the ability to face the future rationally. But in the soothing atmosphere of the nursing home, fussed over by a solicitous matron, she had managed to calm herself and as her mind cleared she had realized that the best way of relieving her feelings of guilt for having testified against him was to devote herself to procuring Stoner's freedom. When she had spoken to the doctor that afternoon she had been sure that she would be able to help him and she had begun to view the future with optimism. But later that same day she had written, "If only I thought it would help Stoner I would stay on, but it has been pointed out to me all too vividly that I cannot help him."

Later that evening, after the doctor had returned home well satisfied with Alma's progress, she had had another visitor and there can be little doubt that this was the person who pointed out so vividly that there was nothing Alma could do to save Stoner.

Known only to the matron as a friend of Mrs. Rattenbury's, the woman had sat talking for several hours. At about 9:30 the matron remembered that the evening post had arrived and sorting through it found several letters for Alma. She had taken them up to her room and had been surprised to find Alma and her friend still engaged in what seemed to be a very serious conversation.

About a half an hour later the woman had come downstairs and said, "She's going."

Hardly able to take this in the matron had replied, "No she's not. She can't be. She's going to sleep for the night."

"She's going and no one can stop her," the woman said.

The matron remonstrated. Alma was in a very delicate state of health. It would be foolish, if not dangerous, for her to go.

Alma's mind was made up and nothing would stop her, the woman said. She realized that she was taking a terrible responsibility, she continued, but she would arrange for a nurse to be with Alma at all times. She had been vague about where she and Alma planned to go, saying only that perhaps they would take a flat together, or failing that take a room at an hotel.

The matron pronounced the plan ridiculous and went upstairs to talk to Alma. She found her out of bed, dressed, her packing almost finished. She tried to reason with her. It was late, too late to try to find a flat, too late to easily find an hotel room.

"Just go back to bed tonight and have a long sleep," she coaxed. "You'll feel much better in the morning. Then you can move in comfort."[5]

But Alma, her mind made up, had been adamant, crossly pointing out that no one could keep her there against her will.

Moments later Alma and the woman had driven away from the nursing home in a private car. They were not together for long. Later that night, when Alma arrived at the door of the Elizabeth Fullcher nursing home on Devonshire road she was alone.

At about 2:30 the next afternoon, she had borrowed £2 from one of the nurses saying that she was going out for a while and promising to return by nine o'clock that night. Instead she had used the money to buy a knife, caught a train to the south coast and stabbed herself to death in a lonely spot on the banks of the Avon.

At the coroner's inquest into her death held in Christchurch on the 7th of June, Dr. Geoffrey Jones related the results of his post mortem examination. He had discovered six stab wounds in the left breast. Five had been large wounds passing inwards and downwards between the ribs. Judging by the shape and direction of the wounds, the doctor concluded that they had been self-inflicted by a sharp instrument held in the right hand. The heart had been punctured three times. Death had been almost instantaneous, in fact Alma had probably died before entering the water.

No attempt was made to identify the woman who had called on Alma the night before her death nor was Mrs. Maude McClellan, the matron of the Elizabeth Fullcher nursing home, asked if prior arrangements had been made for Alma's admittance.

Calling Alma's suicide notes neurotic statements the coroner read them into the record and then announced his verdict. "The deceased not being of sound mind did kill herself."

Alma was buried in the Wimbourne Road cemetery in Bournemouth just a few steps away from the unmarked grave of her husband, Francis Mawson Rattenbury.

Long before the funeral was due to take place hundreds of people gathered at the cemetery where they chatted contentedly, leaning against headstones as they waited for the arrival of Alma's coffin. When the funeral began the crowd, by then numbering over three thousand, surged toward the chapel eager to be admitted to the service. Alma's burial had to be delayed while the handful of mourners waited for the arrival of the Bournemouth police who had been called in to clear a path through the mob from the chapel to the gravesite.

Reverend Freeman of St. Peter's church in Bournemouth who conducted the service was disgusted by the behaviour he witnessed that day. He found the crowd of curiosity seekers to be entirely without restraint.

"It would have made me happier," he said, "if there had been some show of respect or sorrow, but it was a gathering without devotion and without sympathy, and only moved apparently by morbid curiosity."[6]

Curious sightseers pushed and jostled each other trying to get a better look and Irene Riggs, supported by her father, sobbed uncontrollably as Alma's coffin was slowly lowered into the grave lined with her favourite pink and mauve flowers.

Going almost unnoticed as he mingled among the crowd was a quiet little man collecting signatures on a petition form. He was campaigning for the reprieve of George Percy Stoner.

The campaign for Stoner's reprieve had begun only hours after Justice Humphreys had passed sentence of death. With Stoner's execution scheduled for June 18th, the members of the small committee headed by F. W. Thistleton, a Bournemouth accountant, had known that they had little time to lose. They sought a commutation of the death sentence to one of life imprisonment bringing with it the possibility that Stoner might sometime in the future be released. Their appeal for clemency was based on nine points which included every possible argument the committee could muster to support their plea for mercy.

George Percy Stoner is a boy.
He was subjected to undue influence.
He was a victim of drugs.
He was probably under their influence when the crime was committed.
He showed by his behaviour at the trial that he was capable of better things.
His execution, while strictly legal, benefits the community in no respect.
He might, if reprieved, turn out to be a successful member of society, and be an asset to the state.
He was temporarily insane when the crime was committed, though not legally so.
He might have been the son of any of us.[7]

The Committee had ordered the printing of 2,000 petition forms, enough for 144,000 signatures, and was preparing for a door-to-door canvas of the Bournemouth area when newspapers, their grim headlines reading "Mrs. Rattenbury Found Dead," hit the streets. Overnight a local campaign became a national *cause célèbre*.

Alma's suicide was a bonanza to the national press. Reporters recounted with relish the events of the trial long after interest in the case would normally have waned. Sifting through the details of her early life, they created of her an artistic and tragic heroine; a brilliant and talented musician and composer whose first love was her art; a gay young wife plunged into heartbreaking widowhood by the untimely death of her gallant officer-husband on the battlefields of France; a bereaved young widow searching for her husband's grave while serving with devotion and dedication as a war nurse. One article which appeared in the *Daily Mirror* surrounded by a heavy black border was particularly maudlin.

Alma had been driven to suicide by utter hopelessness convinced that nothing she could do would help Stoner. If it had occurred to her that her death might save him, she would not have slipped away to an isolated spot where her body might not have been found for days. Now sympathy felt for her was directed to Stoner. No longer held back by the unpalatable prospect of a freed Stoner rushing into the arms of his waiting mistress, volunteers flocked to Thistleton's office. The Mayor of Bournemouth publicly signed the petition as did several aldermen. From Westminster the Member of Parliament for East Dorset, G. R. Hall Caine, recognizing a popular cause when he saw one, pledged his support and offered to deliver the petition to the Home Secretary personally. Bournemouth clergymen announced from their pulpits that petition forms would be posted in their churches and encouraged their parishioners to sign. Throughout the city shopkeepers tacked the petition on their doors, among them Mrs. Maude Price, the owner of Villa Madeira, who prominently displayed a form outside her tobacconist's shop on the Old Christchurch road.

Hundreds of vacationers, who had come to enjoy the sun and sand of Bournemouth during the spring Bank Holiday, patiently queued at the temporary booths erected along the seafront waiting to add their names to the petition. One young man who had spent all his holiday Monday on the Bournemouth Pier collecting over 1,000 signatures typified the heady dedication of all the volunteers when

FUNNY STORY FOR TO-DAY!

So they are burying Mrs. Rattenbury to-day.
I was in a lift when I heard she'd killed herself. The liftman told me and laughed. His laughing shocked me.

I can see most jokes, but this one got by me. I couldn't get that last journey of hers out of my head — the journey down to the Sunny South Coast.

* * *

The cruel, monstrous apparatus of publicity had done its best.

The poor, half-crazed woman (are you smiling?) wanted to get away from it all.

The only point was, that there wasn't anywhere to get away to (the liftman would have laughed at this).

Well, as you know, she got to Bournemouth all right. God knows what happened there.

Then on to Christchurch.

At this stage a knife comes into the picture.

"A long thin knife," says one paper; "a stiletto," "a dagger," "a bread knife," "a sort of bowie knife" — the horrible, gloating chorus is a bit out of harmony. (Funny story, eh?)

* * *

Then out into the quiet fields.

Now she sits and the pathetic last letters are scrawled down.
Is she thinking of Stoner? — What is he doing? How are they treating him?

What'll he say when he hears of this . . .

* * *

You know the rest.

The clumsy stabbing, and the attempted drowning just to make sure.

Make sure of what?

To make sure of getting away, not from the law that says she's an innocent woman, but from you and me. And millions like us.

* * *

And, of course, from the liftman who laughed.

he said at the end of a long day, "1 am aching all over but it is in a good cause."

The committee worked late every night answering inquiries from all parts of the country. From Liverpool an Alderman Walker called asking for 100 petition forms. From Brighton, from Swansea, from London, from Manchester came a flood of telephone calls and telegrams asking for all the forms the committee could spare. From Weymouth a writer called the committee pledging to collect 5,000 signatures in his area and from Altrincham the secretary of a political club called asking for forms and voicing the common opinion when he told the committee, "I am convinced the lad was led astray."

On June 11, a week before Stoner's execution was scheduled to take place, E. W. Marshall Harvey, Stoner's Bournemouth solicitor lodged a notice of appeal on his behalf. Although heartened by this news, the volunteers thought it best to be prudent and proceed according to their original schedule.

Shortly before 11 o'clock on the morning of June 14 a car drew up outside the Home Office. Out stepped three men; two members of Parliament, Hall Caine and Sir Henry Page Croft and the campaign organizer, F. W. Thistleton. They struggled up the steps carrying four brown paper packages each labelled "Stoner Petition." Sir John Simon, the Home Secretary, was discreetly absent enjoying a "brief respite from his official duties." And so the three presented the petition to his private secretary and left telling the press that the signatures numbered over 305,000.

And more petitions were arriving by the hour. Thirteen thousand signatures had arrived by morning post and the committee was still receiving requests for petition forms. Late the night before an elderly woman had travelled to Bournemouth from her home in London hoping to deliver her petition forms before the deadline. A schoolboy had arrived at Thistleton's office that morning with 173 signatures he had collected himself.

The pressure on the Home Secretary was mounting daily and he cannot have been sorry that he could delay any decision until after the hearing of Stoner's appeal.

*　　*　　*

Midsummer's Day brought with it clear bright skies and the highest temperatures of the year. In Bournemouth where the mercury hovered near 90 degrees holiday makers sought relief from the heat, lolling idly at the water's edge or sipping iced drinks beneath the wide trees of the pleasure grounds. Some stoical Bournemouth businessmen went about in stiff collars and bowler hats, but most loosened their ties, shed their jackets and then their vests as the temperature continued to climb.

In London people grumbled through the hottest day recorded since 1878. The sun blazed down on Mrs. Violet Van der Elst and her little band of sandwichmen as they gathered outside the Court of Criminal Appeal to continue their fight against capital punishment. "STONER MUST BE REPRIEVED," "STOP THE LAW KILLING THIS BOY," "STOP ILLEGAL KILLING," "END CAPITAL PUNISHMENT" their placards read as they paraded up and down outside the court where Stoner's application for a new trial would be heard.

Despite the stuffy heat of the courtroom, Stoner's face was white with tension as he took his place in the dock accompanied by three warders. He wore his only good clothes, the grey suit which Alma had bought for him at Harrod's and which he had worn throughout the trial. Not daring to look at the three judges, he let his eyes wander about the courtroom. He seemed to be searching for a familiar face among the throng of spectators fidgeting uncomfortably in the oppressive heat of the public gallery.

Calling Rattenbury's murder a clumsy crime, Casswell who had defended Stoner at the Old Bailey began his arguments. Carefully and slowly he detailed the evidence presented at the trial. Not even the smallest detail escaped his attention as he plodded on. Twice he was interrupted by the Lord Chief Justice who asked with sweaty impatience, "What is the proposition in law that you are putting forward? It may be my fault but I do not understand the relevancy of these observations."

Casswell answered that the point he was trying to make was there ought to have been separate trials, that joint trials had presented a serious possibility of a miscarriage of justice. And then inexorably he returned to a blow by blow account of the evidence presented at the Old Bailey.

Finally an exasperated Chief Justice interrupted again.

"Does it appear to you that all this is so interesting that it is our duty to hear it twice?"

And Casswell apologized. He was not aware that the justices were familiar with the evidence, he said.

To which the Chief Justice replied with no small amount of sarcasm, "We have spent a pleasant weekend, you know, reading this sort of thing. Please remember we know the evidence on this case."

Casswell, finally taking the hint, made an effort to summarize. He repeated his contention that separate trials should have been granted. Stoner had not known, Casswell said, that Alma would take the stand and throw the blame on him. He had been unwilling to testify as he had not wanted to implicate Alma. If separate trials had been held, Alma would have been tried first as her name appeared first on the indictment. Then Stoner at his own trial would have felt free to tell his side of the story knowing that nothing he said could harm Alma.

After a short consultation, the Lord Chief Justice put forward the court's point of view. The defence had not argued that there had been insufficient evidence to convict Stoner. Stoner's appeal had been based solely on the contention that separate trials should have been ordered. The court was being asked to believe that Justice Humphreys with all the evidence before him had erred in his decision to let joint trials proceed and "Anyone who would believe that would believe anything," the Chief Justice scolded.

He found Stoner's request to testify now that Mrs. Rattenbury was dead "almost sinister" and he refused Stoner's application to take the stand and "swear what he would not swear, and was not prepared to swear while she was alive."

Calling the case sordid and squalid, the Chief Justice concluded, "The fact, if it be a fact, that a lad of good character was corrupted by an abandoned woman old enough to be his mother raises no question of law that can be employed as a ground of appeal. The court has neither the power, nor the inclination, to alter the law as regard to that. The case is dismissed."[8]

Stoner pale and dazed remained standing in the dock seemingly unaware that his appeal was over until a warder touched him on the shoulder and led him through the curtained doorway behind the dock to the stairway leading to the cells below.

Now his only hope lay with Sir John Simon. The jury in finding Stoner guilty had recommended mercy. The Home Office had received nearly 350,000 signatures pleading for Stoner's reprieve. There was really little question as to what the Home Secretary's decision would be.

On Tuesday, June 25, three months and one day since the murder of Francis Mawson Rattenbury, he announced his decision. Stoner would not hang, his sentence was commuted to one of penal servitude for life.

Notes

1 Reverend Gervase Smith, D.D. "Memorial Sketch" *The John Rattenbury Memorials,* (ed.) Reverend H. Owen Rattenbury, T. Woolmer, London, 1884.

2 *Ibid.*

3 *Ibid.*

4 Reverend H. Owen Rattenbury, *op. cit.*

5 Obituary Notice, *Minutes of Conference 1904,* Wesleyan Methodist Book-Room, London, 1904.

6 Reverend H. Owen Rattenbury, *op. cit.*

7 John Rattenbury, *Memoirs of a Smuggler, compiled from his Diary and Journal: containing the principal events in the life of John Rattenbury, of Beer, Devonshire; Commonly called "The Rob Roy of the West,"* J. Harvey, London, 1837.

8 Later generations took a kinder view. Recalling this incident Harold Rattenbury (Mary Owen's grandson) adds ". . . it was long years before other copies of his diary became our proud possession again. Whether he was a direct ancestor or not may perhaps be left in doubt. We never wanted to check the matter up; but we certainly claimed him as our own." Harold B. Rattenbury, *China-Burma Vagabond,* Fred. Muller Ltd., London, 1946.

9 Saltaire, today, remains a model of a planned community. Although the suburbs of Bradford have crept up to and encircled Saltaire, the town planned by Lockwood and Mawson retains its distinct identity.

10 W. E. Forster, M.P., cited by A. H. Robinson, "Lockwood and Mawson. The story of a Great Partnership," *Bradford Bystander,* November 1971.

11 *Yorkshire Daily Observer,* December 12, 1904.

12 *Ibid.*

13 *Bradford Daily Telegraph,* December 10, 1904.

14 *The Architect,* January 17, 1890.

15 *The Architect,* May 8, 1891.

16 *The British Architect,* April 29, 1892.

17 *Daily Colonist,* March 17, 1893.

18 *The British Architect,* April 29, 1892.

CHAPTER TWO

1 Gastown's official name was Granville.

2 Douglas Sladen, On the Cars and Off . . . , London, 1895 and W. G. Blaikie, Summer Suns in the Far West, London 1890, cited by Margaret Ormsby, *British Columbia: A History*, Macmillan, 1958.

3 Vancouver *Province*, May 3, 1975.

4 J. S. Helmcken, *Daily Colonist*, January 1, 1891.

5 *British Colonist*, July 20, 1859.

6 Dorothy Blakey Smith, *The Parliament Buildings: A Postscript to Parkinson*, May 1962, mss. (PABC).

7 *Daily Colonist*, March 16, 1893.

8 *Daily Colonist*, November 8, 1892.

9 Judges' Report (PABC).

10 *Vancouver Daily World*, March 18, 1893.

11 "Victoria the Capital City of British Columbia," The West Shore, Portland, June 1889 reprinted in *Victoria Historical Review*, Victoria Celebrations Society, 1962.

12 Rudyard Kipling, *From Sea to Sea and Other Sketches*, (copyright 1899, 1907) Mandalay Edition, Doubleday, 1927.

13 *Daily Colonist*, March 18, 1894.

14 *Seattle Post-Intelligencer*, March 14, 1894.

15 *Daily Colonist*, March 18, 1894.

16 F. M. Rattenbury, Report Upon Tenders for New Parliament Buildings, December 1, 1893 (PABC).

17 F. M. Rattenbury, notes assembled to defend his rejection of Koksilah stone, November 1894 (PABC).

18 Theodore Davie (Attorney General) to Adams, November 22, 1894 (PABC).

19 *Ibid.*

20 F. M. Rattenbury to G. B. Martin (C.C. of L. and W.) November 22, 1894 (PABC).

21 G. B. Martin to Adams, November 27, 1894 (PABC).

22 F. M. Rattenbury to G. B. Martin, December 3, 1894 (PABC).

23 Adams to G. B. Martin, December 10, 1894 (PABC).

24 *Daily Colonist*, October 11, 1898.

25 *Daily Colonist*, September 27, 1896.

CHAPTER THREE

1 F. M. Rattenbury, "Report upon Tenders . . . , December 1, 1893 (PABC).

2 F. M. Rattenbury to G. B. Martin, November 13, 1895 (PABC).

3 F. M. Rattenbury to G. B. Martin, April 9, 1897 (PABC).

[4] Extract from Minutes of meeting of Executive Council of May 19, 1897 (PABC).

[5] F. M. Rattenbury to G. B. Martin September 19, 1897 (PABC).

[6] W. S. Gore to F. M. Rattenbury, October 5, 1897 (PABC).

[7] F. M. Rattenbury to W. S. Gore, October 5, 1897 (PABC).

[8] W. S. Gore to G. B. Martin, October 7, 1897 (PABC).

[9] F. M. Rattenbury to G. B. Martin, November 14, 1987 (PABC).

[10] F. M. Rattenbury to G. B. Martin, December 26, 1897 (PABC).

[11] *Daily Colonist*, February 10, 1898.

[12] Although improved by the salmon net, the acoustic properties of the hall remained a problem, the members having "great difficulty" in hearing one another — prompting one member to suggest, "As the salmon net has not proved a success perhaps a fish trap might prove more effectual." *Daily Colonist*, May 1, 1903.

[13] Rigan (Chief Caretaker) to J. E. Griffith (Public Works Engineer) May 27, 1913 (PABC).

CHAPTER FOUR

[1] Edwin Tappan Adney, *The Klondike Stampede of 1897-1898*. Harper and Brothers, New York, 1900.

[2] John Rattenbury's stay in B.C. and the Yukon was brief. His cousin, Methodist missionary Harold B. Rattenbury reports that he became "a steamship captain, running between Malaya and the China Coast. When I reached China in 1902 expecting to meet him, I was met by his widow instead, who took me to see his grave in the famous 'Happy Valley' in Hong Kong." Harold B. Rattenbury, *op. cit.*

[3] F. M. Rattenbury to T. M. Potts, June 26, 1898 reprinted in the *Daily Colonist*, July 9, 1898.

[4] Martha Louise Black, *My Ninety Years*, ed. Flo Whyard, Alaska Northwest Publishing Co., 1976.

[5] From Skagway to Dawson. A Talk with Mr. T. [*sic.*] M. Rattenbury, *The Mining Record*, 1898.

[6] Col. S. B. Steele, *Forty Years in Canada*. Dodd, Mead & Co., New York, 1915 (facsimilie edition Coles, Toronto, 1973).

CHAPTER FIVE

[5] The fact that Princess Louise (wife of the Marquis of Lorne, Governor General of Canada) found the residence in any way heavenly seems to have been due to her husband's absence rather than any celestial pretensions enjoyed by Cary Castle. According to Elizabeth Longford (*Victoria R.I.*, London, 1964) "The Princess had suffered an appalling sleigh accident ... she was dragged by the hair for several minutes and lost one ear. To this shock the Queen attributed an aversion to her husband which had to be accepted as a sad but inescapable fact ..."

2 F. M. Rattenbury to W. C. Wells (C.C. of L. and W.) August 27, 1900 (PABC).

3 Thomas Hooper to W. C. Wells, August 28, 1900 (PABC).

4 F. M. Rattenbury to W. C. Wells, August 14, 1901 (PABC).

5 F. M. Rattenbury to W. C. Wells, September 11, 1901 (PABC).

6 *Daily Colonist*, April 21, 1903.

7 *Daily Colonist*, April 28, 1903. The day after Muir's letter was printed in full in the *Colonist* the following item appeared in the same paper. "To Build a Bungalow" "F. M. Rattenbury is calling for tenders up to Monday next for the erection of a bungalow residence on Belcher street." Muir's reaction to this piece of news was not recorded.

8 *Daily Colonist*, April 30, 1903.

9 Award in the matter of Drake vs. the Government of B.C., n.d. but probably December 1903 (PABC).

10 F. M. Rattenbury to R. Green (C.C. of L. and W.) December 17, 1903 (PABC).

11 At Sir Henri's suggestion Cary Castle was equipped with an unusual shower, a white marble enclosure with an array of pipes and taps which afforded a bather the luxury of being sprayed from all angles with temperature controlled jets of water. The design so impressed Rattenbury that he ordered a similar unit for his own home.

12 The hearing of the legislative committee were reported at length in the *Daily Colonist*, February 5-12, 1904.

13 Journals of the Legislative Assembly of the province of British Columbia, session 1903-1904.

CHAPTER SIX

1 Vancouver *Province*, February 19, 1901.

2 *Daily Colonist*, November 26, 1902.

3 *Daily Colonist*, May 23, 1903.

4 Rattenbury had calculated that an Inner Harbour completed according to his plans would have an immediate impact on every visitor no matter how well-travelled and blase he might be. And he was quite right. Rudyard Kipling visited Victoria for a second time shortly before the Empress was completed and later wrote, "There is a view, when the morning mists peel off the harbour where the steamers tie up, of the Houses of Parliament on one hand, and a huge hotel on the other, which as an example of cunningly-fitted-in waterfronts and facades is worth a very long journey." *op. cit.* A correspondent attached to the Prince of Wales' 1919 tour was equally impressed. "The bay goes squarely up to a promenade. Behind the stone balustrade is a great lawn, and beyond that . . . is a finely decorated building, a fitted background to any romance, though it is actually an 'hotel deluxe' . . . To the right is a rambling building, ornate and attractive, with low, decorated domes and outflung and rococo wings . . . The whole of this square grouping of green grass and white buildings . . . gives a glamorous air to the scene." W. Douglas Newton, *Westward with the Prince of Wales*, 1920.

[5] *Daily Colonist*, May 23, 1903.

[6] *Daily Colonist*, August 17, 1905.

[7] *Daily Colonist*, November 3, 1906.

[8] *Daily Colonist*, November 25, 1902.

CHAPTER SEVEN

[1] Oliver to Newcombe, January 4, 1906 Newcombe Collection, (PABC).

[2] *Victoria Times*, February 3, 1906.

[3] Virtue's first hotel, the Mount Baker, had burned down two years earlier. The new hotel, known as the Oak Bay, designed by Rattenbury and erected in only 19 working days was later renamed the Old Charming Inn and survived until the 1960's when it was demolished to make way for an apartment building, the Rudyard Kipling.

[4] Shortly after he purchased Mary Tod Island, Rattenbury agreed to lease it to Virtue for one dollar a year. When Virtue died 23 years later, in 1929, he had come to think of the island as his own and he bequeathed it to the municipality for use as a park. Rattenbury generously agreed to abide by Virtue's wishes.

[5] *Victoria Illustrated*, 1891.

[6] Margaret Williams, *Daily Colonist*, November 27, 1966.

[7] *Victoria Times*, January 4, 1907.

[8] *Daily Colonist*, January 24, 1907.

[9] F. M. Rattenbury to W. Scott (Premier) September 5, 1906 (SAB).

[10] Scott to Rattenbury November 1, 1906 (SAB).

[11] Rattenbury to Scott November 5, 1906 (SAB).

[12] Rattenbury to Scott October 31, 1907 (SAB).

[13] Rattenburg [*sic*] to Scott November 15, 1907 (SAB).

CHAPTER EIGHT

[1] *Daily Colonist*, August 8, 1905.

[2] *Victoria Times*, June 10, 1908.

[3] *Daily Colonist*, December 18, 1897.

[4] *Victoria Times*, June 25, 1908.

[5] *Daily Colonist*, January 14, 1913.

[6] *Daily Colonist*, January 11, 1913.

[7] *Daily Colonist*, January 11, 1913.

CHAPTER NINE

[1] Cited by Phyllis Bowman, *Muskeg, Rocks and Rain*, 1973.

[2] *Ibid.*

[3] *Victoria Times*, February 22, 1918.

4 In the late 1880's Mrs. Baillie-Grohman stayed briefly at the Rae Street house while her husband visited the Kootenays to oversee his canal building scheme. "I could not very well stay at the Driard, as a good deal of drinking went on there in the evening," she wrote. "... we went for a short time to a little bungalow opposite the Cathedral, owned by a Mrs. Howard. She was a widow and a pretty daughter lived with her. They let rooms to bachelors. This place I found would not do very well either, as I felt the three or four men living there would rather have it to themselves." cited by J. K. Nesbitt, *Daily Colonist*, October 27, 1968.

5 Kyrle C. Symons, *That Amazing Institution*, n.d.

6 Ratz took a similar interest in his daughter's school, St. Margaret's. In 1911 he prepared plans for the new school buildings erected the following year on two acres of land at the corner of Fort and Fern streets.

7 Oak Bay Council refused to accept his resignation — suggesting instead that he take a three month leave of absence.

8 Colonel H. M. Urquart, History of the Sixteenth Battalion, cited Williams, *Daily Colonist*, November 27, 1966.

CHAPTER TEN

1 *Sunday Dispatch*, June 9, 1935.

2 Raymond Massey, *When I Was Young*, McClelland & Stewart, Toronto, 1976.

3 Miss C. Maclure, Interview, January 3, 1975.

4 *Sunday Dispatch*, June 9, 1935.

5 *Ibid.*

6 *Vancouver News Herald*, April 20, 1935.

7 *Daily Express*, June 6, 1935.

8 Miss C. Maclure.

9 Miss C. Maclure.

10 Miss C. Maclure.

11 Frank B. Rattenbury, Interview, August 1974.

12 Mrs. E. Burton (Mary Rattenbury), Interview, November 9, 1974.

13 F. M. Rattenbury to P. L. James, May 28, 1925 (PABC).

14 *Victoria Times*, June 11, 1925.

15 B. Gardom to P. L. James, June 11, 1925 (PABC).

16 Frank B. Rattenbury.

17 Mrs. E. Burton.

18 In 1935 the net value of his estate amounted to only $2,610.

19 *Vancouver Sun*, April 17, 1935.

CHAPTER ELEVEN

1 W. H. K. Wright, ed. *Some Account of the Barony and Town of Okehampton: Its Antiquities and Institutions. Including the Journals kept by Messrs. Rattenbury and Shebbeare, Gents. and Burgesses, from the 21, James I, to the death of William III*, Masland, 1889.

[2] *Sunday Dispatch*, June 9, 1935.

[3] F. Tennyson Jesse, ed. *Trial of Alma Victoria Rattenbury and George Percy Stoner*, Notable British Trials Series, William Hodge and Co. Ltd., London, 1935. (Unless otherwise indicated all other direct quotations in Chapter Eleven are taken from this transcript of the trial.)

[4] Bert Parsons, Interview, June 7, 1975.

[5] Eliot Crawshay-Williams, *Stay of Execution*, Jarrolds, London, 1933.

[6] *Dark-Haired Marie*, words by Edward Lockton, music by Lozanne Keith Prowse and Co. Ltd., London, 1932.

CHAPTER TWELVE

[1] F. Tennyson Jesse, *op. cit.* (All other direct quotations in Chapter Twelve are taken from this transcript of the trial).

CHAPTER THIRTEEN

[1] *The Western Morning News and Daily Gazette*, June 8, 1935.

[2] Dixie Dean, Interview, June 9, 1975.

[3] *Sunday Dispatch*, June 9, 1935.

[4] *Ibid.*

[5] *Ibid.*

[6] *Bournemouth Daily Echo*, June 10, 1935.

[7] *Bournemouth Daily Echo*, June 7, 1935.

[8] *Bournemouth Daily Echo*, June 24, 1935.

Bibliography

NEWSPAPERS

Bournemouth Daily Echo
Bradford Daily Telegraph
Daily Express
Daily Mirror
Sunday Dispatch
Western Morning News and Daily Gazette
Yorkshire Daily Observer

Vancouver Daily World
Vancouver News Herald
Vancouver *Province*
Vancouver Sun
Victoria *Daily Colonist*
Victoria Times

Seattle-Post Intelligencer

PERIODICALS

The Architect
The British Architect
The Illustrated London News

BOOKS AND PERIODICALS

Adney, Edwin Tappan. *The Klondike Stampede of 1897-1898*. Harper and Brothers, New York, 1900.

Berton, Pierre. *Klondike.* McClelland & Stewart, Toronto, 1963.

Bissley, Paul. *Early and Late Victorians. A History of the Union Club of British Columbia.* 1969.

Black, Martha Louise. *My Ninety Years.* ed. Flo Whyard. Alaska Northwest Publishing Co., Anchorage, 1976.

Bowman, Phyllis. *Muskeg, Rocks and Rain,* 1973.

Cotton, Peter. "The Stately Capitol," *RAIC Journal,* April 1958.

Curl, James Stevens. "A Victorian Model Town," *Country Life,* March 9, 1972.

Debrett's *Peerage.* London, Odhams, 1970.

Fieldhouse, Joseph. *Bradford.* Local History Series. London, 1972.

First Biennial Report of the State Capitol Commission of the State of Washington, December 31, 1894 (Washington State Library).

Hamilton, Walter J. *The Yukon Story.* Mitchell Press, 1967.

Jesse, F. Tennyson, ed. *Trial of Alma Victoria Rattenbury and George Percy Stoner.* Notable British Trials series. W. Hodge, London, 1935.

Kalman, Harold D. *The Railway Hotels and the Development of the Chateau Style in Canada.* University of Victoria Maltwood Museum Studies in Architectural History, 1968.

Large, R. G. *Prince Rupert — a Gateway to Alaska and the Pacific.* Mitchell Press, 1973.

Lower, J. A. "The Construction of the Grand Trunk Pacific Railway in British Columbia," *British Columbia Historical Quarterly,* July 1940.

Minute Book, Oak Bay Council Meetings, Oak Bay Municipal Hall.

Minutes of the Conference 1904, 1962 Wesleyan Methodist Book-Room, London.

Morgan, Murray. *One Man's Gold Rush.* J. J. Douglas Ltd., Vancouver, 1973.

Murdoch, George. *A History of the Municipality of Oak Bay from Prehistoric Times to the Present.* 1968. Oak Bay Municipal Hall (typescript).

Ormsby, Margaret. *British Columbia: A History.* Macmillan, 1958.

Public Schools Year Book, 1914.

Rattenbury, T. [*sic*] M., A Talk with. "From Skagway to Dawson." *The Mining Record,* 1898.

Rattenbury, Harold B. *China-Burma Vagabond.* Muller Ltd., 1946.

Rattenbury, H. Owen (Rev.), ed. *The John Rattenbury Memorials,* T. Woolmer, London, 1884.

Rattenbury, John. *Memoirs of a Smuggler, compiled from his Diary and Journals containing the principal events in the life of John Rattenbury, of Beer, Devonshire; commonly called the "Rob Roy of the West."* J. Harvey, London, 1837.

Robinson, Bart. *Banff Springs. The Story of a Hotel.* Summerthought, Banff, 1973.

Robinson, A. H. "Lockwood and Mawson. The Story of a Great Partnership," *Bradford Bystander,* September, November 1971.

Sampson, Mrs. Curtis. *Reminiscences of Bygone Days at Government House.* typescript (PABC).

Satterfield, Archie. *Chilkoot Pass. Then and Now.* Alaska Northwest Publishing Co., Anchorage, 1973.

Scholefield, E. O. S. and F. W. Howay. *British Columbia from earliest times to the present.* Vancouver, 1914.

Shiels, Bob. *Calgary.* The Calgary Herald, 1975.

Sproule, Albert F. *The Role of Patrick Burns in the Development of Western Canada.* M.A. Thesis, University of Alberta, 1962.

Steele, Colonel S. B. *Forty Years in Canada.* Dodd, Mead and Co., New York, 1915.

Symons, Kyrle. *That Amazing Institution.* 1948.

Victoria Historical Review, Victoria Celebrations Society, 1962.

Victoria Illustrated. The Colonist, 1891.

Wilson Edmund, ed. *Leeds Grammar School Admission Books 1820-1900.* Leeds, 1906.

Wright, W. H. K., ed. *Some Account of the Barony and Town of Okehampton, Its Antiquities and Institutions. Including the Journals kept by Messrs. Rattenbury and Shebbeare, Gents. and Burgesses, from the 21, James I, to the Death of William III.* Masland, 1889.

Index